Lecture Notes in Comput

3

Commenced Publication in 1973
Founding and Former Series Editors:
Gerhard Goos, Juris Hartmanis, and Jan va

Ricardo Peña   Rex Page (Eds.)

Trends
in Functional
Programming

12th International Symposium, TFP 2011
Madrid, Spain, May 16-18, 2011
Revised Selected Papers

 Springer

Volume Editors

Ricardo Peña
Universidad Complutense de Madrid
Facultad de Informática
Departamento de Sistemas Informáticos y Computación
C/ Profesor Jose Garcia Santesmases s/n, 28040 Madrid, Spain
E-mail: ricardo@sip.ucm.es

Rex Page
University of Oklahoma
School of Computer Science
110 West Boyd Street, Norman, OK 73019, USA
E-mail: page@ou.edu

ISSN 0302-9743   e-ISSN 1611-3349
ISBN 978-3-642-32036-1   e-ISBN 978-3-642-32037-8
DOI 10.1007/978-3-642-32037-8
Springer Heidelberg Dordrecht London New York

Library of Congress Control Number: 2012942732

CR Subject Classification (1998): D.1.1, D.1.3, D.3.2-3, E.1, F.3.3

LNCS Sublibrary: SL 1 – Theoretical Computer Science and General Issues

Typesetting: Camera-ready by author, data conversion by Scientific Publishing Services, Chennai, India

Printed on acid-free paper

Springer is part of Springer Science+Business Media (www.springer.com)

Preface

The 12th International Symposium on Trends in Functional Programming (TFP) was held in Madrid, Spain, during May 16–18, 2011. It was hosted by the Computer Science Faculty of the Universidad Complutense de Madrid. In this edition, TFP was co-located with the Second International Workshop on Foundational and Practical Aspects of Resource Analysis (FOPARA 2011).

The TFP symposium is an international forum for researchers with interest in all aspects of functional programming, taking a broad view of current and future trends in the area of functional programming. It aspires to be a lively environment for presenting the latest research results, and other contributions, described in draft papers submitted prior to the symposium. A formal post-symposium refereeing process then selects a high-quality set of articles between those presented at the symposium and submitted for formal publication. This year, 21 papers were submitted and 12 of them were accepted by the Program Committee. These are the ones included in this volume.

The TFP symposium is the heir of the successful series of Scottish Functional Programming Workshops. Previous TFP symposia were held in Edinburgh (UK) in 2003, in Munich (Germany) in 2004, in Tallinn (Estonia) in 2005, in Nottingham (UK) in 2006, in New York (USA) in 2007, in Nijmegen (The Netherlands) in 2008, in Komarno (Slovakia) in 2009, and in Oklahoma (USA) in 2010.

TFP pays special attention to PhD students—acknowledging their role in developing new trends—reflected in several ways. In the first place, there is a *student paper* category to identify works that are mainly produced by students. These works receive an extra round of feedback by the Program Committee before they are submitted to the standard review process for formal publication. In this way, students can upgrade their papers before they are put to compete with more 'professional' ones. Also, every year there is a *best student paper award* to acknowledge the best work done by PhD students. This year, the award went to Laurence E. Day and his supervisor Graham Hutton for their paper "Towards Modular Compilers for Effects."

We thank all the speakers, the authors, the rest of the participants, the Program Committee, and the TFP Steering Committee for contributing to the success of TFP 2011. We also acknowledge the generous funding and support of our sponsors the Spanish *Ministry of Science and Innovation*, the *Computer Science Faculty* of the Universidad Complutense, and the *Fundación General de la Universidad Complutense*.

March 2012
Ricardo Peña
Rex Page

Conference Organization

Program Committee

Peter Achten	Radboud University Nijmegen, The Netherlands
Ana Bove	Chalmers University of Technology, Sweden
Olaf Chitil	University of Kent, UK
Marko van Eekelen	Radboud University Nijmegen and Open University, The Netherlands
Robert B. Findler	Northwestern University, USA
Víctor Gulías	University of La Coruña, Spain
Jurriaan Hage	University of Utrecht, The Netherlands
Kevin Hammond	University of St. Andrews, UK
Michael Hanus	Christian Albrechts University of Kiel, Germany
Zoltán Horváth	Eötvös Loránd University, Hungary
Frank Huch	Christian Albrechts University of Kiel, Germany
Mauro Jaskelioff	National University of Rosario, Argentina
Rita Loogen	Philipps University Marburg, Germany
Jay McCarthy	Brigham Young University, USA
Henrik Nilsson	University of Nottingham, UK
Rex Page	University of Oklahoma, USA
Ricardo Peña (PC Chair)	Complutense University of Madrid, Spain
John Reppy	University of Chicago, USA
Konstantinos Sagonas	Uppsala University, Sweden
Simon Thompson	University of Kent, UK
Germán Vidal	Polytechnical University of Valencia, Spain

External Reviewers

Zoltán Csörnyei	Wouter Swierstra
Peter Divianszky	Melinda Toth
Tamás Kozsik	

Sponsoring Institutions

GOBIERNO DE ESPAÑA
MINISTERIO DE CIENCIA E INNOVACIÓN

Facultad de Informática

FUNDACIÓN GENERAL
UNIVERSIDAD COMPLUTENSE
MADRID

Table of Contents

Miscellaneous

Constraint-Free Type Error Slicing

Thomas Schilling

School of Computing
University of Kent, UK
ts319@kent.ac.uk

Abstract. Type error messages for ML-based languages tend to suffer from imprecise error locations – the type checker reports only one of many possible locations of an error. The notion of a *type error slice* corrects this by reporting *all* program locations that contribute to a given error (and no more).

Previous work on producing type error slices required the use of a constraint-based type checker implementation. For most existing systems this would require substantial changes to well-tested and subtle pieces of code. In this work we show how to produce useful type error slices with an unmodified type checker. Other tools, such as automatic correction systems, can be layered on top of our system.

We have implemented this technique on top of the Glasgow Haskell Compiler (GHC) and report our experiences.

1 Introduction

Consider the following ill-typed Haskell definition:

$$f = \lambda x \rightarrow \texttt{length (x '*' ++ x [True])}$$

The widely used Glasgow Haskell Compiler[1] (GHC) reports the error:

```
Couldn't match expected type 'Char' with actual type '[t0]'
```

The associated location is the expression [True]. GHC somehow decided that the "expected type" of x's argument should be Char. If we swap the two calls of x, however, GHC changes its mind and decides that it expects type [Bool]:

$$f = \lambda x \rightarrow \texttt{length (x [True] ++ x '*')}$$

```
Couldn't match expected type '[Bool]' with actual type 'Char'
```

While one might argue that the wording of the message could be improved, the real problem is more fundamental. GHC only reports *one* location for the error. In a language based on the Hindley/Milner typing discipline [7, 1], however, it is impossible to always report the single correct location of an error; there are

---

[1] Version 7.0.2.

R. Peña and R. Page (Eds.): TFP 2011, LNCS 7193, pp. 1–16, 2012.
© Springer-Verlag Berlin Heidelberg 2012

several possible locations where changes can be made to fix an error, depending on the intended semantics of the program.

A better notion of location for error messages in such languages are *type error slices* [2, 11]: the location of an error includes *all* parts of the program that contribute to it (and no more). For the first example above this would be:

$$f = \lambda \boxed{x} \rightarrow \text{length} (\boxed{x} \ [\text{True}] \ ++ \ \boxed{x} \ \text{'*'})$$

All the highlighted parts of the program together cause the error, and only changes to these locations may remove the error. It is also possible to provide a textual representation of error slices:

$$..(\lambda x \ \rightarrow \ ..(x \ [..])..(x \ \text{'*'})..)..$$

In this particular case, no changes to other parts of the program can possibly fix the error.[2] In general there may be multiple type error slices and finding them all is not always feasible (see Section 2.2), but all the locations included in a single type error slice will always be relevant to the error.

While type error slices are no replacement for a carefully worded error message they can provide helpful complementary information and can give hints about possible ways to understand and fix the error. From the above type error slice we can deduce quite a bit of useful information about the error. First, it is important that x is λ-bound and therefore has a monomorphic type. Second, it is used as a function in two different applications. Third, the fact that the literal True is not highlighted indicates that it is not important that x is applied to a list of booleans, but merely that x is applied to *some* list.

Existing methods for constructing type error slices are based on a constraint-based implementation of the type checker. The source program is parsed and then translated into constraints expressing the typing rules. If the source program had a type error then these constraints are unsolvable and it is then possible to find a minimal unsolvable constraint set. These are the constraints that are in a sense essential to the error. An unsolvable constraint set is minimal if removing any constraint would make it solvable. Finally, this set is translated back into source code locations which then form the type error slice.

While it is known that type-checking for Hindley-Milner corresponds to constraint-solving, most implementations generate and solve these constraints on the fly. This is insufficient for the way type error slices are constructed in the aforementioned systems. For example, Rahli *et al.* [9] re-implemented a full type checker for SML. Type checkers are complicated pieces of code and are hard to get right. Having to maintain two implementations is usually unacceptable.

Even type checkers that *are* implemented in terms of explicit constraint-generation are not immediately suitable for the construction of type error slices.

---

[2] We could insert a shadowing binding of x, but this means actually changing the use sites of x since they now refer to a different variable. There is indeed a presentation issue of slices containing several variables with the same name. Such variables could be distinguished, for instance, with colour.

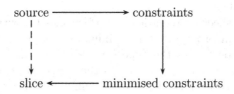

Fig. 1. Our method (dashed line) in relation to existing method (solid lines) of constructng type error slices

In order to construct the type error slice, it is necessary to accurately associate source code locations with the constraints they introduced.

In this work we present a simple method of constructing accurate type error slices without special requirements on the type checker. Instead of translating the source program into a set of constraints, our method works directly on the source program. Our approach is in a sense more direct as shown in Figure 1. Instead of translating the program into constraints, minimising these and translating things back into an expression (solid arrows), we construct slices directly by transforming the program itself (dashed arrow). Our approach is based on an idea from the SEMINAL project [6, 5]: in order to check whether a program location is part of the type error slice, we modify the program in a way that removes any type constraints introduced by that location. If the modified program type checks (or uncovers a different error), the location must be part of the type error slice.

Coming back to our first example, to test whether the first use site of x should be part of the error slice, we replace x by a term ⊥ that type checks in any context. A possible such term in Haskell is (let y = y in y), but any term of type $\forall \alpha.\alpha$ will do. We obtain the following program which is sent to the type checker.

$$f = \lambda x \rightarrow \text{length } (\bot \text{ [True] } \mathbin{++} x \text{ '*')}$$

This program does indeed type check, so we conclude that the first use site of x must be part of the error slice. To test whether the call to length takes part in the error we send this program to the type checker:

$$f = \lambda x \rightarrow \bot \text{ (x [True] } \mathbin{++} x \text{ '*')}$$

This program does not type check, which means that "disabling" the reference to length did not fix the error, and thus it is not part of the error slice. To test whether the application of x to [True] contributes to the error, (x [True]) is rewritten to (⊥ x [True]). That is, we keep both function and argument, but we remove all constraints that were introduced by applying one to the other. We obtain the program:

$$f = \lambda x \rightarrow \bot \text{ (⊥ x [True] } \mathbin{++} x \text{ '*')}$$

The resulting program now type checks, hence this application site must be part of the type error slice.

Our type error slicer systematically performs such rewriting steps for every location of the input program until a minimal set of program locations is found which are then reported as the type error slice. Eventually we arrive at the following program, which corresponds to the expected error slice. (The call to ++ has been removed because it has been found irrelevant to the error.)

$$\bot \ (\lambda x \ \rightarrow \ \bot \ (\bot \ x \ [\bot]) \ (x \ \text{'*'}))$$

Because this technique is purely source-based it can also quite easily be adapted to support some extensions to the Hindley/Milner type system.

This work makes the following contributions:

- We show how constraint-based type error slicing can be implemented while treating the type checker as a black box (Section 2). This is predicated upon the existence of a source-level rewriting function that simulates removal of type checker constraints.
- As a concrete example we define such a function for a core subset of ML, named Mini-ML (Section 3).
- We describe our findings after implementing this approach for Haskell (Section 4).

2   From Constraint-Based to Source-Based Type Error Slicing

Previous work [2, 9, 12] used a constraint-based type checker to construct type error slices. Type checking is split into a constraint generation phase and a separate constraint solving phase. Each generated constraint is annotated with a label to relate it back to the input program.

For instance, the program (with subscripts denoting labels / source locations)

$$(\lambda x_{l_1} \rightarrow (f_{l_3} \ (x_{l_4} \ 0_{l_5})_{l_6} \ (x_{l_7} \ +_{l_8} \ 0_{l_9})_{l_{10}})_{l_{11}})_{l_2}$$

is translated into the following constraints:

$$\{(t_2 \equiv_{l_2} t_{x2} \rightarrow t_{11}), (t_{x2} \equiv_{l_1} t_{x4}), (t_{x2} \equiv_{l_1} t_{x7}), (t_3 \equiv_{l_{11}} t_6 \rightarrow t_{10} \rightarrow t_{11}),$$
$$(t_4 \equiv_{l_6} t_5 \rightarrow t_6), (t_4 \equiv_{l_4} t_{x4}), (t_5 \equiv_{l_5} \text{Int}), (t_8 \equiv_{l_{10}} t_7 \rightarrow t_9 \rightarrow t_{10}),$$
$$(t_8 \equiv_{l_8} \text{Int} \rightarrow \text{Int} \rightarrow \text{Int}), (t_7 \equiv_{l_7} t_{x7}), (t_9 \equiv_{l_9} \text{Int})\}$$

Because the input program is ill-typed, this constraint set is unsolvable. Each unsolvable constraint set has at least one *minimal* unsolvable subset which can be found in a number of ways. The algorithm used by Haack and Wells [2] and Wazny [12] is based on a simple idea. Solve constraints one by one until the constraint set becomes unsatisfiable. The constraint that was added last must be part of the minimal unsolvable subset. Figure 2 shows the full algorithm.

```
 1: function MINIMISE₁(D)
 2:     M ← ∅
 3:     while satisfiable(M) do
 4:         C ← M
 5:         while satisfiable(C) do
 6:             e ∈ D − C
 7:             C ← C ∪ {e}
 8:         end while
 9:         D ← C        ▷ Discard constraints that no longer need to be considered.
10:         M ← M ∪ {e}
11:     end while
12:     return M
13: end function
```

Fig. 2. Constraint minimisation algorithm after Wazny [12] and Haack and Wells [2]. It takes a constraint set D and returns a minimal unsolvable subset $M \subseteq D$.

The returned constraint set M is minimal because removing any constraint from it makes it solvable. (For a proof see [2].) For the example constraints above, the only minimal set would be:

$$\{(t_{x2} \equiv_{l_1} t_{x4}), (t_{x2} \equiv_{l_1} t_{x7}), (t_4 \equiv_{l_6} t_5 \rightarrow t_6), (t_4 \equiv_{l_4} t_{x4}),$$
$$(t_8 \equiv_{l_{10}} t_7 \rightarrow t_9 \rightarrow t_{10}), (t_8 \equiv_{l_8} \text{Int} \rightarrow \text{Int} \rightarrow \text{Int}), (t_7 \equiv_{l_7} t_{x7})\}$$

To construct the type error slice the labels of the minimal unsatisfiable set are extracted ($\{l_1, l_4, l_6, l_7, l_8, l_{10}\}$) and the relevant locations of the source program are highlighted. Locations not part of the slice are replaced by "...":

$$\dots \text{x} \rightarrow \dots (\text{x} \ \dots) \ \dots (\text{x} + \dots) \ \dots$$

Note that the λ of the abstraction is not shown. This is because only one of the two labels (l_1 and l_2) is part of the error slice. Each label has different constraints attached. In Mini-ML label l_1 has been chosen to encode the requirement that x is bound monomorphically; label l_2 is attached to the constraint that the expression must have an arrow type. In this example, therefore, the error occurs because x is monomorphic.[3] It is up to the compiler writer to decide how many labels to attach to each expression type and which constraints attach to each label. In this example we chose to include the arrow to indicate monomorphic binding as at issue and λ only if the function as a whole is at issue.

2.1   Source-Based Type Error Slicing

Because we only need the constraint *labels* and not the constraints itself, the algorithm from Figure 2 actually does more work than we need. Instead of

---

[3] It would be perfectly fine to not make this distinction; the notion of a type error slice is independent of such details. However, more fine-grained placement of labels can give the user more information about the cause of an error.

```
 1: function MINIMISE₂(D)
 2:     L ← ∅
 3:     while satisfiable(filter(D, L)) do
 4:         L' ← L
 5:         while satisfiable(filter(D, L')) do
 6:             l ∈ labels(D) − L'
 7:             L' ← L' ∪ {l}
 8:         end while
 9:         D ← filter(D, L')
10:         L ← L ∪ {l}
11:     end while
12:     return L
13: end function
```

Fig. 3. Label minimisation algorithm. The *filter* function is defined as: $filter(C, L) = \{\tau_1 \equiv_l \tau_2 \in C \mid l \in L\}$

minimising constraint sets the algorithm should instead minimise label sets. A modified version of the algorithm to do just that is shown in Figure 3.

This algorithm keeps track of a set of labels instead of a set of constraints and uses *filter* to only pass the constraints with the selected labels to *satisfiable*. The functions *filter* and *satisfiable* are indeed the only parts of the algorithm that directly deal with constraints. For a given (Hindley/Milner-based) programming language the implementation of *satisfiable* is provided in the form of the type checker. If we can simulate the effect of *filter* by rewriting the input program, we can construct type error slices without the need for a constraint-based type checker implementation! It is useful to have a constraint-based *specification* to define which constraints are associated with which labels, but a full implementation is not needed.

To formalise this idea we use a function $e \rightsquigarrow C$ that translates a closed expression e into a set of constraints C. The type checker is a function from expressions to a success-or-failure type.

$$typecheck : Expr \rightarrow \{\mathsf{ok}, \mathsf{error}\}$$

Since we are dealing only with type errors, we assume that C is unsatisfiable. We require three properties. First, type checking must correspond exactly to solving the constraints.

Proposition 1. *Let* $e \rightsquigarrow C$ *then* $typecheck(e) = \mathsf{ok}$ *if and only if satisfiable(C).*

Second, we have a source-level rewriting function $filter_E$ which takes an expression and a set of labels occurring in the expression, and returns a rewritten expression. This function must accurately simulate the effect of *filter*:

Proposition 2. *If* $e \rightsquigarrow C$, $filter_E(e, L) \rightsquigarrow C'$ *and* $filter(C, L) = C''$, *then* $satisfiable(C')$ *if and only if* $satisfiable(C'')$.

Note that we do not require the constraints of the filtered expression to be the same, but only to be equivalent under *satisfiable*. Finally, we require that $filter_E(e, L)$ leaves labels intact.

Proposition 3. *Let* $L = labels(e)$ *and* $L' \subseteq L$, *then* $labels(filter_E(e, L')) = L'$.

Given these assumptions it is now straightforward to show that the source-based label minimisation algorithm of Figure 4 is equivalent to the constraint-based algorithm of Figure 3 by simple syntactic substitution.

```
 1: function MINIMISE3(e)
 2:     L ← ∅
 3:     while typecheck(filter_E(e, L)) = ok do
 4:         L' ← L
 5:         while typecheck(filter_E(e, L')) = ok do
 6:             l ∈ labels(e) − L'
 7:             L' ← L' ∪ {l}
 8:         end while
 9:         e ← filter_E(e, L')
10:         L ← L ∪ {l}
11:     end while
12:     return L
13: end function
```

Fig. 4. Source-based Label minimisation algorithm

In Section 3 we give an example of an implementation of $filter_E$ for the simple ML-like language Mini-ML.

A note on efficiency: assuming that *satisfiable/typecheck* takes time (in practise) linear in the size of its input, then the algorithm is quadratic in the number of labels.

2.2   Multiple Type Error Slices

The algorithms in Figures 2, 3, 4 are all non-deterministic because the order in which constraints (resp. labels) are picked is undefined. Furthermore, each algorithm will only find a single minimal unsolvable subset, but there may in fact be (and often are) multiple minimal unsolvable constraint sets and thus type error slices. Consider the following ill-typed program::

$$\lambda \ x \ \rightarrow \ (x \ 123, \ x \ \text{'a'}, \ x \ [])$$

This program has three possible type error slices:

$$\lambda \text{ x } \rightarrow \text{ ..(x 123)..(x 'a')..}$$
$$\lambda \text{ x } \rightarrow \text{ ..(x 123)..(x [])..}$$
$$\lambda \text{ x } \rightarrow \text{ ..(x 'a')..(x [])..}$$

Which one is returned by the algorithms depends on the order in which the constraints or labels are explored. In order to find *all* minimal unsolvable subsets essentially all subsets of the input constraint/label set need to be explored. There is room for some optimisations [12], but finding all minimal unsolvable subsets is not feasible in general as there may be exponentially many for some input programs [2].

Nevertheless, searching for several type error slices, perhaps coupled with a timeout, can be helpful to the user because slices may cover different program points. Program points that are part of many error slices may also indicate the most likely source of an error (and can be highlighted with more intensity). In the above example the binding site of x occurs in all slices. This suggests that changing x to be `let`-bound or changing the function's type to a higher-rank type may be the most suitable action for fixing the error.

If an expression contains multiple errors it will contain as many (or more) type error slices.

3 Source-Based Type Error Slicing for Mini-ML

Figure 5 defines the syntax of Mini-ML, a simple functional language with integers and polymorphic let-bindings.[4] Expressions in Mini-ML are annotated with unique labels l which identify each sub-expression. In a full language implementation this may be source location information from the parser. The typing rules for Mini-ML are almost completely standard Hindley/Milner and are omitted here for space reasons. The only feature is the addition of $\perp$ which behaves like a variable of type $\forall \alpha.\alpha$ (and can be implemented by adding it to the initial environment).

A constraint-based type checker translates a source program into a set of constraints, which are then solved in a separate step. If the constraints are solvable, then the program type checks. If they are unsolvable, the program has a type error.

Figure 6 defines rules for generating equality constraints for Mini-ML (adapted from Haack and Wells [2]). These can then be solved using standard unification. The translation returns three components:

- τ is the type assigned to the input expression.
- C is a set of equality constraints. Each equality constraint is annotated with a label.
- Γ is a bottom-up environment It maps each free variable in the input expression to a set of type variables, one per use site.

---

[4] This is the same language that Haack and Wells [2] used to introduce type error slices for Hindley/Milner.

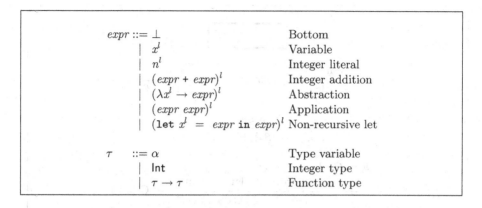

Fig. 5. Expression and type syntax for Mini-ML. Expressions are annotated with unique labels l.

The rules in Figure 6 may look a bit dense, but they all follow quite simple patterns. We use rule C-APP to describe the basic ideas. The first step is to generate constraints for both the expression in the function position (e_1) and the expression in the argument position (e_2). The application site now creates three additional constraints: (1) the type of e_1 must be of function shape, (2) the argument type of this function type must match the type of e_2, and (3) the result type of the application expression matches the result type of e_1. These three constraints are returned together with the combined constraints of both e_1 and e_2, as well as their combined environments. In fact, every constraint-based typing rule returns all the constraints of its sub-expressions plus the additional constraints imposed by the given syntactic construct.

The rules for C-LIT, C-BOT, C-VAR and C-ADD should now be straightforward to understand. The result of C-LIT is a type variable, and not simply Int, so that it is possible to associate the label of the expression with a constraint. This is also done in rule C-VAR for the same reason.

Abstraction has two associated labels hence rule C-ABS creates constraints annotated with different labels. Label l_1 is used with the constraints that enforce monomorphic variable binding. The constraints labelled with l_1 accordingly ensure that each occurrence of the bound variable gets the same (mono-)type. The label l_2 encodes the requirement that the type of a lambda-abstraction is of function shape.

Rule C-LET looks a bit daunting, but the ideas are very similar to those of C-ABS. For each of the n use sites of the bound variable x, the constraints generated from the expression e_1 are copied and connected to the corresponding type variables. This is equivalent to a capture avoiding substitution (i.e., inlining) of e_1 for every occurrence of x in e_2. It implements the requirement that every use site of x must be an instance of the (generalised) type of e_1 and is labelled with l_1. The constraint labelled with l_2 requires that the context must expect a type compatible with e_2's type. The use of $max(1, n)$ ensures that there is at

$$\boxed{expr \Downarrow \tau, C, \Gamma}$$

$$\frac{\beta \text{ fresh}}{n^l \Downarrow \beta, \{\beta \equiv_l \text{Int}\}, \emptyset} \text{ C-Lit} \qquad \frac{\beta \text{ fresh}}{\bot \Downarrow \beta, \emptyset, \emptyset} \text{ C-Bot}$$

$$\frac{\beta, \beta_x \text{ fresh}}{x^l \Downarrow \beta, \{\beta \equiv_l \beta_x\}, \{x : \{\beta_x\}\}} \text{ C-Var}$$

$$\frac{e_1 \Downarrow \tau_1, C_1, \Gamma_1 \qquad e_2 \Downarrow \tau_2, C_2, \Gamma_2 \qquad \beta \text{ fresh}}{C_0 = \{\tau_1 \equiv_l \text{Int}, \tau_2 \equiv_l \text{Int}, \beta \equiv_l \text{Int}\}}{(e_1 + e_2)^l \Downarrow \beta, C_0 \cup C_1 \cup C_2, \Gamma_1 \cup \Gamma_2} \text{ C-Add}$$

$$\frac{e_1 \Downarrow \tau_1, C_1, \Gamma_1 \qquad e_2 \Downarrow \tau_2, C_2, \Gamma_2 \qquad \beta, \beta_1, \beta_2 \text{ fresh}}{C_0 = \{\tau_1 \equiv_l \tau_2 \to \beta\}}{(e_1\ e_2)^l \Downarrow \beta, C_0 \cup C_1 \cup C_2, \Gamma_1 \cup \Gamma_2} \text{ C-App}$$

$$\frac{e \Downarrow \tau, C, \Gamma \qquad \beta, \beta_x \text{ fresh}}{C_0 = \{\beta_x \equiv_{l_1} \tau \mid \tau \in \Gamma(x)\} \cup \{\beta \equiv_{l_2} \beta_x \to \tau\}}{(\lambda\ x^{l_1} \to e)^{l_2} \Downarrow \beta, C_0 \cup C, \Gamma \setminus x} \text{ C-Abs}$$

$$\frac{\begin{array}{c} e_1 \Downarrow \tau, C, \Gamma \qquad e_2 \Downarrow \tau', C', \Gamma' \qquad \beta, \beta_1, \beta_2 \text{ fresh} \\ \{\tau'_1, ..., \tau'_n\} = \Gamma'(x) \qquad k = max(1, n) \\ \tau_1, C_1, \Gamma_1 \ ...\ \tau_k, C_k, \Gamma_k \text{ fresh variants of } \tau, C, \Gamma \\ \Gamma'' = \Gamma_1 \cup ... \cup \Gamma_k \cup \Gamma' \setminus x \\ C_0 = \{\beta \equiv_{l_2} \tau'\} \cup \{\tau'_1 \equiv_{l_1} \tau_1, ..., \tau'_n \equiv_{l_1} \tau_n\} \\ C'' = C_0 \cup C_1 \cup ... \cup C_k \end{array}}{(\texttt{let } x^{l_1} = e_1 \texttt{ in } e_2)^{l_2} \Downarrow \beta, C \cup C' \cup C'', \Gamma''} \text{ C-Let}$$

$$(\Gamma_1 \cup \Gamma_2)(x) := \Gamma_1(x) \cup \Gamma_2(x)$$

Fig. 6. Constraint-based typing rules for Mini-ML

least one copy of the constraints generated for e_1. Thus, even if there is no use of x in e_2, e_1 has to type check on its own. Duplicating these constraints many times will make a direct implementation of this constraint-generation scheme very inefficient. A more efficient implementation can be achieved by using let-bindings at the constraint level [8, 9].

Figure 7 defines a rewriting function satisfying Proposition 2 for the Mini-ML language. For abstraction and `let`-bindings we have four rules because each construct contains two labels. For abstractions, label l_1 encodes to the monomorphic nature of the binding. The corresponding rewrite rules therefore shadow the binding of x with a `let` and thus remove the constraint. Label l_2 links the type of the context with the type of the body e. By rewriting the body to $(\bot\ e)$ this

$$\mathcal{F}[x^l]_L = \bot \qquad l \notin L$$
$$\mathcal{F}[x^l]_L = x^l \qquad l \in L$$
$$\mathcal{F}[n^l]_L = \bot \qquad l \notin L$$
$$\mathcal{F}[n^l]_L = n^l \qquad l \in L$$
$$\mathcal{F}[(e_1 + e_2)^l]_L = \bot \ \mathcal{F}[e_1]_L \ \mathcal{F}[e_2]_L \qquad l \notin L$$
$$\mathcal{F}[(e_1 + e_2)^l]_L = (\mathcal{F}[e_1]_L + \mathcal{F}[e_2]_L)^l \qquad l \in L$$
$$\mathcal{F}[(e_1 \ e_2)^l]_L = \bot \ \mathcal{F}[e_1]_L \ \mathcal{F}[e_2]_L \qquad l \notin L$$
$$\mathcal{F}[(e_1 \ e_2)^l]_L = (\mathcal{F}[e_1]_L \ \mathcal{F}[e_2]_L)^l \qquad l \in L$$
$$\mathcal{F}[(\lambda x^{l_1} \to e)^{l_2}]_L = (\lambda x \to \texttt{let } x = \bot \texttt{ in } \bot \ \mathcal{F}[e]_L) \quad l_1 \notin L, l_2 \notin L$$
$$\mathcal{F}[(\lambda x^{l_1} \to e)^{l_2}]_L = (\lambda x^{l_1} \to \bot \ \mathcal{F}[e]_L) \qquad l_1 \in L, l_2 \notin L$$
$$\mathcal{F}[(\lambda x^{l_1} \to e)^{l_2}]_L = (\lambda x \to \texttt{let } x = \bot \texttt{ in } \mathcal{F}[e]_L)^{l_2} \quad l_1 \notin L, l_2 \in L$$
$$\mathcal{F}[(\lambda x^{l_1} \to e)^{l_2}]_L = (\lambda x^{l_1} \to \mathcal{F}[e]_L)^{l_2} \qquad l_1 \in L, l_2 \in L$$
$$\mathcal{F}[(\texttt{let } x^{l_1} = e_1 \texttt{ in } e_2)^{l_2}]_L = (\texttt{let } x = \bot \ \mathcal{F}[e_1]_L \texttt{ in } \bot \ \mathcal{F}[e_2]_L) \ l_1 \notin L, l_2 \notin L$$
$$\mathcal{F}[(\texttt{let } x^{l_1} = e_1 \texttt{ in } e_2)^{l_2}]_L = (\texttt{let } x^{l_1} = \mathcal{F}[e_1]_L \texttt{ in } \bot \ \mathcal{F}[e_2]_L) \ l_1 \in L, l_2 \notin L$$
$$\mathcal{F}[(\texttt{let } x^{l_1} = e_1 \texttt{ in } e_2)^{l_2}]_L = (\texttt{let } x = \bot \ \mathcal{F}[e_1]_L \texttt{ in } \mathcal{F}[e_2]_L)^{l_2} \ l_1 \notin L, l_2 \in L$$
$$\mathcal{F}[(\texttt{let } x^{l_1} = e_1 \texttt{ in } e_2)^{l_2}]_L = (\texttt{let } x^{l_1} = \mathcal{F}[e_1]_L \texttt{ in } \mathcal{F}[e_2]_L)^{l_2} \ l_1 \in L, l_2 \in L$$

Fig. 7. Rewritings to filter constraints associated with a label set. Omitted labels on expressions on the right hand side are intended to be filled with fresh labels.

connection is broken thereby disabling the constraint. All constraints introduced by e are of course kept – only constraints labelled with l_2 are removed. The same technique is used for label l_1 of a let expression which links the use sites of x with the type of e_1.

Whether it is possible to find a rewrite function satisfying Proposition 2 depends in part on the syntactic flexibility of the target programming language. We were interested in creating a type error slicer for Haskell. The following section describes the experiences we obtained by doing this.

4   Type Error Slicing for Haskell

We have implemented a source-based type error slicer on top of the Glasgow Haskell Compiler (GHC). Haskell is quite a large language and contains several (main) syntactic categories: expressions, patterns, types, and statements (in do-notation, list comprehensions, pattern guards). Implementing a full type checker for Haskell is a large undertaking and keeping up with and supporting GHC's many extensions is even harder. A source-based type error slicer therefore seems like a very promising approach. Applying our technique to a fully-fledged language like Haskell can thus tell us if the technique is indeed practical.

The main questions we were trying to answer were whether the additional syntactic categories would present problems, and how efficiently type error slices can be generated.

Type error slicing is only useful for type errors that are the result of too many conflicting constraints. Haskell's type system also allows programs to contain

```
 1: function MINIMISE₄(e)
 2:     L ← ∅
 3:     for l ∈ labels(e) do
 4:         e' ← disableₑ(e, l)
 5:         if typecheck(e') = ok then
 6:             L ← L ∪ {l}
 7:         else
 8:             e ← e'                    ▷ Permanently exclude label l.
 9:         end if
10:     end for
11:     return L
12: end function
```

Fig. 8. Minimisation Algorithm. The input e is the expression to minimise, the output is L, the set of labels for a type error slice.

ambiguity errors that cannot be resolved by *removing* constraints by the type checker. For example, in Haskell the expression **show (read ''42'')** does not type check. The problem is that **read** has type **String** $\rightarrow \alpha$ for any type α that is an instance of the **Read** type class. Similarly, **show** has type $\beta \rightarrow$ **String** for any type β that is an instance of the **Show** type class. The typechecker adds the constraint $\alpha \equiv \beta$, but that is still not enough information to decide which instance of **Read** or **Show** to use. This error can only be resolved by adding *more* constraints, for example by adding a type annotation. Because of this limitation, our type error slicer only produces errors for two (very common) types of errors: unification errors ("Cannot match") and occurs check errors.

Our type error slicer is invoked after GHC has type checked the program (and produced errors). The user then selects an error and a slice is produced by performing additional calls to the GHC type checker (via the GHC compiler API). The resulting slice is then highlighted in the editor or presented in text form.

Alternative Slicing Algorithm. We currently do not change the reported error message. This causes some interesting problems. As mentioned in Section 2.2, there are often multiple possible error slices. It is therefore important that the reported slice does in fact correspond to the same error that GHC found. Another problem is that due to the problem of ambiguity the type checker may fail with a different kind of error. For this reason we actually use a different algorithm from those in Section 2 for constructing type error slices.

Figure 8 shows our modified algorithm. The idea is to keep removing constraints (labels) until removing any constraint would make the constraint set solvable. This, by definition, gives us a minimal unsolvable constraint set. Removal of constraints is again simulated using a source-level rewriting function $disable_E$ which can be implemented in terms of $filter_E$:

$$disable_E(e, l) = filter_E(e, labels(e) - \{l\})$$

In our implementation we define $disable_E$ directly, rather than using a definition based on $filter_E$.

This algorithm is more reliable because, in a sense, it works "outside in" by starting with the full constraint set which is known to produce the same error. If removing a constraint changes the error message significantly (e.g., a different error class or a different error location) then we consider the constraint to be *not* relevant to the given error. That is, we treat the type checker result as ok instead of as error. An error message in GHC may contain inferred types and type variables. We consider a error messages that only change slightly (e.g., renamed type variable) to be equal and thus refer to the same error.

Performance Considerations. One disadvantage of the algorithm of Figure 8 is that it is to some extent less efficient than that of Figure 4 because it needs to traverse *all* labels of the input expression. The algorithm of Figure 4 only needs to traverse the labels until the constraints first become unsolvable. No matter which algorithm we choose, however, a few optimisations are required to produce type error slices for realistic programs.

Most top-level bindings are not relevant to a particular error. The body of a top-level function with a type annotation is also initially not relevant to the type error as the function will enter the scope of the erroneous expression with the type specified in the signature. This gives rise to two optimisations:

- We replace the bodies of top-level bindings with type signatures with $\bot$. If such a use of a function f ends up in the error slice then we can expand the search space to the body of f. We only do this if the user requests, this, however. It will only lead to a more helpful slice if the type signature is wrong.
- Top-level bindings without a type signature are handled using two strategies. First, by taking advantage of a dependency analysis performed before type checking by GHC we can remove all bindings not required by the erroneous expression. Second, we can move all bindings required by the erroneous expression into a separate module M and rewrite the original module to import M and remove all other bindings.[5] The type checker now needs to type check only a module containing a single function definition.

With these optimisations constructing type error slices can be produced in acceptable time for interactive use (a few seconds).

Slicing Type Signatures. A second potential issue is whether source-level rewritings can actually be implemented. This essentially depends on the syntax of the language. Haskell has four main syntactic categories: expressions, types, patterns, and statements. Expressions present no problems; they can be handled the same way as in Mini-ML. Statements occurring in do blocks also cause no

---

[5] Because GHC can report multiple type errors some of these bindings may contain type errors. We "fix" these errors using the same strategy that GHC uses which in effect amounts to replacing the body of the erroneous binding by $\bot$.

further issues as they can be translated into expressions. Patterns are a bit trickier because there is no equivalent of ⊥ in the constructor position. Consider a pattern match expression:

$$\textsf{case}\ \ldots\ \textsf{of}\ C\ x\ y \rightarrow \ldots$$

Similarly to function application, the constructor C may impose constraints on the possible types of x and y. We can remove these constraints by rewriting the program to:[6]

$$\textsf{case}\ \ldots\ \textsf{of}\ C\ \_\ \_\ \rightarrow\ \textsf{case}\ \bot\ \textsf{of}\ (x, y) \rightarrow \ldots$$

Type signatures are trickier, this time because there is no type-level equivalent of ⊥ for any component. Type variables bound by ∀ are bound "rigidly", that is such a variable can only be unified with itself. What is needed is instead an existentially bound variable, i.e., a variable that can be unified with anything. Such variables can be simulated using source-level transformations. However, this rewriting is rather complicated.

The basic idea is as follows. Assume we have a function $\textsf{unify} :: \forall \alpha. \alpha \rightarrow \alpha \rightarrow$ () and a binding f. We now want to declare that f has type $\textsf{Either Int Char}$. There are two ways we can do this. Either by using a type signature, or using $\textsf{unify}$:

```
-- Same effect as declaring   f :: Either Int Char
f = (42, 'x')
  where () = unify f (⊥ :: Either Int Char)
```

This method is clearly overly complicated, but we can now introduce a (∀-quantified) type variable and it will behave like an existential (or unification) variable. That is, the following program will type check:

```
f = (42, 'x')
  where () = unify f (⊥ :: c Int Char)
```

For this to work with types involving type variables we also need GHC's "scoped type variables" extension. Because of the complexity involved in constructing such slices we currently do not slice type signatures. Type signatures are either fully part of a type error slice or not at all.

5   Related Work

Many different approaches have been tried to improve error messages for Hindley-Milner based programming languages. For space reasons we cannot list all of them here. Instead we refer the interested reader to Heeren's excellent summary [4] which covers work published up to 2005. Below we list related work using type error slices and work on error messages published after 2005.

---

[6] Recall that "_" in Haskell is the wildcard pattern.

Type error slicing for ML-like languages was first introduced by Haack and Wells [2]. Their work defines the concept of a type error slice and presents an algorithm for constructing slices for Mini-ML. Rahli et al. [9] later extended this work to cover full Standard ML by reimplementing a complete constraint-based type checker.

Stuckey et al. [11] used type error slices to construct type error messages for their Haskell-like language CHAMELEON. CHAMELEON's type checker fully embraced the notion of constraint-based type checking and used it to introduce concepts from the constraint-solving area such as constraint-handling rules (CHR) into its dialect of Haskell. Stuckey et al. also modified the constraint minimisation algorithm to find minimal constraints that imply certain other constraints. They use this algorithm to give hints which source code locations may be annotated to resolve ambiguity errors. Many ideas and concepts of CHAMELEON are explained in more detail in Wazny's Ph.D. thesis [12].

Heeren's type graphs [3] are also quite similar to type error slicing. Heeren uses them to find a maximal consistent subset and uses such to pinpoint the most likely source of an error. A maximal consistent subset can be obtained from a minimal unsolvable subset by removing any constraint.

Our inspiration for a purely source-based approach to type error slicing came from Lerner et al.'s SEMINAL project [6, 5]. This work uses the type checker as a black box to search for a single type error message. SEMINAL searches through possible rewritings and reports the smallest change that could fix an error. The result is a very constructive error message (as it includes a way to fix the error), but if an expression contains multiple independent errors, this approach would return a single error often with a fix suggestion high up in the syntax tree, far removed from the actual errors. To deal with these cases SEMINAL uses a triage mode which may can be computationally expensive. A message produced by SEMINAL, according to a user study, is better than the default (Caml) error message in 13% - 19% of the cases, but also to a worse in 17% of the cases [5].

Both Heeren and SEMINAL produce error messages with a *single* suggestion for a fix. This works great if the suggested fix is indeed the one intended by the user, but it can be very misleading if this is not the case. Type error slices are more objective in that they list a set of possible locations to apply a fix to, but do not guess which one. Suggested fixes could be a complementary feature to type error slices.

6   Future Work

Type error slices are based on the assumption that an error is caused by conflicting constraints. If an error is caused by missing information, then removing constraints obviously cannot fix the error. In Haskell this is the case, e.g., for ambiguity errors (e.g., $\bot \mathbin{>\!\!>\!=} \bot$), or when adding a type class instance would help. Such errors need to be handled differently, although type error slices can still be used to indicate the places where *additional* information (e.g., type annotations) would be helpful [12]. We plan to explore this in a type-checker implementation agnostic way.

Recent implementations of GHC now use a constraint-based type checker [10]. For efficiency reasons, this type checker does not generate constraints in a form that is immediately suitable for type error slicing; for example, a constraint may be tagged with multiple source locations. Source-based type error slicing could be used to implement a hybrid approach. First, the constraint solver returns the source locations of all constraints it used to arrive at an error. A source-based slicer then minimises these constraints to derive an accurate error slice.

References

[1] Damas, L., Milner, R.: Principal type-schemes for functional programs. In: POPL 1982: Proceedings of the 9th ACM SIGPLAN-SIGACT Symposium on Principles of Programming Languages, pp. 207–212. ACM (1982)

[2] Haack, C., Wells, J.B.: Type Error Slicing in Implicitly Typed Higher-Order Languages. In: Degano, P. (ed.) ESOP 2003. LNCS, vol. 2618, pp. 284–301. Springer, Heidelberg (2003)

[3] Hage, J., Heeren, B.: Heuristics for Type Error Discovery and Recovery. In: Horváth, Z., Zsók, V., Butterfield, A. (eds.) IFL 2006. LNCS, vol. 4449, pp. 199–216. Springer, Heidelberg (2007)

[4] Heeren, B.J.: Top Quality Type Error Messages. Ph.D. thesis, Universiteit Utrecht (2005)

[5] Lerner, B.S., Flower, M., Grossman, D., Chambers, C.: Searching for Type-Error Messages. In: Proceedings of the 2007 ACM SIGPLAN Conference on Programming Language Design & Implementation, PLDI 2007, pp. 425–434. ACM (2007)

[6] Lerner, B.S., Grossman, D., Chambers, C.: Seminal: Searching for ML Type-Error Messages. In: Proceedings of the 2006 ACM SIGPLAN Workshop on ML 2006, pp. 63–73. ACM (2006)

[7] Milner, R.: A Theory of Type Polymorphism in Programming. Journal of Computer and System Sciences 17, 348–375 (1978)

[8] Pottier, F., Rémy, D.: The Essence of ML Type Inference. In: Pierce, B. (ed.) Advanced Topics in Types and Programming Languages, ch. 10, The MIT Press (2005)

[9] Rahli, V., Wells, J.B., Kamareddine, F.: Challenges of a type error slicer for the SML language. Tech. rep., Heriot-Watt University, Edinburgh, UK (2009)

[10] Schrijvers, T., Peyton Jones, S., Sulzmann, M., Vytiniotis, D.: Complete and Decidable Type Inference for GADTs. In: Proceedings of the 14th ACM SIGPLAN International Conference on Functional Programming, ICFP 2009, pp. 341–352. ACM (2009)

[11] Stuckey, P.J., Sulzmann, M., Wazny, J.R.: Improving Type Error Diagnosis. In: Proceedings of the 2004 ACM SIGPLAN Workshop on Haskell 2004, pp. 80–91. ACM (2004)

[12] Wazny, J.R.: Type inference and type error diagnosis for Hindley/Milner with extensions. Ph.D. thesis, The University of Melbourne (January 2006)

Subtyping by Folding an Inductive Relation into a Coinductive One

Vladimir Komendantsky

School of Computer Science
University of St Andrews
St Andrews, KY16 9SX, UK
vk10@st-andrews.ac.uk

Abstract. In this paper we show that a prototypical subtype relation that can neither be defined as a least fixed point nor as a greatest fixed point can nevertheless be defined in a dependently typed language with inductive and coinductive types. The definition proceeds alike a fold in functional programming, although a rather unusual one: that is not applied to any starting object. There has been a related construction of bisimilarity in Coq by Nakata and Uustalu recently, however, our case is not concerned with bisimilarity but a weaker notion of similarity that corresponds to recursive subtyping and has it's own interesting problems.

1 Introduction

It is common in practice to have datatypes formed by nested least and greatest fixed points. For example, consider a grammar and parse trees of derivations in that grammar that are allowed to be infinite only below certain non-terminal nodes. Or, a semantic model of a programming language where we distinguish between termination and diverging computation. With dependent types, it is possible to define types such as of grammars or parse trees. However, it is not straightforward to define nested fixed points using implementations of inductive and coinductive type definitions. This is mainly because these type definitions are subject to strong syntactic checks in current implementations of dependently typed languages. A strong restriction is made by type-checkers that require coinductive type definitions to satisfy syntactic soundness constraints simple enough to be machine-checkable. A common form of such syntactic constraints is known simply as *guards*. It is often a programming challenge to avoid guardedness issues and yet define a meaningful coinductive type. There are at least two different methods to encode nested fixed points in type-theoretic proof assistants that are both known as *mixed induction-coinduction*, the first is defined in [8] and the second, in [18]. The former uses a programming construct of suspension computation monad, while the latter seems to rely on a variant of fold function. Suspension monad is efficient and intuitive, however, it has to be supported by the programming language rather than simply implemented on top of it, for which many dependently typed provers would require substantial re-engineering. Not having a sufficient resource for rewriting the implementation of a prover,

R. Peña and R. Page (Eds.): TFP 2011, LNCS 7193, pp. 17–32, 2012.

we choose the second, probably not so efficient but maybe a bit more portable method and apply the fold pattern on top of the language.

The language in question is Coq [19]. It has dependent products of the form $\forall\,(x : A).\,B$ where x is a variable which is bound in B; the case when x is not free in B is denoted $A \to B$ and is a simple, non-dependent type. Also, Coq features inductive and coinductive type definitions. For the sake of presentation, we do not provide listings of Coq code, which would be plain ASCII. Instead, throughout the paper, we use a human-oriented type-theoretic notation, where Type denotes the universe of types (which is predicative), and inductive and coinductive definitions are displayed in natural-deduction style with single and, respectively, double lines.

Contribution. We develop a method for inductive-coinductive encoding for a class of similarity relations exemplified in the paper by recursive subtyping of μ-types. A mechanised version of our proofs formalised in Coq is also presented without going through too many technical details. The method allows to internalise, in type theory, similarity relations that can neither be defined as an inductive relation nor as a coinductive relation alone but as a relation formed by nesting an inductive relation inside a coinductive relation or vice versa.

The motivation for this work is a better understanding of termination issues in subtyping as an exercise in the higher-order programming style with iteration and coiteration schemes [1] with a possibility of extensions to formalisms such as *extended regular expressions* (with variables that approximate behaviour of backreferences), and paving the way for further extensions and provably correct practical applications. The generic approach to terms with variables allows to completely redefine the structure of substitution for extended cases and yet keep the same fundamental approach to subtyping (or, more generally, similarity).

Outline. In Sec. 2 we explain the subtyping relation construction method. In Sec. 3 we define the object language of recursive types formally, using Coq as the meta-language. In Sec. 4 we define subtyping in the meta-language. Sec. 5 contains the statement and a proof of soundness and completeness of our definition of recursive subtyping with respect to containment of finite and infinite trees. The powerful method of monadic substitution is described in Sec. 6. In fact, this technical section contains precise function definitions used in the earlier sections 3 and 4. Related work on subtyping for recursive types and methods for decision procedures is summarised in Sec. 7 where the *alter ego* mixed induction-coinduction method is described as well. Finally, in Sec. 8 we give concluding remarks. The interested reader can also refer to the accompanying Coq script with definitions and proofs constructed for this paper at the author's web page by the URL `http://www.cs.st-andrews.ac.uk/~vk/doc/subfold.v`. The script requires Coq with the Ssreflect [10] extension that are available as packages in common operating systems. The Ssreflect extension does not change the type-theoretic foundation of Coq but rather provides enhancements for the tactic language and handy type definitions and lemmas for bounded numbers and tuples used in our formalisation. Therefore a proof without Ssreflect is also possible by routine redefinition of notions already available.

Notational conventions. In the paper, we use a natural-deduction style notation for inductive and coinductive definitions. For example, the inductive definition of the type Σ of dependent sum is written in two steps. First, we define the *universe*, of which our type is inhabitant (to the right of the semicolon):

$$\Sigma \quad : \quad \forall\, (A : \mathsf{Type}).\ (A \to \mathsf{Type}) \to \mathsf{Type}$$

and second, we define the *constructors* of the type by providing a natural deduction rule for each constructor. In the case of Σ, there is only one constructor, and so, only one rule:

$$\frac{\dfrac{x : A}{p : P\,x}}{\mathsf{exist}\ x\ p : \Sigma\ A\ P}$$

with exist being the name of the constructor. The structure of a rule is a finite tree whose root contains the conclusion of the rule. Let us define the *level* of the root of a rule to be 0. If the level of a given node in a tree is n then the level of the roots of its immediate subtrees is $n + 1$. The constructor exist requires three levels, from 0 to 2, because the variable p defined at level 1 depends on another variable x which should be defined first, at level 2. It is standard [19] to define first the notion a *dependent type* (any type $\forall\, (x : A).\ B$ where x is free in B), and then the notion of an *inductive type*. The latter can be quite involving. As a light-weight alternative, we can define and visualise a *dependent inductive type* starting from our presentation of inductive types in terms of rules as follows:

A *dependent inductive type* is an inductive type with at least one of its constructors defined by a natural deduction rule containing more than 2 levels.

An inductive type corresponds to the least fixed point of the inference operator generated by the set of rules of the type definition. On the other hand, a coinductive type is supposed to approximate the greatest fixed point of the inference operator. At present, the type theory of Coq does not have mixed inductive-coinductive type definitions. Types can be defined either inductively or coinductively, and never both at the same time. This makes it easier to write rules because we do not have a choice of rule notation once it is fixed that a type is inductive or coinductive.

In the case of the definition of the non-dependent inductive relation tylei in Sec. 4, constructor names are omitted for brevity especially because they do not carry information other than that involved in theorem proving only, and we do not refer to these names the paper.

We make an exclusion from the general level pattern by writing lines above roots of 0-level rules, for example,

$$\frac{}{0 : \mathbb{N}}$$

to indicate whether these rules are inductive or coinductive, because any 0-level rule, even though it defines a *value*, is typechecked differently by Coq depending on whether it appears in an inductive or coinductive definition.

2   The Fold Pattern

Here is the polymorphic type of the familiar list-based left fold function:

$$\mathsf{foldl} : \forall\ (S\ T : \mathsf{Type})\ (f : T \to S \to T)\ (a : T)\ (l : \mathsf{list}\ S).\ T$$

(On a fundamental approach to fold, the reader is advised to refer to [4].) The result of iterative computation of an appropriately typed function f on values from the list l starting from a given value a is aggregated on the left.

Let us now drop the requirement that the fold starts from some object. This removes the first argument of the function f altogether. The fold function that we are going to construct has two dependent arguments: a function f and a collection l (which is not quite a list) of objects of S. This description fits the definition of the following operator $\leq_{\mathrm{intro}}$ generating a coinductive relation $\leq$:

$$\frac{f : (\forall\ E\ F.\ R\ E\ F \to E \leq F) \qquad l : E \leq_R F}{\leq_{\mathrm{intro}}\ R\ E\ F\ f\ l : E \leq F}$$

We can see that the arguments R, E and F can be inferred from the types of f and l. The constructor $\leq_{\mathrm{intro}}$ has two dependent arguments, f and l, and yields an object (in fact, a proof) inhabiting a particular case of relation. The function f can indeed be seen as a mapping of a proof that from an object E we can access another object F by the relation R to a corresponding proof that from E we can also reach F by $\leq$. In other words, f is an inclusion of R into $\leq$. The interpretation of the argument l is a bit more involved. Think of $\leq_R$ as a finite relation encapsulating another, infinite one in such a way that an infinite number of steps is possible only finitely. The latter sounds rather speculative, however, the intuition is that $E \leq_R F$ is alike a type of finite list of certain abstract, possibly infinite objects. Moreover, proofs of $E \leq_R F$ can be perceived as paths from E to F. So, the function $\leq_{\mathrm{intro}}\ R\ E\ F\ f$ collapses the finite list l of possibly infinite paths to a certain infinite coinductively defined object. Thanks to the premises of $\leq_{\mathrm{intro}}$ we are able to compare elements of pairs in the domain of $\leq$ in a finite number of steps possibly infinitely.

It is worth noting that having a coinductive type definition such as that of $\leq$ is nothing close to requiring an infinite amount of memory for objects of that type. The shape of such an object is a regular tree which may have an infinite unfolding but in itself is a finitely presented entity.

3   Recursive Types

Below in this section we give a proper inductive definition of recursive types, our object language, in Coq as the the meta-language. However, first recall a *traditional* definition of the set of recursive types that uses a grammar [5,3]:

$$E, F ::= \bot \mid \top \mid X \mid E \rightarrow F \mid \mu X.\ E \rightarrow F$$

where X is a symbolic variable taken from a set of variables. The least fixed point operator μ binds free occurrences of the variable X in $E \rightarrow F$. This definition has neither products nor sums that are needed for practical programming. However, we do not consider product or sum types in this schematic implementation because their treatment follows a similar pattern compared to $\rightarrow$, see, e.g., [3]. Moreover, we choose to replace named variables in the definition by nameless de Brujin variables, which yields an equivalent and yet more tangible construction.

A nameless variable is essentially a number m with an upper bound n where m represents the depth of the variable under binders in a term with at most n free variables. We will now define an appropriate notion of bounded number. First, take the usual inductive definition of the type of (unary) natural number:

$$\mathbb{N} : \mathsf{Type}$$

$$\frac{}{0 : \mathbb{N}} \qquad \frac{n : \mathbb{N}}{S\ n : \mathbb{N}}$$

Further on in the paper, $1 + n$ is assumed to be convertible to $S\ n$. Natural numbers enjoy a decidable less-than relation. It can be defined via the usual truncated subtraction and decidable equality, that is, a relation with values true or false of type bool. Let us recall the equality relation on natural numbers as follows:

$$\_ == \_\quad :\quad \mathbb{N} \rightarrow \mathbb{N} \rightarrow \mathsf{bool}$$
$$0 == 0 \quad = \quad \mathsf{true}$$
$$S\ m == S\ n \quad = \quad m == n$$
$$0 == S\ n \quad = \quad \mathsf{false}$$
$$S\ m == 0 \quad = \quad \mathsf{false}$$

The less-then relation is then a function

$$m < n \quad = \quad S\ m - n == 0$$

The type of bounded number can be defined now:

$$\mathcal{I} : \mathbb{N} \rightarrow \mathsf{Type}$$

$$\frac{\begin{array}{c} m : \mathbb{N} \\ \hline p : m < n \end{array}}{\mathsf{num}\ n\ m\ p : \mathcal{I}_n}$$

So, we have a dependent inductive type here, with the type of the variable p depending on the value m. The type $\mathcal{I}_n$ is a special dependent pair type, simpler than Σ from the Introduction, specified on the concrete boolean predicate $\lambda\ m.\ m < n$. The proof of $m < n$ is encoded as a boolean value. This has two outcomes. From one side, since it is easier to reason by cases on boolean-valued relations than on more general relations with values in Type, this definition of bounded number greatly facilitates proof by cases. On the other hand, compared to the algebraic type of finite number employed, for example, in the construction of [8], the type $\mathcal{I}_n$ is a subtype of $\mathbb{N}$ by the coercion

$$\mathsf{N\_of\_num}\ (n : \mathbb{N})\ (i : \mathcal{I}_n)\quad =\quad \textbf{let num}\ m\ \_ = i$$
$$\textbf{in}\ m$$

This permits application of lemmas for $\mathbb{N}$ to statements about $\mathcal{I}_n$ without recursive conversion of finite numbers to natural numbers. The question of automation of insertion of the coercion $\mathsf{N\_of\_nat}$ is inessential for the constructions in the paper.

Now we can give our working definition of *recursive types* by induction as follows:

$$\mathsf{ty} : \mathbb{N} \to \mathsf{Type}$$

$$\frac{}{\bot : \mathsf{ty}\ n} \qquad \frac{}{\top : \mathsf{ty}\ n} \qquad \frac{i : \mathcal{I}_n}{X_i : \mathsf{ty}\ n} \qquad \frac{E : \mathsf{ty}\ n \qquad F : \mathsf{ty}\ n}{E {\to} F : \mathsf{ty}\ n}$$

$$\frac{E : \mathsf{ty}\ (1+n) \qquad F : \mathsf{ty}\ (1+n)}{\mu\ E {\to} F : \mathsf{ty}\ n}$$

where the constructors are, respectively, the empty type $\bot$, the unit type $\top$, the variable constructor X (indeed, we later use it without an index), the function type constructor $\to$ and the least fixed point arrow type constructor $\mu\ \_{\to}\_$.

Recursive types have a correspondence with non-wellfounded (finite or infinite) trees with the following definition by coinduction:

$$\mathsf{tree} : \mathbb{N} \to \mathsf{Type}$$

$$\frac{}{\bot^\infty : \mathsf{tree}\ n} \qquad \frac{}{\top^\infty : \mathsf{tree}\ n} \qquad \frac{i : \mathcal{I}_n}{X_i^\infty : \mathsf{tree}\ n} \qquad \frac{t : \mathsf{tree}\ n \qquad t : \mathsf{tree}\ n}{t {\to}^\infty u : \mathsf{tree}\ n}$$

Intuitively, trees are views of μ-types unfolded *ad infinitum*. We denote the tree corresponding to a type E by $[\![E]\!]$. It is interesting to see now what is the exact connection of types with trees. We give a definition that uses a piece of notation from later on in this paper. We define $[\![\_]\!]$ corecursively using the function sbst (see the definition in Sec. 6) of capture avoiding substitution of the second argument for all occurrences of variable 0 in the first argument as follows:

$$
\begin{array}{lcl}
[\![\bot]\!] & = & \bot^\infty \\
[\![\top]\!] & = & \top^\infty \\
[\![X_i]\!] & = & X_i^\infty \\
[\![E {\to} F]\!] & = & [\![E]\!] \to^\infty [\![F]\!] \\
[\![\mu\ E {\to} F]\!] & = & [\![\mathsf{sbst}\ E\ (\mu\ E {\to} F)]\!] \to^\infty [\![\mathsf{sbst}\ F\ (\mu\ E {\to} F)]\!]
\end{array}
$$

The straightforward subtree relation $\mathsf{tle}\ n$ on $\mathsf{tree}\ n$ is denoted by $\leq^\infty$ (omitting the implicit argument n):

$$\mathsf{tle}\ n : \mathsf{tree}\ n \to \mathsf{tree}\ n \to \mathsf{Type}$$

$$\frac{}{\bot^\infty \leq^\infty t} \qquad \frac{}{t \leq^\infty \top^\infty} \qquad \frac{i : \mathcal{I}_n}{X_i^\infty \leq^\infty X_i^\infty} \qquad \frac{u_1 \leq^\infty t_1 \qquad t_2 \leq^\infty u_2}{(t_1 {\twoheadrightarrow}^\infty t_2) \leq^\infty (u_1 {\twoheadrightarrow}^\infty u_2)}$$

Thus, two recursive types are in the subtype relation when their potentially infinite unfoldings are in the subtree relation. Traditionally, subtyping theorems are stated in terms of inductive limits of sequences of approximations of unfoldings of recursive types (e.g., in [3]). Instead of using explicit induction in that way, we rather rely on dependent types of the CIC which allow to define a powerful monadic structure encapsulating unfolding *ad infinitum*. The point here, similar to an observation made by Amadio and Cardelli in [3], is that unfoldings of recursive types are *regular* trees, which we treat using a mix of induction and coinduction.

4   Definition of Recursive Subtyping

We define the weak similarity relation tyle $n \subseteq$ ty $n \times$ ty n by folding the inductive part of the definition into the coinductive one. Our technique is an illustration of a generic method for folding one relation into another. For the purpose of having notational correspondence to the Coq proofs, we decide to keep both the Coq name for a relation and introduce a mnemonic denotation for it at the same time for readability. In what follows, $\leq_R$ denotes tylei n R, and $\leq$ denotes tyle n for an implicit parameter n.

First, we define the inductive part tylei n R of the subtyping relation (denoting tylei n R E F by $E \leq_R F$, suppressing the implicit argument n):

$$\text{tylei} : \forall\, n.\ (\text{ty } n \to \text{ty } n \to \text{Type}) \to \text{ty } n \to \text{ty } n \to \text{Type}$$

$$\frac{}{\bot \leq_R E} \qquad \frac{}{E \leq_R \top} \qquad \frac{R\ E\ F \qquad R\ G\ H}{F{\twoheadrightarrow}G \leq_R E{\twoheadrightarrow}H} \qquad \frac{}{\mu\ E{\twoheadrightarrow}F \leq_R \text{unfld } E\ F}$$

$$\frac{}{\text{unfld } E\ F \leq_R \mu\ E{\twoheadrightarrow}F} \qquad \frac{}{E \leq_R E} \qquad \frac{E \leq_R F \qquad F \leq_R G}{E \leq_R G}$$

where unfld is the operation that unfolds a μ-redex by substituting the term $\mu\ E{\twoheadrightarrow}F$ for the variable 0 in the term $E{\twoheadrightarrow}F$. This operation is defined in Sec. 6. Having the rules for reflexivity and transitivity in the inductive part of the subtype relation is essential for this construction. Indeed, by having these rules explicitly, we are able to compare elements of pairs in the domain of the subtype relation in a *finite* number of steps possibly *infinitely*. Leaving transitivity out of the definition would collapse finite and infinite transitivity chains to infinite ones only.

Next step is to fold the inductive relation and produce a weak similarity. This is done by the single-constructor coinductive type:

$$\text{tyle } n : \text{ty } n \to \text{ty } n \to \text{Type}$$

We denote tyle n E F by $E \leq F$. In the rule below, we keep arguments n, R, E, F of the constructor despite that we can infer these from the types of other parameters because, in the proofs, we have to make partial applications of the constructor to arguments:

$$r : \text{reflexive } R \qquad t : \text{transitive } R \qquad f : \forall\, E\, F.\ R\, E\, F \to E \leq F \qquad l : E \leq_R F$$
$$\overline{} \atop \leq_{\text{intro}} n\ R\, r\, t\, E\, F\, f\, l : E \leq F$$

The only introduction rule for $\leq$ has four hypotheses, namely, that R is reflexive, transitive and a subrelation of $\leq$, and that F is $\leq_R$-accessible from E in finitely many steps (since $\leq_R$ is an inductive relation).

5 Soundness and Completeness

Below we give a proof outline for the Main Theorem. For particular details, the reader can refer to the accompanying script.

Main Theorem (Soundness and completeness)

$$\forall\, (n : \mathbb{N})\ (E\, F : \text{ty } n).\ E \leq F \leftrightarrow [\![E]\!] \leq^{\infty} [\![F]\!]$$

Proof. *"Only if" (completeness).* Suppose that the following coinductive hypothesis H holds:

$$\forall\, (n : \mathbb{N})\ (E\, F : \text{ty } n).\ [\![E]\!] \leq^{\infty} [\![F]\!] \to E \leq F$$

Let us first define the following *coinduction principle P*:

$$\leq_{\text{intro}}\ n\ Q\ Q_{\text{refl}}\ Q_{\text{trans}}$$

where Q is the relation $\lambda\, E\, F : \text{ty } n.\ [\![E]\!] \leq^{\infty} [\![F]\!]$ (note that we abstract over types here, not trees), and Q_{refl} and Q_{trans} are respectively a reflexivity lemma and a transitivity lemma (each proved by straightforward coinduction). The coinduction principle P allows us to prove statements of the kind

$$\forall\, E\, F : \text{ty } n.\ \Big(\forall\, E\, F : \text{ty } n.\ [\![E]\!] \leq^{\infty} [\![F]\!] \to E \leq F\Big) \to E \leq_Q F \to E \leq F$$

We reason by simple case analysis on $[\![E]\!]$. The case $\perp^{\infty}$ is proved by an application of P to E, F, H and the constructor for $\perp$. Most other cases are proved by case analysis on F and either a similar argument involving the coinductive principle P applied to a single constructor or proof by contradiction. The three remaining cases are

1. $[\![E_1 \to E_2]\!] \leq^{\infty} [\![\mu\ F_1 \twoheadrightarrow F_2]\!] \to (E_1 \to E_2) \leq (\mu\ F_1 \twoheadrightarrow F_2)$
2. $[\![\mu\ E_1 \twoheadrightarrow E_2]\!] \leq^{\infty} [\![F_1 \to F_2]\!] \to (\mu\ E_1 \twoheadrightarrow E_2) \leq (F_1 \to F_2)$
3. $[\![\mu\ E_1 \twoheadrightarrow E_2]\!] \leq^{\infty} [\![\mu\ F_1 \twoheadrightarrow F_2]\!] \to (\mu\ E_1 \twoheadrightarrow E_2) \leq (\mu\ F_1 \twoheadrightarrow F_2)$

These are proved by the application of the coinduction principle to E, F, H and the transitivity constructor of $\leq_Q$ with the explicitly unfolded μ-term.

"If" (soundness). We start by admitting the coinductive hypothesis H:

$$\forall\, (n : \mathbb{N})\ (E\, F : \text{ty } n).\ E \leq F \to [\![E]\!] \leq^{\infty} [\![F]\!]$$

We eliminate the assumption $E \leq F$ by inverse application of the rule $\leq_{\text{intro}}$. Thus we obtain a relation R on trees and 4 respective premises. By inductive elimination of the premiss $E \leq_R F$ we arrive at the following 4 cases:

1. $E = \bot$;
2. $F = \top$;
3. there exist E_1, E_2, F_1 and F_2 such that $E = E_1 \to E_2$, $F = F_1 \to F_2$, $R\ F_1\ E_1$ and $R\ E_2\ F_2$;
4. there exists E_1 such that $E_1 = E = F$.

This is proved by application of the rules of $\leq_R$ and the premises of $\leq_{\text{intro}}$ saying that R is reflexive and transitive. (Thus we solve the guardedness issue that would have arisen should we attempt to use reflexivity and transitivity of the coinductive relation $\leq^\infty$ instead of these two premises.) Hence we have four possibilities when $E \leq^\infty F$ can hold. The first two cases are proved by the $\bot$ and $\top$ constructors of $\leq^\infty$. The third case is proved by applying the $\to$ constructor, the hypothesis H, and the premiss saying that R is a subrelation of $\leq$. The last case is proved by reflexivity of $\leq^\infty$ (whose proof coinsides with the proof of Q_{refl} from the completeness part). $\qquad\square$

6   Monadic Substitution

Definitions in this technical section have implicit arguments being systematically omitted for conciseness. We implemented in Coq a generic notion of symbolic substitution introduced in [2] for untyped lambda terms. It is based on the notion of *universe of types*, that is, a function space $A \to$ Type where A can be any given type. The type A is said to *index* the type Type. For effective indexing, the index type should be countable, and for that, it suffices to consider the type $\mathbb{N}$ of natural numbers. The terminology and basic notation are similar to those of McBride [15], although we do not use the notion of a context of types of in the definition of the universe, which makes it more generic. We call the resulting universe *stuff* (referring to its abstract character):

$$\text{stuff : Type}$$

$$\text{stuff} = \mathbb{N} \to \text{Type}$$

For a given n, the intended meaning of stuff n is *stuff with n variables*. The intention is to have a general category of objects such as formulas with n free variables. Yet objects of this category are not endowed with structure making it applicable to an as wide variety of situations as possible.

In the foundation of the method is a type of monadic structure called *kit*. Here we modify the version of [15] by removing the notion of a context of types:

$$\text{kit : stuff} \to \text{stuff} \to \text{Type}$$

$$\dfrac{var : \forall\, n.\ \mathcal{I}_n \to U\ n \qquad lift : \forall\, n.\ U\ n \to T\ n \qquad wk : \forall\, n.\ U\ n \to U\ (1 + n)}{\text{Kit}\ var\ lift\ wk : \text{kit}\ U\ T}$$

A *substitution* of type sub T m n is such that it applies to stuff with at most m variables and yields stuff with at most n variables. Hence a substitution is essentially an m-tuple of T n, that is,

$$\mathsf{sub} : \mathsf{stuff} \to \mathbb{N} \to \mathbb{N} \to \mathsf{Type}$$

$$\mathsf{sub}\ T\ m\ n = m\text{-}\mathsf{tuple}\ (T\ n)$$

Here are basic functions on substitutions, with their types. We need a function to lift a substitution to the next order. This is implemented in the function lift_sub of type

$$\forall\ (T\ U : \mathsf{stuff})\ (K : \mathsf{kit}\ T\ U)\ m\ n.\ \mathsf{sub}\ T\ m\ n \to \mathsf{sub}\ T\ (1+m)\ (1+n)$$

whose definition is by case analysis on K.

Next function to consider is the identity substitution id_sub:

$$\mathsf{id\_sub} : \forall\ (T\ U : \mathsf{stuff})\ (K : \mathsf{kit}\ T\ U)\ n.\ \mathsf{sub}\ T\ n\ n$$

It is defined by induction on n, applying lift_sub on the inductive step.

We define a substitution function sub_0 that applies to stuff T with $1+n$ variables, substitutes a given term E for the variable 0, and returns stuff T with n free variables:

$$\mathsf{sub}_0 : \forall\ (T\ U : \mathsf{stuff})\ (K : \mathsf{kit}\ T\ U)\ n\ (E : T\ n).\ \mathsf{sub}\ T\ (1+n)\ n$$

and the definition is simply by consing E with id_sub K n.

The weakening function

$$\mathsf{wkn\_sub} : \forall\ m\ n\ T\ U\ (K : \mathsf{kit}\ T\ U).\ \mathsf{sub}\ T\ n\ (m+n)$$

is defined by induction on m, applying id_sub on the inductive basis, and tuple mapping on the inductive step.

Substitutions can be easily endowed with structure of composition because they take stuff and return stuff. In order to establish compositionality on substitutions, we define applicative structure on substitutions which is called subApp:

$$\mathsf{subApp} : \mathsf{stuff} \to \mathsf{Type}$$

$$\frac{var : \forall\ n.\ \mathcal{I}_n \to T\ n \qquad app : \forall\ U\ m\ n.\ \mathsf{kit}\ U\ T \to T\ m \to \mathsf{sub}\ U\ m\ n \to T\ n}{\mathsf{SubApp}\ var\ app : \mathsf{subApp}\ T}$$

Our next goal is to define a concrete kit on stuff T given an applicative structure of substitutions on T. This is done in stuffKit below. We need three components of a kit: variables, lifting and weakening. For variables, we can simply reuse those of the applicative structure. Lifting is simply the identity here. Only weakening requires further definitions for substitution of variables.

Define a kit for variables as follows:

$$\mathsf{varKit} : \forall\ (T : \mathsf{stuff}).\ (\forall\ n.\ \mathcal{I}_n \to T\ n) \to \mathsf{kit}\ \mathcal{I}\ T$$

$$\text{varKit } vr = \text{Kit } (\lambda\, n.\ \text{id } \mathcal{I}_n)\ vr\ (\text{rshift } 1)$$

where rshift 1 is the operation of increment of the upper bound by 1. Substitution of variables is defined below:

$$\text{varSub} : \forall\, m\ n\ (T : \text{stuff}).\ \text{subApp } T \to T\ m \to \text{sub } \mathcal{I}\ m\ n \to T\ n$$

$$\text{varSub } a = \textbf{let } \text{SubApp } vr\ ap = a \textbf{ in } ap\ \mathcal{I}\ m\ n\ (\text{varKit } vr)$$

The required kit on stuff T has the following type:

$$\text{stuffKit} : \forall\, (T : \text{stuff}).\ \text{subApp } T \to \text{kit } T\ T$$

Its variables and lifting are as defined above. Weakening is derived from substitution of variables.

$$\text{stuffKit } a \quad = \quad \textbf{let } \text{SubApp } vr\ \_ = a \textbf{ in}$$
$$\text{Kit } vr\ (\lambda\, \_.\ \text{id})\ (\lambda\, n\ E.\ (\text{varSub } a)\ E\ (\text{wkn\_sub } 1\ n\ (\text{varKit } vr)))$$

Finally, for the generic applicative structure, the canonical weakening function wkstuff from stuff with n variables to stuff with $1 + n$ variables is defined as follows:

$$\text{wkstuff} : \forall\, T\ (K : \text{kit } T\ T)\ (a : \text{subAppT})\ n.\ \text{sub } T\ n\ (1+n) \to T\ n \to T\ (1+n)$$

$$\text{wkstuff } K\ a\ s \quad = \quad \textbf{let } \text{SubApp } \_\ ap = a \textbf{ in}$$
$$\lambda\, E.\ (ap\ T\ n\ (1+n)\ K)\ E\ s$$

A straightforward substitution strategy is implemented by the function trav below that traverses a term E and applies a given substitution s. Note that, since s is a tuple, s_i is a consistent notation for the i-th element of s.

trav	:	$\forall\, T\ m\ n.\ \text{kit } T\ \text{ty} \to \text{ty } m \to \text{sub } T\ m\ n \to \text{ty } n$
trav $K\ \bot\ s$	=	$\bot$
trav $K\ \top\ s$	=	$\top$
trav $K\ X_i\ s$	=	$\textbf{let } \text{Kit } \_\ li\ \_ = K \textbf{ in } li\ \_\ s_i$
trav $K\ (F{\to}G)\ s$	=	$(\text{trav } K\ F\ s){\to}(\text{trav } K\ G\ s)$
trav $K\ (\mu\ F{\to}G)\ s$	=	$\mu\ (\text{trav } K\ F\ (\text{lift\_sub } K\ s)){\to}(\text{trav } K\ G\ (\text{lift\_sub } K\ s))$

The traverse function allows to define an instance of the applicative structure on ty that we call tyApp, in Figure 1. In the definition of tyApp, we denoted the constructor of nameless variables by X. This is a consistent notation since we defined, in Sec. 3, that X_i is of type ty n for a given natural number n and a bounded number i of type $\mathcal{I}_n$. So, X is a function of type $\forall\, n.\ \mathcal{I}_n \to \text{ty } n$. The monadic structure on ty can now be defined as a stuff kit specified on type ty. The function subty$_0$ substitutes a given μ-type E for the 0-th variable. It is defined using the generic substitution sub$_0$ we defined above. Weakening is specialised on ty by the function wkty. The function sbst is capture-avoiding substitution of

$$
\begin{array}{lll}
\text{tyApp} & : & \text{subApp ty} \\
\text{tyApp} & = & \text{SubApp } X \text{ trav} \\
\text{tyKit} & : & \text{kit ty ty} \\
\text{tyKit} & = & \text{stuffKit tyApp} \\
\text{subty}_0 & : & \forall\, n\ (E : \text{ty } n).\ \text{sub ty } (1+n)\ n \\
\text{subty}_0 & = & \text{sub}_0 \text{ tyKit} \\
\text{wkty} & : & \forall\, n.\ \text{sub ty } n\ (1+n) \to \text{ty } n \to \text{ty } (1+n) \\
\text{wkty} & = & \text{wkstuff tyKit tyApp} \\
\text{subKit} & : & \text{kit ty ty} \\
\text{subKit} & = & \text{Kit } X\ (\lambda\, n.\ \text{id (ty } n))\ (\lambda\, n.\ \text{wkty (wk\_sub } n \text{ tyKit)}) \\
\text{sbst} & : & \forall\, n.\ \text{ty } (1+n) \to \text{ty } n \to \text{ty } n \\
\text{sbst } E\ F & = & \text{trav subKit } E\ (\text{subty}_0\ F) \\
\text{unfld} & : & \forall\, n.\ \text{ty } (1+n) \to \text{ty } (1+n) \to \text{ty } n \\
\text{unfld } E\ F & = & \text{sbst } (E{\to}F)\ (\mu\ E{\to}F)
\end{array}
$$

Fig. 1. The structure of substitution on ty

a given term F for all occurrences of the 0-th variable of a term E. At last, unfld unfolds a μ-redex.

Unlike monadic presentations, named presentations of terms *with holes* can be cumbersome and have limited application. Among the closest nameless but not monadic presentations are Capretta's polynomial expressions with metavariables [6]. They require proving equality of substitutions in a context. Monadic presentations of terms allow to have substitutions as part of the construction and also allow for free to have a notion of a term with a hole. For example, it can be seen that Capretta's tree expressions with metavariables have the same expressive power as monadic substitutions on polynomial trees.

7   Related Work

In their seminal paper [3], Amadio and Cardelli extended the partial order on finite types to possibly infinite recursive types and showed that it is sound and complete with respect to a certain partial order on finite and infinite trees. The partial order on trees was defined by an infinite sequence of finite approximations created by truncating trees at a finite depth. Two trees were defined to be in subtree relation if and only if the partial order holds between their finite approximations at all finite depths. The time complexity of this subtyping algorithm is exponential.

The authors of [3] stated that a relation of recursive subtyping to decidable problems on automata was not known. More exactly, the word used was "well-known", which may create some space for speculation. However, shortly after, such connection was found. An efficient, $O(n^2)$-time subtyping algorithm for recursive types was defined in [14] using regular term semantics. The algorithm works by reduction of a subtyping problem to the emptiness problem of a special automaton called *term automaton*. It was shown there that the automaton-theoretic approach can be productively applied to subtyping.

It was spelt out by the authors of [5] that the interpretation of subtyping and equality in terms of, respectively, simulation and bisimulation leads to an inference system with coinductively motivated fixpoint rules for the term language of coercions between μ-types. This coinductive view also has a straightforward application to regular languages [11,12] given that containment (in other words, subtyping) and equivalence there correspond to simulation and bisimulation on finite automata.

From the point of view of higher-order programming, nested type definitions can be seen as instances of iteration or coiteration schemes. This view was developed in [1]. The definition of tyle is related to type definitions by *Mendler coiteration for higher ranks*, a relationship that can be investigated further in future work. In this paper, the connection is not made explicit as it would eventually require an implementation of generalised iteration and coiteration schemes in the proof assistant. In comparison, the aim of our work is to use a minimalist and standard set of tools allowing to state the soundness and completeness result without going through a more general theory.

The soundness and completeness result allows us to tell that our definition of syntactic subtyping is correct with respect to the tree semantics. In a proof assistant this is only a change in representation. Since proof search is undecidable on the universe of types in general, it is impractical, and likely impossible, to use either of the representations for efficient proof search in a prover. Instead, we can use the approach which is known as the *two-level approach* [6] or *small-scale reflection* [10].

We can implement a decision procedure for a class of propositional goals $G \in$ Prop by

1. first defining a type of *codes* goal : Type and an interpretation function $\llbracket \_ \rrbracket$: goal $\to$ Prop surjective on G,
2. and then defining a decision algorithm dec : goal $\to$ bool which can be proved sound and complete with respect to the propositional interpretation, that is,

$$\forall g : \text{goal. dec } g = \text{true} \leftrightarrow \llbracket g \rrbracket$$

As a result, to prove $P \in G$, it is sufficient to compute dec g, where g is the code for P.

Alternatively, soundness and completeness of the decision algorithms is an object of inductive type decidable : Prop $\to$ bool $\to$ Type defined by

$$\frac{p : P}{\text{dT } p \ : \ \text{decidable } P \text{ true}} \qquad \frac{p : \neg P}{\text{dF } p \ : \ \text{decidable } P \text{ false}}$$

Thus decidable P b denotes the fact that provability of P is decidable by the algorithm b. As a side note, the above inductive type can be extended to account for many-valued decision algorithms, for example, three-valued ones, where one of the values stands for the undefined result.

Common decision procedures may be based on various notions of derivative. For example, decision procedures for regular expression containment may be based on deterministic [11] or non-deterministic derivatives [12]. Both kinds of derivative can be implemented in the type theory of Coq [17,13].

Alternative approach to subtyping: suspension monad. A practical approach to nested induction-coinduction is presented in Agda [7]. The authors provide, at the language level, a type function ∞ : Type $\to$ Type which marks a given type as being coinductive. This type function has an interpretation as a suspension type constructor that can be used in functional languages with eager evaluation to model laziness. This interpretation is faithful since ∞ is supplied with delay and force operators $\sharp : \forall A.\ A \to \infty A$ and $\flat : \forall A.\ \infty A \to A$ respectively.

One of the immediate advantages of having the suspension monad supported by the language is efficiency. This has also a positive effect on succinctness of function definitions by recursion-corecursion since the implementation includes an improved termination checker capable of inferring termination guarantees for such function definitions. This leaves behind the more syntactically oriented termination checker of Coq.

On the other hand, without support of suspension monad in Coq, we cannot follow this approach there. This is why it is very interesting to find ways to use type theory effectively without re-engineering the implementation. Also, note that currently the suspension monad does not allow to express directly type definitions which have an outer least fixed point and an inner greatest fixed point because of the way the termination checker of Agda works.

8   Conclusions

We showed how a rather simple fold encoding pattern can be used to define a prototypical subtyping relation: μ-types without products or sums. Our study is closely related to the work of Altenkirch and Danielsson [8] who define subtyping using a suspension computation monad inspired by semantics of programming languages. The method with the suspension monad requires support in the way of dedicated programming language primitives. However, it is not always practically possible for the user of a prover or dependently typed language to amend the implementation. Here, we follow a method that allows to encode infinitary subtyping by folding an inductive relation into a coinductive one, which can be done using standard type-theoretic means. As with the suspension monad method, proving soundness corresponds to the most technically advanced part of work. The soundness argument requires to make the introduction rule for the coinductive wrapper relation parametric not only in an abstract relation R but also in *properties of R*.

It is worth noting that the presented approach of weak similarity is a natural solution to problems arising from declaring closure properties such as transitivity in coinductive relations that were discussed in [9]. Indeed, with our definitions, infinite transitivity chains do not arise.

The paper [16] discusses an issue with the current implementation of most dependently typed systems that does not easily allow to encode bisimilarity into substitutive equality for reasoning about corecursive functions. This can be relevant to mixing induction and coinduction since mixing is essentially a fold method which, in order to work under case analysis (that is, unfolding), has to contain a reference to an abstract unfolded relation. With current implementations of dependent elimination, restoring the concrete relation behind this abstract one corresponds to a major part of work. Meanwhile, if we had elimination being able to unfold this relation automatically, this would be a clear time-saving benefit.

We can see that the traverse function trav defined in the paper is a prototype substitution strategy in the sense that, if we define substitution monads for other term languages and subtype relations of interest, the traverse function may carry some non-trivial operational meaning such as that of various matching strategies for (possibly extended) regular expressions. One of such interesting languages is the language of regular types [15], that is, recursive types with product and sum datatype constructors, which can be viewed as generalising regular expressions with non-terminating left-recursion.

Acknowledgements. I would like to thank Keiko Nakata and Niels Anders Danielsson for their help and advice regarding theorem proving and provers, and my TFP referees for their valuable remarks. The research is supported by the research fellowship EU FP7 Marie Curie IEF 253162 'SImPL'.

References

1. Abel, A., Matthes, R., Uustalu, T.: Iteration and coiteration schemes for higher-order and nested datatypes. Theoretical Computer Science 333(1-2), 3–66 (2005)
2. Altenkirch, T., Reus, B.: Monadic Presentations of Lambda Terms Using Generalized Inductive Types. In: Flum, J., Rodríguez-Artalejo, M. (eds.) CSL 1999. LNCS, vol. 1683, pp. 453–468. Springer, Heidelberg (1999)
3. Amadio, R.M., Cardelli, L.: Subtyping recursive types. ACM Transactions on Programming Languages and Systems 15(4), 575–631 (1993)
4. Bird, R., de Moor, O.: Algebra of programming. Prentice-Hall, Inc., Upper Saddle River (1997)
5. Brandt, M., Henglein, F.: Coinductive Axiomatization of Recursive Type Equality and Subtyping. In: de Groote, P., Hindley, J.R. (eds.) TLCA 1997. LNCS, vol. 1210, pp. 63–81. Springer, Heidelberg (1997)
6. Capretta, V.: Certifying the Fast Fourier Transform with Coq. In: Boulton, R.J., Jackson, P.B. (eds.) TPHOLs 2001. LNCS, vol. 2152, pp. 154–168. Springer, Heidelberg (2001)
7. Danielsson, N.A., Altenkirch, T.: Mixing induction and coinduction, Draft (2009)
8. Danielsson, N.A., Altenkirch, T.: Subtyping, Declaratively. In: Bolduc, C., Desharnais, J., Ktari, B. (eds.) MPC 2010. LNCS, vol. 6120, pp. 100–118. Springer, Heidelberg (2010)

9. Gapeyev, V., Levin, M.Y., Pierce, B.: Recursive subtyping revealed. J. Fun. Prog. 12(6), 511–548 (2002)
10. Gonthier, G., Mahboubi, A., Tassi, E.: A Small Scale Reflection Extension for the Coq system. Research Report RR-6455, INRIA (2011)
11. Henglein, F., Nielsen, L.: Declarative coinductive axiomatization of regular expression containment and its computational interpretation (preliminary version). Technical Report 612, Department of Computer Science, University of Copenhagen (DIKU) (February 2010)
12. Komendantsky, V.: Computable partial derivatives of regular expressions, Draft. Contributed proofs (2011), http://www.cs.standrews.ac.uk/~vk/doc/mir.v
13. Komendantsky, V.: Regular expression containment as a proof search problem. In: Lengrand, S. (ed.) Pre-proceedings of the International Workshop on Proof-Search in Axiomatic Theories and Type Theories, PSATTT 2011 (2011)
14. Kozen, D., Palsberg, J., Schwartzbach, M.I.: Efficient recursive subtyping. In: Proceedings of the 20th ACM SIGPLAN-SIGACT Symposium on Principles of Programming Languages, POPL 1993, pp. 419–428. ACM, New York (1993)
15. McBride, C.: Type-preserving renaming and substitution (2005) (manuscript)
16. McBride, C.: Let's See How Things Unfold: Reconciling the Infinite with the Intensional (Extended Abstract). In: Kurz, A., Lenisa, M., Tarlecki, A. (eds.) CALCO 2009. LNCS, vol. 5728, pp. 113–126. Springer, Heidelberg (2009)
17. Miyamoto, T.: RegExp contribution to Coq (2011)
18. Nakata, K., Uustalu, T.: Resumptions, weak bisimilarity and big-step semantics for While with interactive I/O: An exercise in mixed induction-coinduction. In: Proc. Structural Operational Semantics, SOS 2010 (2010)
19. Coq development team. The Coq proof assistant reference manual, http://coq.inria.fr/refman/

Epic—A Library for Generating Compilers

Edwin Brady

University of St Andrews, KY16 9SX, Scotland/UK
`eb@cs.st-andrews.ac.uk`

Abstract. Compilers for functional languages, whether strict or non-strict, typed or untyped, need to handle many of the same problems, for example thunks, lambda lifting, optimisation, garbage collection, and system interaction. Although implementation techniques are by now well understood, it remains difficult for a new functional language to exploit these techniques without either implementing a compiler from scratch, or attempting to fit the new language around another existing compiler. Epic is a compiled functional language which exposes functional compilation techniques to a language implementor, with a Haskell API. In this paper we describe Epic and outline how it may be used to implement a high level language compiler, illustrating our approach by implementing compilers for the λ-calculus and a dynamically typed graphics language.

1 Introduction

When implementing a new programming language, whether for research purposes or as a realistic general purpose language, we are inevitably faced with the problem of executing the language. Ideally, we would like execution to be as fast as possible, and exploit known techniques from many years of compiler research. However, it is difficult to make use of the existing available back ends for functional langauges, such as the STG [12,15,19] or ABC [18] machines. They may be too low level, they may make assumptions about the source language (e.g., its type system) or there may simply be no clearly defined API. As a result, experimental languages such as Agda [14] have resorted to generating Haskell, using `unsafeCoerce` to bypass the type system. Similarly, Cayenne [1] generated LML bypassing the type checker. This is not ideal for several reasons: we cannot expect to use the full power and optimisations of the underlying compiler, nor can we expect it to exploit any specific features of our new source language, such as the optimisation opportunities presented by rich dependent type systems [4].

Epic is a library which aims to provide the necessary features for implementing the back-end of a functional language — thunks, closures, algebraic data types, scope management, lambda lifting — without imposing *any* design choices on the high level language designer, other than encouraging a functional style. It provides *compiler combinators*, which guarantee that any output code will be syntactically correct and well-scoped. This gives a simple method for building a compiler for a new functional language, e.g., for experimentation with new type systems or new domain specific languages. In this paper, we describe Epic and its API using two example high level languages. More generally, we observe that:

R. Peña and R. Page (Eds.): TFP 2011, LNCS 7193, pp. 33–48, 2012.
© Springer-Verlag Berlin Heidelberg 2012

1. Recent language and type system research has typically been based on extensions of existing languages, notably Haskell. While this makes implementation easier as it builds on an existing language, it discourages significant departures from the existing language (e.g., full dependent types). With Epic, we encourage more radical experiments by providing a standalone path to a realistic, efficient, language implementation.
2. A tool can become significantly more useful if it is embeddable in other systems. A language back end is no different — by providing an API for Epic, we make it more widely applicable. Haskell's expressiveness, particularly through type classes, makes it simple to provide an appropriate API for describing the core language.
3. Epic's small core and clearly defined API makes it a potential platform for experimentation with optimisations and new back ends. Indeed, we avoid implementation details in this paper. Several implementations are possible, perhaps targetting .NET or the JVM as well as native code.

Epic was originally written as a back end for Epigram [7] (the name[1] is short for "**Epi**gram **C**ompiler"). It is now used by Idris [5] and as an experimental back end for Agda. It is specifically designed for reuse by other source languages.

2　The Epic Language

Epic is based on the λ-calculus with some extensions. It supports primitives such as strings and integers, as well as tagged unions. There are additional control structures for specifying evaluation order, primitive loop constructs, and calling foreign functions. Foreign function calls are annotated with types, to assist with marshaling values between Epic and C, but otherwise there are no type annotations and there is no type checking — as Epic is intended as an intermediate language, it is assumed that the high level language has already performed any necessary type checking. The abstract syntax of the core language is given in Figure 1. We use de Bruijn telescope notation, $\vec{x}$, to denote a sequence of x. Variable names are represented by x, and i, b, f, c, and str represent integer, boolean, floating point, character and string literals respectively.

2.1　Definitions

An Epic program consists of a sequence of *untyped* function definitions, with zero or more arguments. The entry point is the function *main*, which takes no arguments. For example:

$$factorial(x) \;=\; \underline{\text{if}}\, x == 0 \,\underline{\text{then}}\, 1$$
$$\underline{\text{else}}\, x \,\times\, factorial(x-1)$$

$$main() \quad=\; putStrLn(intToString(factorial(10)))$$

---

[1] Coined by James McKinna.

$$p ::= \vec{def} \qquad \text{(Epic program)} \qquad def ::= x(\vec{x}) = t \qquad \text{(Definition)}$$

$t ::= x$	(Variable)		$t(\vec{t})$	(Application)
$\mid \lambda x.\, t$	(Lambda binding)		$\underline{\text{let }} x = t \underline{\text{ in }} t$	(Let binding)
$\mid \mathsf{Con}\, i(\vec{t})$	(Constructor)		$t!i$	(Projection)
$\mid t \text{ op } t$	(Infix operator)		$\underline{\text{if }} t \underline{\text{ then }} t \underline{\text{ else }} t$	(Conditional)
$\mid \underline{\text{case }} t \underline{\text{ of }} \vec{alt}$	(Case expressions)		$\underline{\text{lazy}}(t)$	(Lazy evaluation)
$\mid \underline{\text{effect}}(t)$	(Effectful term)		$\underline{\text{while }} t\, t$	(While loops)
$\mid x := t \underline{\text{ in }} t$	(Variable update)		$\underline{\text{foreign }} T\; str\, (t \stackrel{\rightarrow}{:} T)$	(Foreign call)
$\mid \underline{\text{malloc }} t\, t$	(Allocation)		$i \mid f \mid c \mid b \mid str$	(Constants)

$alt ::= \mathsf{Con}\, i(\vec{x}) \mapsto t$	(Constructors)		$i \mapsto t$	(Constants)
$\mid \underline{\text{default}} \mapsto t$	(Match anything)			

$$op ::= + \mid - \mid \times \mid / \mid == \mid < \mid \le \mid > \mid \ge \mid << \mid >>$$

$T ::= \mathsf{Int} \mid \mathsf{Char} \mid \mathsf{Bool} \mid \mathsf{Float} \mid \mathsf{String}$	(Primitives)	
$\mid \mathsf{Unit}$	(Unit type)	
$\mid \mathsf{Ptr}$	(Foreign pointers)	
$\mid \mathsf{Any}$	(Polymorphic type)	

Fig. 1. Epic syntax

The right hand side of a definition is an expression consisting of function applications, operators (arithmetic, comparison, and bit-shifting), bindings and control structures (some low level and imperative). Functions may be partially applied.

Values. Values in an Epic program are either one of the primitives (an integer, floating point number, character, boolean or string) or a *tagged union*. Tagged unions are of the form $\mathsf{Con}\, i(t_1, \ldots, t_n)$, where i is the *tag* and the $\vec{t}$ are the *fields*; the name Con suggests "Constructor". For example, we could represent a list using tagged unions, with $\mathsf{Con}\, 0\,()$ representing the empty list and $\mathsf{Con}\, 1\,(x, xs)$ representing a cons cell, where x is the element and xs is the tail of the list.

Tagged unions are inspected either using field projection ($t!i$ projects the ith field from a tagged union t) or by case analysis. E.g., to append two lists:

$$
\begin{aligned}
append(xs, ys) \;=&\; \underline{\text{case }} xs \underline{\text{ of }} \\
&\mathsf{Con}\, 0() \qquad \mapsto \quad ys \\
&\mathsf{Con}\, 1(x, xs') \;\mapsto\; \mathsf{Con}\, 1(x, append(xs', ys))
\end{aligned}
$$

Evaluation Strategy. By default, expressions are evaluated eagerly (in applicative order), i.e. arguments to functions and tagged unions are evaluated immediately, left to right. Evaluation can instead be delayed using the lazy construct. An expression $\underline{\text{lazy}}(t)$ builds a thunk for the expression t which will not be evaluated until it needs to be inspected, typically by one of: inspection in a case expression or the condition in an if statement; field projection; being passed to a foreign function; explicit evaluation with effect. An expression effect(t) evaluates the thunk t *without* updating the thunk with the result. This is to facilitate evaluation of side-effecting expressions.

Higher Order Functions. Finally, expressions may contain λ and let bindings. Higher order functions such as *map* are also permitted:

$$map(f, xs) = \underline{case}\ xs\ \underline{of}$$
$$\mathsf{Con}\ 0() \qquad \mapsto \quad \mathsf{Con}\ 0()$$
$$\mathsf{Con}\ 1(x, xs') \mapsto \quad \mathsf{Con}\ 1(f(x), map(f, xs'))$$

$$evens(n) = \underline{let}\ nums = take(n, countFrom(1))\ \underline{in}$$
$$map(\lambda x.\ x \times 2, nums)$$

2.2   Foreign Functions

Most programs eventually need to interact with the operating system. Epic provides a lightweight foreign function interface which allows interaction with external C code. Since Epic does no type checking or inference, a foreign call requires the argument and return types to be given explicitly. e.g. the C function:

```
double sin(double x);
```

We can call this function from Epic by giving the C name, the return type (an Epic Float, which corresponds to a C double) and the argument type (also an Epic Float).

$$sin(x) = \underline{foreign}\ \mathsf{Float}\ "\mathsf{sin}"\ (x\ :\ \mathsf{Float})$$

2.3   Low Level Features

Epic emphasises control over safety, and therefore provides some low level features. A high level language may wish to use these features in some performance critical contexts, whether for sequencing side effects, implementing optimisations, or to provide run-time support code. Epic allows sequencing, while loops and variable update, and provides a malloc construct for manual memory allocation (by default memory is garbage collected). The behaviour of malloc $n\ t$ is to create a fixed pool of n bytes, and allocate only from this pool when evaluating t. Due to space restrictions we will not discuss these constructs further.

2.4   Haskell API

The primary interface to Epic is through a Haskell API which is used to build expressions and programs with higher order abstract syntax (HOAS) [17]. Implementing a compiler for a high level language then involves converting the abstract syntax of a high level program into an Epic program, through these "compiler combinators", and implementing any run-time support as Epic functions.

Programs and Expressions. The API allows the building of Epic programs with an Embedded Domain Specific Language (EDSL) style interface, i.e. we try to exploit Haskell's syntax as far as possible. There are several possible representations of Epic expressions. `Expr` is the internal abstract representation, and `Term` is a representation which carries a name supply. We have a type class `EpicExpr` which provides a function `term` for building a concrete expression using a name supply:

```
type Term = State NextName Expr
class EpicExpr e where
    term :: e -> Term
```

There are straightforward instances of `EpicExpr` for the internal representations `Expr` and `Term`. There is also an instance for `String`, which parses concrete syntax, which is beyond the scope of this paper. More interestingly, we can build an instance of the type class which allows Haskell functions to be used to build Epic functions. This means we can use Haskell names for Epic references, and not need to worry about scoping or ambiguous name choices.

```
instance EpicExpr e => EpicExpr (Expr -> e) where
```

Alternatively, function arguments can be given explicit names, constructed with `name`. A reference to a name is built with `ref`, and `fn` composes `ref` and `name`.

```
name :: String -> Name
ref  :: Name   -> Term
fn   :: String -> Term
```

We provide an instance of `EpicExpr` to allow a user to give names explicitly. This may be desirable when the abstract syntax for the high level language we are compiling has explicit names.

```
instance EpicExpr e => EpicExpr ([Name], e) where
```

For example, the identity function can be built in either of the following ways:

```
id1, id2 :: Term
id1 = term (\x -> x)
id2 = term ([name "x"], fn "x")
```

Both forms, using Haskell functions or explicit names, can be mixed freely in an expression. A program is a collection of named Epic expressions built using the `EpicExpr` class:

```
type Program = [EpicDecl]
data EpicDecl = forall e. EpicExpr e => EpicFn Name e
```

The library provides a number of built-in definitions for some common operations such as outputting strings and converting data types:

```
basic_defs :: [EpicDecl]
```

In this paper we use *putStr* and *putStrLn* for outputting strings, *append* for concatenating strings, and *intToString* for integer to string conversion. We can compile a collection of definitions to an executable, or simply execute them directly. Execution begins with the function called *main* — Epic reports an error if this function is not defined:

```
compile :: Program -> FilePath -> IO ()
run     :: Program -> IO ()
```

Building Expressions. We have seen how to build λ bindings with the EpicExpr class, using either Haskell's λ or pairing explicitly bound names with their scope. We now add further sub-expressions. The general form of functions which build expressions is to create a `Term`, i.e. an expression which manages its own name supply by combining arbitrary Epic expressions, i.e. instances of EpicExpr. For example, to apply a function to an argument, we provide an EpicExpr for the function and the argument:

```
infixl 5 @@
(@@) :: (EpicExpr f, EpicExpr a) => f -> a -> Term
```

Since `Term` itself is an instance of `EpicExpr`, we can apply a function to several arguments through nested applications of `@@`, which associates to the left as with normal Haskell function application. We have several arithmetic operators, including arithmetic, comparison and bitwise operators, e.g.:

```
op_ :: (EpicExpr a, EpicExpr b) => Op -> a -> b -> Term
plus_, minus_, times_, divide_ :: Op
```

We follow the convention that Epic keywords and primitive operators are represented by a Haskell function with an underscore suffix. This convention arises because we cannot use Haskell keywords such as `if`, `let` and `case` as function names. For consistency, we have extended the convention to all functions and operators. `if...then...else` expressions are built using the `if_` function:

```
if_ :: (EpicExpr a, EpicExpr t, EpicExpr e) => a -> t -> e -> Term
```

For <u>let</u> bindings, we can either use HOAS or bind an explicit name. To achieve this we implement a type class and instances which support both:

```
class LetExpr e where
    let_ :: EpicExpr val => val -> e -> Term

instance EpicExpr sc => LetExpr (Name, sc)
instance                 LetExpr (Expr -> Term)
```

To build a constructor form, we apply a constructor with an integer *tag* to its arguments. We build a constructor using the `con_` function, and provide a shorthand `tuple_` for the common case where the tag can be ignored — as the name suggests, this happens when building tuples and records:

```
con_   :: Int -> Term
tuple_ :: Term
```

Case Analysis. To inspect constructor forms, or to deconstruct tuples, we use case expressions. A case expression chooses one of the alternative executions path depending on the value of the scrutinee, which can be any Epic expression:

```
case_ :: EpicExpr e => e -> [Case] -> Term
```

We leave the definition of `Case` abstract (although it is simply an Epic expression carrying a name supply) and provide an interface for building case branches. The scrutinee is matched against each branch, in order. To match against a constructor form, we use the same trick as we did for λ-bindings, either allowing Haskell to manage the scope of constructor arguments, or giving names explicitly to arguments, or a mixture. For convenience, we make `Expr` and `Term` instances to allow empty argument lists.

```
class Alternative e where
    mkAlt :: Tag -> e -> Case

instance Alternative Expr
instance Alternative Term
instance Alternative e => Alternative (Expr -> e)
instance Alternative e => Alternative ([Name], e)
```

We can build case alternatives for constructor forms (matching a specific tag), tuples, or integer constants (matching a specific constant), and a default case if all other alternatives fail to match. In the following, `e` is an expression which gives the argument bindings, if any, and the right hand side of the match.

```
con          :: Alternative e => Int -> e -> Case
tuple        :: Alternative e =>        e -> Case
constcase    :: EpicExpr e    => Int -> e -> Case
defaultcase  :: EpicExpr e    =>        e -> Case
```

3   Example—Compiling the λ-Calculus

In this section we present a compiler for the untyped λ-calculus using HOAS, showing the fundamental features of Epic required to build a complete compiler.

3.1   Representation

Our example is an implementation of the untyped λ-calculus, plus primitive integers and strings, and arithmetic and string operators. The Haskell representation uses higher order abstract syntax (HOAS). We also include global references (`Ref`) which refer to top level functions, function application (`App`), constants (`Const`) and binary operators (`Op`):

```
data Lang = Lam (Lang -> Lang)
          | Ref Name
          | App Lang Lang
          | Const Const
          | Op Infix Lang Lang
```

Constants can be either integers or strings:

```
data Const = CInt Int | CStr String
```

There are infix operators for arithmetic (Plus, Minus, Times and Divide), string manipulation (Append) and comparison (Eq, Lt and Gt). The comparison operators return an integer — zero if the comparison is true, non-zero otherwise:

```
data Infix = Plus | Minus | Times | Divide | Append | Eq | Lt | Gt
```

A complete program consists of a collection of named Lang definitions:

```
type Defs = [(Name, Lang)]
```

3.2   Compilation

Our aim is to convert a collection of Defs into an executable, using the compile or run function from the Epic API. Given an Epic Program, compile will generate an executable, and run will generate an executable then run it. Recall that a program is a collection of named Epic declarations:

```
data EpicDecl = forall e. EpicExpr e => EpicFn Name e
type Program = [EpicDecl]
```

Our goal is to convert a Lang definition into something which is an instance of EpicExpr. We use Term, which is an Epic expression which carries a name supply. Most of the term construction functions in the Epic API return a Term.

```
build :: Lang -> Term
```

The full implementation of build is given in Figure 2. In general, this is a straightforward traversal of the Lang program, converting Lang constants to Epic constants, Lang application to Epic application, and Lang operators to the appropriate built-in Epic operators.

```
build :: Lang -> Term
build (Lam f)          = term (\x -> build (f (EpicRef x)))
build (EpicRef x)      = term x
build (Ref n)          = ref n
build (App f a)        = build f @@ build a
build (Const (CInt x)) = int x
build (Const (CStr x)) = str x
build (Op Append l r)  = fn "append" @@ build l @@ build r
build (Op op l r)      = op_ (eOp op) (build l) (build r)
     where eOp Plus    = plus_
           eOp Minus   = minus_
           ...
```

Fig. 2. Compiling Untyped λ-calculus

Using HOAS has the advantage that Haskell can manage scoping, but the disadvantage that it is not straightforward to convert the abstract syntax into another form. The Epic API also allows scope management using HOAS, so we need to convert a function where the bound name refers to a Lang value into a function where the bound name refers to an Epic value. The easiest solution is to extend the Lang datatype with an Epic reference:

```
data Lang = ...
          | EpicRef Expr

build (Lam f) = term (\x -> build (f (EpicRef x)))
```

To convert a Lang function to an Epic function, we build an Epic function in which we apply the Lang function to the Epic reference for its argument. Every reference to a name in Lang is converted to the equivalent reference to the name in Epic. Although it seems undesirable to extend Lang in this way, this solution is simple to implement and preserves the desirable feature that Haskell manages scope. Compiling string append uses a built in function provided by the Epic interface in basic_defs:

```
build (Op Append l r) = fn "append" @@ build l @@ build r
```

Given build, we can translate a collection of HOAS definitions into an Epic program, add the built-in Epic definitions and execute it directly. Recall that there must be a *main* function or Epic will report an error — we therefore add a main function which prints the value of an integer expression given at compile time.

```
main_ exp = App (Ref (name "putStrLn"))
                (App (Ref (name "intToString")) exp)

mkProgram :: Defs -> Lang -> Program
mkProgram ds exp = basic_defs ++
                   map (\ (n, d) -> EpicFn n (build d)) ds ++
                   [(name "main", main_ exp)]

execute :: Defs -> Lang -> IO ()
execute p exp = run (mkProgram p exp)
```

Alternatively, we can generate an executable. Again, the entry point is the Epic function *main*:

```
comp :: Defs -> Lang -> IO ()
comp p exp = compile "a.out" (mkProgram p exp)
```

This is a compiler for a very simple language, but a compiler for a more complex language follows the same pattern: convert the abstract syntax for each named definition into a named Epic Term, add any required primitives (we have just used basic_defs here), and pass the collection of definitions to run or compile.

4   Atuin—A Dynamically Typed Graphics Language

In this section we present a more detailed example language, Atuin[2], and outline
how to use Epic to implement a compiler for it. Atuin is a simple imperative
language with higher order procedures and dynamic type checking, with primitive operations implementing turtle graphics. The following example illustrates
the basic features of the language. The procedure `repeat` executes a code block
a given number of times:

```
repeat(num, block) {
  if num > 0 {
    eval block
    repeat(num-1, block)
  }
}
```

Using `repeat`, `polygon` draws a polygon with the given number of sides, a size
and a colour:

```
polygon(sides, size, col) {
  if sides > 2 {
    colour col
    angle = 360/sides
    repeat(sides, {
      forward size
      right angle
    })
  }
}
```

Programs consist of a number of procedure definitions, one of which must be
called `main` and take no arguments:

```
main() {
  polygon(10,25,red)
}
```

4.1   Abstract Syntax

The abstract syntax of Atuin is defined by algebraic data types constructed by a
Happy-generated parser. Constants can be one of four types: integers, characters,
booleans and colours:

```
data Const = MkInt Int   | MkChar Char
           | MkBool Bool | MkCol Colour

data Colour = Black | Red | Green | Blue | ...
```

Atuin is an imperative language, consisting of sequences of commands applied
to expressions. We define expressions (`Exp`) and procedures (`Turtle`) mutually.

---

[2] http://hackage.haskell.org/package/atuin

Expressions can be constants or variables, and combined by infix operators. Expressions can include code blocks to pass to higher order procedures.

```
data Exp = Infix Op Exp Exp | Var Id
         | Const Const      | Block Turtle
data Op = Plus | Minus | Times | Divide | ...
```

Procedures define sequences of potentially side-effecting turtle operations. There can be procedure calls, turtle commands, and some simple control structures. Pass defines an empty code block:

```
data Turtle = Call Id [Exp]     | Turtle Command
            | Seq Turtle Turtle | If Exp Turtle Turtle
            | Let Id Exp Turtle | Eval Exp
            | Pass
```

The turtle can be moved forward, turned left or right, or given a different pen colour. The pen can also be raised, to allow the turtle to move without drawing.

```
data Command = Fd Exp     | RightT Exp | LeftT Exp
             | Colour Exp | PenUp      | PenDown
```

As with the λ-calculus compiler in Section 3, a complete program consists of a collection of definitions, where definitions include a list of formal parameters and the program definition:

```
type Proc = ([Id], Turtle)
type Defs = [(Id,  Proc)]
```

4.2 Compiling

While Atuin is a different kind of language from the λ-calculus, with complicating factors such as a global state (the turtle), imperative features, and dynamic type checking, the process of constructing a compiler follows the same general recipe, i.e. define primitive operations as Epic functions, then convert each Atuin definition into the corresponding Epic definition.

Compiling Primitives. The first step is to define primitive operations as Epic functions. The language is dynamically typed, therefore we will need primitive operations to check dynamically that they are operating on values of the correct type. We define functions which construct Epic code for building values, effectively using a single algebraic datatype to capture all possible run-time values (i.e. values are "uni-typed" [20]).

```
mkint  i = con_ 0 @@ i
mkchar c = con_ 1 @@ c
mkbool b = con_ 2 @@ b
mkcol  c = con_ 3 @@ c
```

Correspondingly, we can extract the concrete values safely from this structure, checking that the value is the required type, e.g.

```
getInt x  = case_ x [con 0 (\ (x :: Expr) -> x),
                     defaultcase (error_ "Not an Int")]
```

Similarly, `getChar`, `getBool` and `getCol` check and extract values of the appropriate type. Using these, it is simple to define primitive arithmetic operations which check that they are operating on the correct type, and report an error if not.

```
primPlus   x y = mkint $ op_ plus_   (getInt x) (getInt y)
primMinus  x y = mkint $ op_ minus_  (getInt x) (getInt y)
primTimes  x y = mkint $ op_ times_  (getInt x) (getInt y)
primDivide x y = mkint $ op_ divide_ (getInt x) (getInt y)
```

Graphics Operations. We use the Simple DirectMedia Layer[3] (SDL) to implement graphics operations. We implement C functions to interact with SDL, and use Epic's foreign function interface to call these functions. For example:

```
void* startSDL(int x, int y);
void  drawLine(void* surf, int x, int y, int ex, int ey,
               int r, int g, int b, int a);
```

The `startSDL` function opens a window with the given dimensions, and returns a pointer to a *surface* on which we can draw; `drawLine` draws a line on a surface, between the given locations, and in the given colour, specified as red, green, blue and alpha channels.

We represent colours as a 4-tuple (r, g, b, a). Drawing a line in Epic involves extracting the red, green, blue and alpha components from this tuple, then calling the C `drawLine` function. To make a foreign function call, we use `foreign_`, giving the C function name and explicit types for each argument so that Epic will know how to convert from internal values to C values:

```
drawLine :: Expr -> Expr -> Expr -> Expr -> Expr -> Expr -> Term
drawLine surf x y ex ey col
    = case_ (rgba col)
        [tuple (\ r g b a ->
            foreign_ tyUnit "drawLine"
             [(surf, tyPtr),
              (x, tyInt), (y, tyInt), (ex, tyInt), (ey, tyInt),
              (r, tyInt), (g, tyInt), (b, tyInt), (a, tyInt)]) ]
```

The turtle state is a tuple (s, x, y, d, c, p) where s is a pointer to the SDL surface, (x, y) gives the turtle's location, d gives its direction, c gives the colour and p gives the pen state (a boolean, false for up and true for down). Note that this state is not accessible by Atuin programs, so we do not dynamically check each component. To implement the `forward` operation, for example, we take the current state, update the position according to the distance given and the current direction, and if the pen is down, draws a line from the old position to the new position.

---

[3] http://libsdl.org/

```
forward :: Expr -> Expr -> Term
forward st dist = case_ st
  [tuple (\ (surf :: Expr) (x :: Expr) (y :: Expr)
            (dir :: Expr) (col :: Expr) (pen :: Expr) ->
     let_ (op_ plus_ x (op_ times_ (getInt dist) (esin dir)))
        (\x' -> let_ (op_ plus_ y (op_ timesF_ (getInt dist) (ecos dir)))
        (\y' -> if_ pen (fn "drawLine" @@ surf @@ x @@ y
                                        @@ x' @@ y' @@ col) unit_ +>
                tuple_ @@ surf @@ x' @@ y' @@ dir @@ col @@ pen)))]
```

Here we have applied getInt, esin and ecos as Haskell functions, so they will be inlined in the resulting Epic code. In contrast, drawLine is applied as a separately defined Epic function, using Epic's application operator (@@).

Compiling Programs. Programs return an updated turtle state, and possibly perform side-effects such as drawing. An Atuin definition with arguments $a_1 \ldots a_n$ is translated to an Epic function with a type of the following form:

$$f \; : \; State \to a_1 \to \ldots \to a_n \to State$$

To compile a complete program, we add the primitive functions we have defined above (line drawing, turtle movement, etc) to the list of basic Epic definitions, and convert the user defined procedures to Epic.

```
prims = basic_defs ++ [EpicFn (name "initSDL") initSDL,
                       EpicFn (name "drawLine") drawLine,
                       EpicFn (name "forward") forward, ... ]
```

We define a type class to capture conversion of expressions, commands and full programs into Epic terms. Programs maintain the turtle's state (an Epic Expr), and return a new state, so we pass this state to the compiler.

```
class Compile a where
    compile :: Expr -> a -> Term
```

In general, since we have set up all of the primitive operations as Epic functions, compiling an Atuin program consists of directly translating the abstract syntax to the Epic equivalent, making sure the state is maintained. For example, to compile a call we build an Epic function call and add the current state as the first argument. Epic takes strings as identifiers, so we use fullId :: Id -> String to convert an Atuin identifier to an Epic identifier.

```
compile state (Call i es) = app (fn (fullId i) @@ state) es
    where app f [] = f
          app f (e:es) = app (f @@ compile state e) es
```

Where operations are sequenced, we make sure that the state returned by the first operation is passed to the next:

```
compile state (Seq x y)
    = let_ (compile state x) (\state' -> compile state' y)
```

Atuin has higher order procedures which accept code blocks as arguments. To compile a code block, we build a function which takes the turtle state (that is, the state at the time the block is executed, not the state at the time the block is created). Epic's `effect_` function ensures that a closure is evaluated, but the result is not updated. Evaluating the closure may have side effects which may need to be executed again — consider the `repeat` function above, for example, where the code block should be evaluated on each iteration.

```
compile state (Block t) = term (\st -> compile st t)
compile state (Eval e)  = effect_ (compile state e @@ state)
```

The rest of the operations are compiled by a direct mapping to the primitives defined earlier. Finally, the main program sets up an SDL surface, creates an initial turtle state, and passes that state to the user-defined `main` function:

```
init_turtle surf = tuple_ @@ surf @@ int 320 @@ int 240 @@
                                   int 180 @@ col_white @@ bool True

runMain :: Term
runMain = let_ (fn "initSDL" @@ int 640 @@ int 480)
           (\surface ->
              (fn (fullId (mkId "main")) @@ (init_turtle surface)) +>
              flipBuffers surface +> pressAnyKey)
```

The full source code for Atuin and its compiler is available from Hackage.

5   Related Work

Epic is currently used by Agda and Idris [5], as well as the development version of Epigram [7]. Initial benchmarking [6] shows that the code generated by Epic can be competitive with Java and is not significantly worse than C. Epic uses techniques from other functional language back ends [12,15,18] but deliberately exposes its core language as an API to make it as reusable as possible. Although there is always likely to be a trade off between reusability and efficiency, exposing the API will make it easier for other language researchers to build a new compiler quickly. As far as we are aware, Epic occupies a unique point in the design space of code generation tools — it is sufficiently high level that it captures common functional language abstractions without being so high level that it imposes constraints such as a type system on the language it is compiling. Alonzo, for example, is a prototype compiler for Agda [2] which compiles via GHC, but requires coercions in the generated code in order for it to be accepted by GHC's type checker. Coq's program extraction tool [10] also aims to generate executable code via a high level language, similarly requiring coercions where Coq terms can not be given a type in the high level language. In contrast, systems such as the Lazy Virtual Machine [9], C-- [16] and LLVM [8] are designed as lower level target languages rather than high level APIs. We could nevertheless consider using these tools for Epic code generation.

6   Conclusion

Epic provides a simple path for language researchers to convert experimental languages (e.g. experimenting with new type systems or domain specific language design) into larger scale, usable tools, by providing an API for generating a compiler, dealing with well-understood but difficult to implement problems such as naming and scope management, code generation, interfacing with foreign functions and garbage collection. In this paper we have seen two examples of languages which can be compiled via Epic, both functionally based, but with different features. The high-level recipe for each is the same: define primitive functions as run-time support, then translate the abstract syntax into concrete Epic functions, using a combinator style API. In addition, we have implemented a compiler for λ_Π [11], a dependently typed language, which shows how Epic can handle languages with more expressive type systems[4].

Future Work. Since Epic is currently used in practice by a number of dependently typed functional languages, future work will have an emphasis on providing an efficient executable environment for these and related languages. An interesting research question, for example, is whether the rich type systems of these languages can be used to guide optimisation, and if so how to present the information gained by the type system to the compiler.

Currently, Epic compiles to machine code via C, using the Boehm conservative garbage collector [3]. While this has been reasonably efficient in practice, we believe that an LLVM based implementation [8,19] with accurate garbage collection would be more appropriate as it could take advantage of functional language features such as immutability of data.

Perhaps more importantly, as a very simple functional language Epic is a convenient platform with which to experiment with functional compilation techniques. For example, we are developing an evaluator which will be a starting point for experimenting with supercompilation [13] and partial evaluation. Of course, any language which uses Epic as a back end will stand to gain from future optimisation efforts!

Acknowledgments. This work was partly funded by the Scottish Informatics and Computer Science Alliance (SICSA) and by EU Framework 7 Project No. 248828 (ADVANCE). Thanks to the anonymous reviewers for their constructive suggestions.

References

1. Augustsson, L.: Cayenne - a language with dependent types. In: Proc. 1998 International Conf. on Functional Programming (ICFP 1998), pp. 239–250 (1998)
2. Benke, M.: Alonzo — a compiler for Agda, Talk at Agda Implementors Meeting 6 (2007)

---

[4] http://www.idris-lang.org/examples/LambdaPi.hs

3. Boehm, H.-J., Demers, A.J.: Xerox Corporation Silicon Graphic, and Hewlett-Packard Company. A garbage collector for C and C++ (2001)
4. Brady, E.: Practical Implementation of a Dependently Typed Functional Programming Language. PhD thesis, University of Durham (2005)
5. Brady, E.: Idris — Systems programming meets full dependent types. In: PLPV, pp. 43–54 (2011)
6. Brady, E., Hammond, K.: Scrapping your inefficient engine: using partial evaluation to improve domain-specific language implementation. In: ICFP 2010: Proceedings of the 15th ACM SIGPLAN International Conference on Functional Programming, pp. 297–308. ACM, New York (2010)
7. Chapman, J., Dagand, P.-E., McBride, C., Morris, P.: The gentle art of levitation. In: ICFP 2010: Proceedings of the 15th ACM SIGPLAN International Conference on Functional Programming, pp. 3–14. ACM, New York (2010)
8. Lattner, C.: LLVM: An infrastructure for multi-stage optimization. Master's thesis, Computer Science Dept. University of Illinois at Urbana-Champaign (December 2002)
9. Leijen, D.: LVM, the Lazy Virtual Machine. Technical Report UU-CS-2004-05, Institute of Information and Computing Sciences, Utrecht University (August 2005)
10. Letouzey, P.: A New Extraction for Coq. In: Geuvers, H., Wiedijk, F. (eds.) TYPES 2002. LNCS, vol. 2646, pp. 200–219. Springer, Heidelberg (2003)
11. Löh, A., McBride, C., Swierstra, W.: A tutorial implementation of a dependently typed lambda calculus. Fundam. Inform. 102(2), 177–207 (2010)
12. Marlow, S., Peyton Jones, S.: How to make a fast curry: push/enter vs eval/apply. In: International Conference on Functional Programming, Snowbird, pp. 4–15 (2004)
13. Mitchell, N.: Rethinking supercompilation. In: Proceedings of the 15th ACM SIGPLAN International Conference on Functional Programming, ICFP 2010, pp. 309–320. ACM, New York (2010)
14. Norell, U.: Towards a practical programming language based on dependent type theory. PhD thesis, Chalmers University of Technology (September 2007)
15. Peyton Jones, S.: Implementing lazy functional languages on stock hardware – the Spineless Tagless G-machine. Journal of Functional Programming 2(2), 127–202 (1992)
16. Jones, S.L.P., Nordin, T., Oliva, D.: C–: A Portable Assembly Language. In: Clack, C., Hammond, K., Davie, T. (eds.) IFL 1997. LNCS, vol. 1467, pp. 1–19. Springer, Heidelberg (1998)
17. Pfenning, F., Elliot, C.: Higher-order abstract syntax. In: Proceedings of the ACM SIGPLAN 1988 Conference on Programming Language Design and Implementation, PLDI 1988, pp. 199–208. ACM, New York (1988)
18. Smetsers, S., Nöcker, E., van Groningen, J., Plasmeijer, R.: Generating Efficient Code for Lazy Functional Languages. In: Hughes, J. (ed.) FPCA 1991. LNCS, vol. 523, pp. 592–617. Springer, Heidelberg (1991)
19. Terei, D.A., Chakravarty, M.M.: An LLVM backend for GHC. In: Proceedings of the Third ACM Haskell Symposium, Haskell 2010, pp. 109–120. ACM, New York (2010)
20. Wadler, P., Findler, R.B.: Well-Typed Programs Can't Be Blamed. In: Castagna, G. (ed.) ESOP 2009. LNCS, vol. 5502, pp. 1–16. Springer, Heidelberg (2009)

Towards Modular Compilers for Effects

Laurence E. Day and Graham Hutton

Functional Programming Laboratory
School of Computer Science
University of Nottingham, UK

Abstract. Compilers are traditionally factorised into a number of separate phases, such as parsing, type checking, code generation, etc. However, there is another potential factorisation that has received comparatively little attention: the treatment of separate language features, such as mutable state, input/output, exceptions, concurrency and so forth. In this article we focus on the problem of modular compilation, in which the aim is to develop compilers for separate language features independently, which can then be combined as required. We summarise our progress to date, issues that have arisen, and further work.

Keywords: Modularity, Haskell, Compilation, Monads.

1 Introduction

The general concept of *modularity* can be defined as the degree to which the components of a system may be separated and recombined. In the context of computer programming, this amounts to the desire to separate the components of a software system into independent parts whose behaviour is clearly specified, and can be combined in different ways for different applications. Modularity brings many important benefits, including the ability to break down larger problems into smaller problems, to establish the correctness of a system in terms of the correctness of its components, and to develop general purpose components that are reusable in different application domains.

In this article we focus on the problem of implementing programming languages themselves in a modular manner. In their seminal article, Liang, Hudak and Jones showed how to implement programming language interpreters in a modular manner, using the notion of monad transformers [9]. In contrast, progress in the area of modular compilers has been more limited, and at present there is no standard approach to this problem. In this article we report on our progress to date on the problem of implementing modular compilers. In particular, the paper makes the following contributions. We show how:

- Modular *syntax* for a language can be defined using the *à la carte* approach to extensible data types developed by Swierstra [15];
- Modular *semantics* for a language can be defined by combining the *à la carte* and modular interpreters techniques, extending the work of Jaskelioff [8];

R. Peña and R. Page (Eds.): TFP 2011, LNCS 7193, pp. 49–64, 2012.

- Modular *compilers* can be viewed as modular interpreters that produce code corresponding to an operational semantics of the source program;
- Modular *machines* that execute the resulting code can be viewed as modular interpreters that produce suitable state transformers.

We illustrate our techniques using a simple expression language with two computational features, in the form of arithmetic and exceptions. The article is aimed at functional programmers with a basic knowledge of interpreters, compilers and monads, but we do not assume specialist knowledge of monad transformers, modular interpreters, or the *à la carte* technique. We use Haskell throughout as both a semantic metalanguage and an implementation language, as this makes the concepts more accessible as well as executable, and eliminates the gap between theory and practice. The Haskell code associated with the article is available from the authors' web pages.

2   Setting the Scene

In this section we set the scene for the rest of the paper by introducing the problem that we are trying to solve. In particular, we begin with a small arithmetic language for which we define four components: syntax, semantics, compiler and virtual machine. We then extend the language with a simple effect in the form of exceptions, and observe how these four components must be changed in light of the new effect. As we shall see, such extensions cut across all aspects and require the modification of existing code in each case.

2.1   A Simple Compiler

Consider a simple language `Expr` comprising integer values and binary addition, for which we can evaluate expressions to an integer value:

```
data Expr      = Val Value | Add Expr Expr

type Value     = Int

eval           :: Expr -> Value
eval (Val n)   = n
eval (Add x y) = eval x + eval y
```

Evaluation of expressions in this manner corresponds to giving a denotational semantics to the `Expr` datatype [14]. Alternatively, expressions can be compiled into a sequence of low-level instructions to be operated upon by a virtual machine, the behaviour of which corresponds to a (small-step) operational semantics [4]. We can compile an expression to a list of operations as follows:

```
type Code         =  [Op]

data Op           =  PUSH Int | ADD

comp              :: Expr -> Code
comp c            =  comp' c []

comp'             :: Expr -> Code -> Code
comp' (Val n)   c =  PUSH n : c
comp' (Add x y) c =  comp' x (comp' y (ADD : c))
```

Note that the compiler is defined in terms of an auxiliary function comp' that takes an additional Code argument that plays the role of an accumulator, which avoids the use of append (++) and leads to simpler proofs [5]. We execute the resulting Code on a virtual machine that operates using a Stack:

```
type Stack         =  [Item]

data Item          =  INT Value

exec               :: Code -> Stack
exec c             =  exec' c []

exec'              :: Code -> Stack -> Stack
exec' []        s =  s
exec' (PUSH n : c) s =  exec' c (INT n : s)
exec' (ADD : c)  s =  let (INT y : INT x : s') = s in
                          exec' c (INT (x + y) : s')
```

The correctness of the compiler can now be captured by stating that the result of evaluating an expression is the same as first compiling, then executing, and finally extracting the result value from the top of the Stack (using an auxiliary function extr), which can be expressed in diagrammatic form as follows:

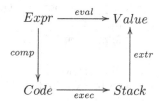

2.2 Adding a New Effect

Suppose now that we wish to extend our language with a new effect, in the form of exceptions. We consider what changes will need to be made to the languages syntax, semantics, compiler and virtual machine as a result of this extension. First of all, we extend the Expr datatype with two new constructors:

```
data Expr = ... | Throw | Catch Expr Expr
```

The Throw constructor corresponds to an uncaught exception, while Catch is a handler construct that returns the value of its first argument unless it is an uncaught exception, in which case it returns the value of its second argument.

From a semantic point of view, adding exceptions to the language requires changing the result type of the evaluation function from Value to Maybe Value in order to accommodate potential failure when evaluating expressions. In turn, we must rewrite the semantics of values and addition accordingly, and define appropriate semantics for throwing and catching.

```
eval                  :: Expr -> Maybe Value
eval (Val n)          =  return n
eval (Add x y)        =  eval x >>= \n ->
                         eval y >>= \m ->
                         return (n + m)
eval Throw            =  mzero
eval (Catch x h)      =  eval x 'mplus' eval h
```

In the above code, we exploit the fact that Maybe is monadic [12,16,17]. In particular, we utilise the basic operations of the Maybe monad, namely return, which converts a pure value into an impure result, (>>=), used to sequence computations, mzero, corresponding to failure, and mplus, for sequential choice.

Finally, in order to compile exceptions we must introduce new operations in the virtual machine and extend the compiler accordingly [6]:

```
data Op               =  ... | THROW | MARK Code | UNMARK

comp                  :: Expr -> Code
comp e                =  comp' e []

comp'                 :: Expr -> Code -> Code
comp' (Val n)       c = PUSH n : c
comp' (Add x y)     c = comp' x (comp' y (ADD : c))
comp' Throw         c = THROW : c
comp' (Catch x h)   c = MARK (comp' h c) : comp' x (UNMARK : c)
```

Intuitively, THROW is an operation that throws an exception, MARK makes a record on the stack of the handler Code to be executed should the first argument of a Catch fail, and UNMARK indicates that no uncaught exceptions were encountered and hence the record of the handler Code can be removed. Note that the accumulator plays a key role in the compilation of Catch, being used in two places to represent the code to be executed after the current compilation.

Because we now need to keep track of handler code on the stack as well as integer values, we must extend the Item datatype and also extend the virtual machine to cope with the new operations and the potential for failure:

```
data Item               =  ... | HAND Code

exec                    :: Code -> Maybe Stack
exec c                  =  exec' c []

exec'                   :: Code -> Stack -> Maybe Stack
exec' []           s =  return s
exec' (PUSH n : c) s =  exec' c (INT n : s)
exec' (ADD : c)    s =  let (INT y : INT x : s') = s in
                          exec' c (INT (x + y) : s')
exec' (THROW : _)  s =  unwind s
exec' (MARK h : c) s =  exec' c (HAND h : s)
exec' (UNMARK : c) s =  let (v : HAND _ : s') = s in
                          exec' c (v : s')
```

The auxiliary unwind function implements the process of invoking handler code in the case of a caught exception, by executing the topmost Code record on the execution stack, failing if no such record exists:

```
unwind                  :: Stack -> Maybe Stack
unwind []               =  mzero
unwind (INT _ : s)      =  unwind s
unwind (HAND h : s)     =  exec' h s
```

2.3 The Problem

As we have seen with the simple example in the previous section, extending the language with a new effect results in many changes to existing code. In particular, we needed to extend three datatypes (Expr, Op and Item), change the return type and existing definition of three functions (eval, exec and exec'), and extend the definition of all the functions involved.

The need to modify and extend existing code for each effect we wish to introduce to our language is clearly at odds with the desire to structure a compiler in a modular manner and raises a number of problems. Most importantly, changing code that has already been designed, implemented, tested and (ideally) proved correct is bad practice from a software engineering point of view [18]. Moreover, the need to change existing code requires access to the source code, and demands familiarity with the workings of all aspects of the language rather than just the feature being added. In the remainder of this paper we will present our work to date on addressing the above problems.

3 Modular Effects

In the previous section, we saw one example of the idea that computational effects can be modelled using monads. Each monad normally corresponds to a single effect, and because most languages involve more than one effect, the issue of how to combine monads quickly arises. In this section, we briefly review the approach based upon *monad transformers* [9].

In Haskell, monad transformers have the following definition:

```
class MonadTrans t where
    lift :: Monad m => m a -> t m a
```

Intuitively, a monad transformer is a type constructor t which, when applied to a monad m, produces a new monad $t\ m$. Monad transformers are also required to satisfy a number of laws, but we omit the details here. Associated with every monad transformer is the operation lift, used to convert from values in the base monad m to the new monad $t\ m$. By way of example, the following table summarises five commonly utilised computational effects, their monad transformer types and the implementations of these types:

Effect	Transformer Type	Implementation
Exceptions	ErrorT m a	m (Maybe a)
State	StateT s m a	$s \rightarrow m\ (a, s)$
Environment	ReaderT r m a	$r \rightarrow m\ a$
Logging	WriterT w m a	m (a, w)
Continuations	ContT r m a	$(a \rightarrow m\ r) \rightarrow m\ r$

The general strategy is to stratify the required effects by starting with a base monad, often the Identity monad, and applying the appropriate transformers. There are some constraints regarding the ordering; for example, certain effects can only occur at the innermost level and certain effects do not commute [9], but otherwise effects can be ordered in different ways to reflect different intended interactions between the features of the language.

To demonstrate the concept of transformers, we will examine the transformer for exceptions in more detail. Its type constructor is declared as follows:

```
newtype ErrorT m a = E { run :: m (Maybe a) }
```

Note that ErrorT Identity is simply the Maybe monad. It is now straightforward to declare ErrorT as a member of the Monad and MonadTrans classes:

```
instance Monad m => Monad (ErrorT m) where
    return      :: a -> ErrorT m a
    return a    = E $ return (Just a)

    (>>=)       :: ErrorT m a -> (a -> ErrorT m b) -> ErrorT m b
    (E m) >>= f = E $ do v <- m
                         case v of
                             Nothing -> return Nothing
                             Just a  -> run (f a)
```

```
instance MonadTrans ErrorT where
   lift        :: m a -> ErrorT m a
   lift m      = E $ m >>= \v -> return (Just v)
```

In addition to the general monadic operations, we would like access to other primitive operations related to the particular effect that we are implementing. In this case, we would like to be able to throw and catch exceptions, and we can specify this by having these operations supported by an error monad class:

```
class Monad m => ErrorMonad m where
   throw :: m a
   catch :: m a -> m a -> m a
```

We instantiate ErrorT as a member of this class as follows:

```
instance Monad m => ErrorMonad (ErrorT m) where
   throw        :: ErrorT m a
   throw        = E $ return Nothing

   catch        :: ErrorT m a -> ErrorT m a -> ErrorT m a
   x 'catch' h = E $ do v <- run x
                        case v of
                           Nothing -> run h
                           Just a  -> return v
```

We can also declare monad transformers as members of effect classes other than their own. Indeed, this is the primary purpose of the lift operation. For example, we can extend StateT to support exceptions as follows:

```
instance ErrorMonad m => ErrorMonad (StateT s m) where
   throw        :: StateT s m a
   throw        = lift . throw

   catch        :: StateT s m a -> StateT s m a -> StateT s m a
   x 'catch' h = S $ \s -> run x s 'catch' run h s
```

In this manner, a monad that is constructed from a base monad using a number of transformers comes equipped with the associated operations for all of the constituent effects, with the necessary liftings being handled automatically.

Returning to our earlier remark that some transformers do not commute, the semantics resulting from lifting in this manner need not be unique for a set of transformers. For example, consider a monad supporting both exceptions and state. Depending on the order in which this monad is constructed, we may or may not have access to the state after an exception is thrown, as reflected in the types s -> (Maybe a, s) and s -> Maybe (a, s). Semantic differences such as these are not uncommon when combining effects, and reflect the fact that the order in which effects are performed makes an observable difference.

Now that we have reviewed how to handle effects in a modular way, let us see how to modularise the syntax of a language.

4   Modular Syntax and Semantics

We have seen that adding extra constructors to a datatype required the modification of existing code. In this section, we review the modular approach to datatypes and functions over them put forward by Swierstra [15], known as *datatypes à la carte*, and show how it can be used to obtain modular syntax and semantics for the language Expr previously described.

4.1   Datatypes à La Carte

The underlying structure of an algebraic datatype such as Expr can be captured by a constructor signature. We define *signature functors* for the arithmetic and exceptional components of the Expr datatype as follows:

```
data Arith  e = Val Int | Add e e

data Except e = Throw | Catch e e
```

These definitions capture the non-recursive aspects of expressions, in the sense that Val and Throw have no subexpressions, whereas Add and Catch have two. We can easily declare Arith and Except as functors in Haskell:

```
class Functor f where
  fmap                 :: (a -> b) -> f a -> f b

instance Functor Arith where
  fmap                 :: (a -> b) -> Arith a -> Arith b
  fmap f (Val n)    =  Val n
  fmap f (Add x y)  =  Add (f x) (f y)

instance Functor Except where
  fmap                 :: (a -> b) -> Except a -> Except b
  fmap f Throw      =  Throw
  fmap f (Catch x h) =  Catch (f x) (f h)
```

For any functor *f*, its induced recursive datatype, Fix *f*, is defined as the least fixpoint of *f*. In Haskell, this can be implemented as follows [11]:

```
newtype Fix f = In (f (Fix f))
```

For example, `Fix Arith` is the language of integers and addition, while `Fix Except` is the language comprising throwing and catching exceptions. We shall see later on in this section how these languages can be combined.

Given a functor f, it is convenient to use a fold operator (sometimes called a *catamorphism*) [10] in order to define functions over `Fix` f [15]:

```
fold           :: Functor f => (f a -> a) -> Fix f -> a
fold f (In t) =  f (fmap (fold f) t)
```

The parameter of type `f a -> a` is called an f-algebra, and can be intuitively viewed as a directive for processing each constructor of a functor. Given such an algebra and a value of type `Fix` f, the `fold` operator exploits both the functorial and recursive characteristics of `Fix` to process recursive values.

The aim now is to take advantage of the above machinery to define a semantics for our expression language in a modular fashion. Such semantics will have type `Fix f -> m Value` for some functor f and monad m; we could also abstract over the value type, but for simplicity we do not consider this here. To define functions of this type using `fold`, we require an appropriate *evaluation algebra*, which notion we capture by the following class declaration:

```
class (Monad m, Functor f) => Eval f m where
    evalAlg :: f (m Value) -> m Value
```

Using this notion, it is now straightforward to define algebras that correspond to the semantics for both the arithmetic and exception components:

```
instance Monad m => Eval Arith m where
    evalAlg               :: Arith (m Value) -> m Value
    evalAlg (Val n)     = return n
    evalAlg (Add x y)   = x >>= \n ->
                          y >>= \m ->
                          return (n + m)

instance ErrorMonad m => Eval Except m where
    evalAlg               :: Except (m Value) -> m Value
    evalAlg (Throw)     = throw
    evalAlg (Catch x h) = x 'catch' h
```

There are three important points to note about the above declarations. First of all, the semantics for arithmetic have now been completely separated from the semantics for exceptions, in particular by way of two separate instance declarations. Secondly, the semantics are parametric in the underlying monad, and can hence be used in many different contexts. And finally, the operations that the underlying monad are required to support are explicitly qualified by class constraints, e.g. in the case of `Except` the monad must be an `ErrorMonad`. The latter two points generalise the work of Jaskelioff [8] from a fixed monad to an arbitrary monad supporting the required operations, resulting in a clean separation of the semantics of individual language components.

With this machinery in place, we can now define a general evaluation function of the desired type by folding an evaluation algebra:

```
eval :: (Monad m, Eval f m) => Fix f -> m Value
eval =  fold evalAlg
```

Note that this function is both modular in the syntax of the language and parametric in the underlying monad. However, at this point we are only able to take the fixpoints of `Arith` or `Except`, not both. We need a way to combine signature functors, which is naturally done by taking their coproduct (disjoint sum) [9]. In Haskell, the coproduct of two functors can be defined as follows:

```
data (f :+: g) e = Inl (f e) | Inr (g e)

instance (Functor f, Functor g) => Functor (f :+: g) where
  fmap          :: (a -> b) -> (f :+: g) a -> (f :+: g) b
  fmap f (Inl x) =  Inl (fmap f x)
  fmap g (Inr y) =  Inr (fmap g y)
```

It is then straightforward to obtain a coproduct of evaluation algebras:

```
instance (Eval f m, Eval g m) => Eval (f :+: g) m where
  evalAlg          :: (f :+: g) (m Value) -> m Value
  evalAlg (Inl x) =  evalAlg x
  evalAlg (Inr y) =  evalAlg y
```

The general evaluation function can now be used to give a semantics to languages with multiple features by simply taking the coproduct of their signature functors. Unfortunately, there are three problems with this approach. First of all, the need to include fixpoint and coproduct tags (`In`, `Inl` and `Inr`) in values is cumbersome. For example, if we wished the concrete expression $1 + 2$ to have type `Fix (Arith :+: Except)`, it would be represented as follows:

```
In (Inl (Add (In (Inl (Val 1))) (In (Inl (Val 2)))))
```

Secondly, the extension of an existing syntax with additional operations may require the modification of existing tags, which breaks modularity. And finally, `Fix (f :+: g)` and `Fix (g :+: f)` are isomorphic as languages, but require equivalent values to be tagged in different ways. The next two sections review how Swierstra resolves these problems [15], and shows how this can be used to obtain modular syntax and semantics for our language.

4.2 Smart Constructors

We need a way of automating the injection of values into expressions such that the appropriate sequences of fixpoint and coproduct tags are prepended. This can be achieved using the concept of a *subtyping relation* on functors, which can be formalised in Haskell by the following class declaration, in which the function `inj` injects a value from a subtype into a supertype:

```
class (Functor sub, Functor sup) => sub :<: sup where
    inj :: sub a -> sup a
```

It is now straightforward to define instance declarations to ensure that f is a subtype of any coproduct containing f, but we omit the details here. Using the notion of subtyping, we can define an injection function,

```
inject      :: (g :<: f) => g (Fix f) -> Fix f
inject      = In . inj
```

which then allows us to define *smart constructors* which bypass the need to tag values when embedding them in expressions:

```
val         :: (Arith :<: f) => Int -> Fix f
val n       = inject (Val n)

add         :: (Arith :<: f) => Fix f -> Fix f -> Fix f
add x y     = inject (Add x y)

throw       :: (Except :<: f) => Fix f
throw       = inject Throw

catch       :: (Except :<: f) => Fix f -> Fix f -> Fix f
catch x h = inject (Catch x h)
```

Note the constraints stating that f must have the appropriate signature functor as a subtype; for example, in the case of val, f must support arithmetic.

4.3 Putting It All Together

We have now achieved our goal of being able to define modular language syntax. Using the smart constructors, we can define values within languages given as fixpoints of coproducts of signature functors. For example:

```
ex1 :: Fix Arith
ex1 =  val 18 'add' val 24

ex2 :: Fix Except
ex2 =  throw 'catch' throw

ex3 :: Fix (Arith :+: Except)
ex3 =  throw 'catch' (val 1337 'catch' throw)
```

The types of these expressions can be generalised using the subtyping relation, but for simplicity we have given fixed types above. In turn, the meaning of such expressions is given by our modular semantics:

```
> eval ex1 :: Value
> 42

> eval ex2 :: Maybe Value
> Nothing

> eval ex3 :: Maybe Value
> Just 1337
```

Note the use of explicit typing judgements to determine the resulting monad. Whilst we have used `Identity` (implicitly) and `Maybe` above, any monad satisfying the required constraints can be used, as illustrated below:

```
> eval ex1 :: Maybe Value
> Just 42

> eval ex2 :: [Value]
> []
```

5 Modular Compilers

With the techniques we have described, we can now construct a modular compiler for our expression language. First of all, we define the `Code` datatype in a modular manner as the coproduct of signature functors corresponding to the arithmetic and exceptional operations of the virtual machine:

```
type Code    = Fix (ARITH :+: EXCEPT :+: EMPTY)

data ARITH  e = PUSH Int e | ADD e

data EXCEPT e = THROW e | MARK Code e | UNMARK e

data EMPTY  e = NULL
```

There are two points to note about the above definitions. First of all, rather than defining the `Op` type as a fixpoint (where `Code` is a list of operations), we have combined the two types into a single type defined using `Fix` in order to allow code to be processed using the generic `fold`; note that `EMPTY` now plays the role of the empty list. Secondly, the first argument to `MARK` has explicit type `Code` rather than general type `e`, which is undesirable as this goes against the idea of treating code in a modular manner. However, this simplifies the definition of the virtual machine and we will return to this point in the conclusion.

The desired type for our compiler is `Fix f -> (Code -> Code)` for some signature functor f characterising the syntax of the source language. To define such a compiler using the generic `fold` operator, we require an appropriate *compilation algebra*, which notion we define as follows:

```
class Functor f => Comp f where
  compAlg :: f (Code -> Code) -> (Code -> Code)
```

In contrast with evaluation algebras, no underlying monads are utilised in the above definition, because the compilation process itself does not involve the manifestation of effects. We can now define algebras for both the arithmetic and exceptional aspects of the compiler in the following manner:

```
instance Comp Arith where
  compAlg              :: Arith (Code -> Code) -> (Code -> Code)
  compAlg (Val n)    =  pushc n
  compAlg (Add x y)  =  x . y . addc

instance Comp Except where
  compAlg              :: Except (Code -> Code) -> (Code -> Code)
  compAlg Throw       =  throwc
  compAlg (Catch x h) = \c -> h c 'markc' x (unmarkc c)
```

In a similar manner to the evaluation algebras defined in section 4.1, note that these definitions are modular in the sense that the two language features are being treated completely separately from each other. We also observe that because the carrier of the algebra is a function, the notion of appending code in the Add case corresponds to function composition. Finally, the smart constructors pushc, addc, etc. are defined in the obvious manner:

```
pushc     :: Int -> Code -> Code
pushc n c =  inject (PUSH n c)

addc      :: Code -> Code
addc c    =  inject (ADD c)
```

The other smart constructors are defined similarly. Finally, it is now straight-forward to define a general compilation function of the desired type by folding a compilation algebra, supplied with an initial accumulator empty:

```
comp     :: Comp f => Fix f -> Code
comp e   =  comp' e empty

comp'    :: Comp f => Fix f -> (Code -> Code)
comp' e  =  fold compAlg e

empty    :: Code
empty    =  inject NULL
```

For example, applying comp to the expression ex3 from the previous section results in the following Code, in which we have removed the fixpoint and coproduct tags In, Inl and Inr for readability:

```
MARK (MARK (THROW NULL) (PUSH 1337 (UNMARK NULL)))
     (THROW (UNMARK NULL))
```

6   Towards Modular Machines

The final component of our development is to construct a modular virtual machine for executing code produced by the modular compiler. Defining the underlying `Stack` datatype in a modular manner is straightforward:

```
type Stack      = Fix (Integer :+: Handler :+: EMPTY)

data Integer e = VAL Int e

data Handler e = HAND Code e
```

As we saw in section 2.1, the virtual machine for arithmetic had type `Code -> Stack -> Stack`, while in section 2.2, the extension to exceptions required modifying the type to `Code -> Stack -> Maybe Stack`. Generalising from these examples, we seek to define a modular execution function of type `Code -> Stack -> m Stack` for an arbitrary monad *m*. We observe that `Stack -> m Stack` is a state transformer, and define the following abbreviation:

```
type StackTrans m a  = StateT Stack m a
```

Using this abbreviation, we now seek to define a general purpose execution function of type `Fix f -> StackTrans m ()` for some signature functor *f* characterising the syntax of the code, and where `()` represents a void result type. In a similar manner to evaluation and compilation algebras that we introduced previously, this leads to the following notion of an *execution algebra*,

```
class (Monad m, Functor f) => Exec f m where
    execAlg :: f (StackTrans m ()) -> StackTrans m ()
```

for which we define the following three instances:

```
instance Monad m => Exec ARITH m where
    execAlg :: ARITH (StackTrans m ()) -> StackTrans m ()
    execAlg (PUSH n st) =  pushs n >> st
    execAlg (ADD st)    =  adds >> st

instance ErrorMonad m => Exec EXCEPT m where
    execAlg :: EXCEPT (StackTrans m ()) -> StackTrans m ()
    execAlg (THROW _)   =  unwinds
    execAlg (MARK h st) =  marks h >> st
    execAlg (UNMARK st) =  unmarks >> st

instance Monad m => Exec EMPTY m where
    execAlg :: EMPTY (StackTrans m ()) -> StackTrans m ()
    execAlg (Null)      =  stop
```

The intention is that pushs, adds, etc. are the implementations of the semantics for the corresponding operations of the machine, and >> is the standard monadic operation that sequences two effectful computations and ignores their result values (which in this case are void). We have preliminary implementations of each of these operations but these appear more complex than necessary, and we are in the process of trying to define these in a more elegant, structured manner.

Folding an execution algebra produces the general execution function:

```
exec :: (Monad m, Exec f m) => Fix f -> StackTrans m ()
exec = fold execAlg
```

7 Summary and Conclusion

In this article we reported on our work to date on the problem of implementing compilers in a modular manner with respect to different computational effects that may be supported by the source language. In particular, we showed how modular syntax and semantics for a simple source language can be achieved by combining the *à la carte* approach to extensible datatypes with the monad transformers approach to modular interpreters, and outlined how a modular compiler and virtual machine can be achieved using the same technology.

However, this is by no means the end of the story, and much remains to be done. We briefly outline a number of directions for further work below.

Challenges: supporting a more modular code type in the virtual machine, as our current version uses a fixed Code type rather than a generic fixpoint type to simplify the implementation; and improving the implementation of the virtual machine operations, by developing a modular approach to case analysis.

Extensions: considering other effects, such as mutable state, continuations and languages with binding constructs, for example using a recent generalisation of the *à la carte* technique for syntax with binders [2]; formalising the idea that some effects may be 'compiled away' and hence are not required in the virtual machine, such as the Maybe monad for our simple language; exploring the extent to which defining compilers in a modular manner admits modular, and hopefully simpler, proofs regarding their correctness; and considering other aspects of the compilation process such as parsing and type-checking.

Other approaches: investigating how the more principled approach to lifting monadic operations developed by Jaskelioff [7] and the modular approach to operational semantics of Mosses [13] can be exploited in the context of modular compilers; the relationship to Harrison's work [3]; considering the compilation to register machines, rather than stack machines; and exploring how dependent types may be utilised in our development (a preliminary implementation of this paper in Coq has recently been produced by Acerbi [1]).

Acknowledgements. We would like to thank Mauro Jaskelioff, Neil Sculthorpe, the participants of BCTCS 2011 in Birmingham and our anonymous referees for useful comments and suggestions; and Matteo Acerbi for implementing our work in Coq.

References

1. Acerbi, M.: Personal Communication (May 2011)
2. Bahr, P., Hvitved, T.: Parametric Compositional Data Types. University of Copenhagen (June 2011)
3. Harrison, W.L.: Modular Compilers and Their Correctness Proofs. PhD thesis, University of Illinois at Urbana-Champaign (2001)
4. Huttel, H.: Transitions and Trees: An Introduction to Structured Operational Semantics. Cambridge University Press (2010)
5. Hutton, G.: Programming in Haskell. Cambridge University Press (2007)
6. Hutton, G., Wright, J.: Compiling Exceptions Correctly. In: Kozen, D. (ed.) MPC 2004. LNCS, vol. 3125, pp. 211–227. Springer, Heidelberg (2004)
7. Jaskelioff, M.: Monatron: An Extensible Monad Transformer Library. In: Scholz, S.-B., Chitil, O. (eds.) IFL 2008. LNCS, vol. 5836, pp. 233–248. Springer, Heidelberg (2011)
8. Jaskelioff, M.: Lifting of Operations in Modular Monadic Semantics. PhD thesis, University of Nottingham (2009)
9. Liang, S., Hudak, P., Jones, M.: Monad Transformers and Modular Interpreters. In: Proceedings of the 22nd ACM Symposium on Principles of Programming Languages. ACM Press (1995)
10. Meijer, E., Fokkinga, M., Paterson, R.: Functional Programming with Bananas, Lenses, Envelopes and Barbed Wire. In: Hughes, J. (ed.) FPCA 1991. LNCS, vol. 523, pp. 124–144. Springer, Heidelberg (1991)
11. Meijer, E., Hutton, G.: Bananas In Space: Extending Fold and Unfold To Exponential Types. In: Proceedings of the 7th SIGPLAN-SIGARCH-WG2.8 International Conference on Functional Programming and Computer Architecture. ACM Press, La Jolla (1995)
12. Moggi, E.: Notions of Computation and Monads. Information and Computation 93, 55–92 (1989)
13. Mosses, P.D.: Modular structural operational semantics (2004)
14. Schmidt, D.A.: Denotational Semantics: A Methodology For Language Development. William C. Brown Publishers, Dubuque (1986)
15. Swierstra, W.: Data Types à la Carte. Journal of Functional Programming 18, 423–436 (2008)
16. Wadler, P.: Comprehending Monads. In: Proc. ACM Conference on Lisp and Functional Programming (1990)
17. Wadler, P.: Monads for Functional Programming. In: Proceedings of the Marktoberdorf Summer School on Program Design Calculi. Springer, Heidelberg (1992)
18. Wadler, P.: The Expression Problem (1998), http://homepages.inf.ed.ac.uk/wadler/papers/expression/expression.txt

Functory: A Distributed Computing Library
for Objective Caml*

Jean-Christophe Filliâtre and K. Kalyanasundaram

CNRS, LRI, Univ Paris-Sud 11, Orsay F-91405
INRIA Saclay - Île-de-France, ProVal, Orsay, F-91893
filliatr@lri.fr, kalyan.krishnamani@inria.fr

Abstract. We present Functory, a distributed computing library for Objective Caml. The main features of this library include (1) a polymorphic API, (2) several implementations to adapt to different deployment scenarios such as sequential, multi-core or network, and (3) a reliable fault-tolerance mechanism. This paper describes the motivation behind this work, as well as the design and implementation of the library. It also demonstrates the potential of the library using realistic experiments.

1 Introduction

This paper introduces Functory, a generic library for distributed computing for a widely used functional programming language, Objective Caml (OCaml for short). This work was initially motivated by the computing needs that exist in our own research team. Our applications include large-scale deductive program verification, which amounts to checking the validity of a large number of logical formulas using a variety of automated theorem provers [7]. Our computing infrastructure consists of a few powerful multi-core machines (typically 8 to 16 cores) and several desktop PCs (typically dual-core). However, for our application needs, no existing library provides a polymorphic API with usual map/fold higher-order operations, built-in fault-tolerance, and the ability to easily switch between multi-core and network infrastructures. Hence we designed and implemented such a library, which is the subject of this paper. The library is available at http://functory.lri.fr/.

The distributed computing library presented in this paper is not a library that helps in parallelizing computations. Rather, it provides facilities for reliable, distributed execution of parallelizable computations. In particular, it provides a set of user-friendly APIs that allows distributed execution of large-scale parallelizable computations, very relevant to our application needs (and also relevant to a variety of real-world applications). Further, the distributed execution could be over multiple cores in the same machine or over a network of machines. The most important features of our library are the following:

---

* This research was partly supported by the French national project U3CAT (*Unification of Critical C Code Analysis Techniques*, ANR-08-SEGI-021).

R. Peña and R. Page (Eds.): TFP 2011, LNCS 7193, pp. 65–81, 2012.

- *Genericity*: it allows various patterns of polymorphic computations;
- *Simplicity*: switching between multiple cores on the same machine and a network of machines is as simple as changing a couple of lines of code;
- *Task distribution and fault-tolerance*: it provides automatic task distribution and a robust fault-tolerance mechanism, thereby relieving the user from implementing such routines.

The application domain of such a distributed computing library is manyfold. It serves a variety of users and a wide spectrum of needs, from desktop PCs to networks of machines. Typical applications would involve executing a large number of computationally expensive tasks in a resource-optimal and time-efficient manner. This is also the case in our research endeavours, that is validating thousands of verification conditions using automated theorem provers, utilizing the computing infrastructure to the maximum. It is worth noting that Functory is not targeted at applications running on server farms, crunching enormous amounts of data, such as Google's MapReduce [6].

In the following, we introduce our approach to distributed computing in a functional programming setting and distinguish it from related work.

Distributed Computing. A typical distributed computing library, as Functory, provides the following (we borrow some terminology from Google's MapReduce):

- A notion of *tasks* which denote atomic computations to be performed in a distributed manner;
- A set of processes (possibly executing on remote machines) called *workers* that perform the tasks, producing results;
- A single process called a *master* which is in charge of distributing the tasks among the workers and managing results produced by the workers.

In addition to the above, distributed computing environments also implement mechanisms for fault-tolerance, efficient storage, and distribution of tasks. This is required to handle network failures that may occur, as well as to optimize the usage of machines in the network. Another concern of importance is the transmission of messages over the network. This requires efficient *marshaling* of data, that is encoding and decoding of data for transmission over different computing environments. It is desirable to maintain architecture independence while transmitting marshalled data, as machines in a distributed computing environment often run on different hardware architectures and make use of different software platforms. For example, machine word size or endianness may be different across machines on the network.

A Functional Programming Approach. Our work was initially inspired by Google's MapReduce[1]. However, our functional programming environment allows us to be more generic. The main idea behind our approach is that workers may implement any polymorphic function:

---

[1] Ironically, Google's approach itself was inspired by functional programming primitives.

worker: $\alpha \rightarrow \beta$

where α denotes the type of tasks and β the type of results. Then the master is a function to handle the results together with a list of initial tasks:

master: $(\alpha \rightarrow \beta \rightarrow \alpha$ list$) \rightarrow \alpha$ list $\rightarrow$ unit

The function passed to the master is applied whenever a result is available. The first argument is the task (of type α) and the second one its result (of type β). It may in turn generate new tasks, hence the return type α list. The master is executed as long as there are pending tasks.

Our library makes use of OCaml's marshaling capabilities as much as possible. Whenever master and worker executables are exactly the same, we can marshal polymorphic values and closures. However, it is not always possible to have master and workers running the same executable. In this case, we cannot marshal closures anymore but we can still marshal polymorphic values as long as the same version of OCaml is used to compile master and workers. When different versions of OCaml are used, we can no longer marshal values but we can still transmit strings between master and workers. Our library adapts to all these situations, by providing several APIs.

Related Work. In order to compare and better distinguish Functory from others work with related goals and motivations, we can broadly classify the related work in this domain into:

1. *Distributed Functional Languages (DFLs)* — functional languages that provide built-in primitives for distribution. Examples include ML5, JoCaml, Glasgow Distributed Haskell, Erlang, etc.
2. *Libraries for existing functional languages* — that could be readily used in order to avoid implementing details like task distribution, fault-tolerance, socket programming, etc.

Functory belongs to the second category. For reasons of completeness, though, we first describe some existing DFLs related to functional programming.

JoCaml is one of the DFLs which provides communication primitives (like channels) for facilitating transmission of computations. However, it does not provide ready-made language features for fault-tolerance, which is indispensable in a distributed setting. The user has to include code for fault-tolerance, as already demonstrated in some JoCaml library [10]. ML5 [11], a variant of ML, is a programming language for distributed computing, specialized for web programming. It provides primitives for transferring control between the client and the server, as well as low-level primitives for marshaling the data. As in the case before, ML5 is a programming language that offers primitives for code mobility, and the code for distribution of computation and fault-tolerance has to be included by the user. ML5 implements type-safe marshaling and Functory does not, though an existing type-safe marshaling library could be used with Functory. Glasgow Distributed Haskell (GdH) [13] is a pure distributed functional language that is built on top of Glasgow Haskell and provides features for distributed computing. It is an extension of both Glasgow Parallel Haskell, that supports only one process and multiple threads and Concurrent Haskell that supports multiple processes. It also offers features for fault-tolerance - error detection and error recovery primitives in the language.

CamlP3l [1] mixes the features of functional programming with predefined patterns for parallel computation to offer a parallel programming environment. Again, it is a programming language offering primitives for distributing computation to parallel processes and also to merge the results from parallel executions. Erlang [3] is a programming language which has features for distribution and fault-tolerance. In particular, it has features for task distribution and is more well-known for its rich error detection primitives and the ability to support hot-swapping. The error detection primitives of Erlang allow nodes to monitor processes in other nodes and also facilitate automatic migration of tasks in failed nodes to recovered or active nodes.

Any DFL above could have been used to implement our library. Our motivation, though, was neither to implement our system using any existing DFL nor to come up with a new DFL. The goal of Functory is rather to provide the users of an *existing* general-purpose functional programming language, namely OCaml, high-level user-friendly APIs that hide the messy details of task distribution and fault-tolerance. We now turn to distributed computing libraries for general purpose functional languages and weed out the distinguishing features of Functory.

There are several implementations of Google's MapReduce in functional programming languages. But Functory was just inspired by Google's MapReduce and is not exactly a MapReduce implementation. The simplest difference comes from the very fact that Functory does not operate on key/value pairs. PlasmaMR [2] is an OCaml implementation of Google's MapReduce on a distributed file system PlasmaFS. It is able to use PlasmaFS to its advantage — the ability of the file system to handle large files and query functions that implement data locality to optimize network traffic. However, PlasmaMR does not support fault-tolerance which is indispensable in any distributed computing application. Another MapReduce implementation in OCaml is Yohann Padioleau's [12]. It is built on top of OCamlMPI [9], while our approach uses a homemade protocol for message passing. Currently, we have less flexibility w.r.t. deployment of the user program than OCamlMPI; on the other hand, we provide a more generic API together with fault-tolerance. We feel that an indispensible need for any distributed computing library is fault-tolerance, and using a homemade protocol enables us to tune our implementation to our needs of fault-tolerance.

The iTask system [8] is a library for the functional language 'Clean' targeted at distributed workflow management. The library provides a set of combinators (some of which perform map/fold operations) that facilitate applications running in different nodes of a distributed system to communicate, exchange information and coordinate their computations in a type-safe manner.

2 API

This section describes our API. We start from a simple API which is reduced to a single higher-order polymorphic function. Then we explain how this function is actually implemented in terms of low-level primitives, which are also provided in our API. Conversely, we also explain how the same function can be used to implement high-level distribution functions for map and fold operations. Finally, we explain how our API is implemented in five different ways, according to five different deployment scenarios.

2.1 A Generic Distribution Function

The generic distribution function in our API follows the idea sketched in the introduction. It has the following signature:

val compute:
    worker:$(\alpha \rightarrow \beta) \rightarrow$
    master:$(\alpha \times \gamma \rightarrow \beta \rightarrow (\alpha \times \gamma)$ list$) \rightarrow (\alpha \times \gamma)$ list $\rightarrow$ unit

Tasks are pairs, of type $\alpha \times \gamma$, where the first component is passed to the worker and the second component is local to the master. The worker function should be pure[2] and is executed in parallel in all worker processes. The function master, on the contrary, can be impure and is only executed sequentially in the master process. The master function typically stores results in some internal data structure. Additionally, it may produce new tasks, as a list of type $(\alpha \times \gamma)$ list, which are then appended to the current set of pending tasks.

2.2 Low-Level Primitives

The function compute above can actually be implemented in terms of low-level primitives, such as adding a task, adding a worker, performing some communication between master and workers, etc. These primitives are provided in our API, such that the user can interact with the execution of the distributed computation. For instance, a monitoring-like application can use these primitives to allow observation and modification of resources (tasks, workers) during the course of a computation. A type for distributed computations is introduced:

type (α, γ) computation

A computation is created with a function create, which accepts the same worker and master as compute:

val create: worker:$(\alpha \rightarrow \beta) \rightarrow$
    master:$(\alpha \times \gamma \rightarrow \beta \rightarrow (\alpha \times \gamma)$ list$) \rightarrow (\alpha, \gamma)$ computation

Contrary to compute, it takes no list of tasks and returns immediately. Tasks can be added later using the following function:

---

[2] We mean *observationally pure* here but we allow exceptions to be raised to signal failures.

val add_task: (α, γ) computation $\to \alpha \times \gamma \to$ unit

A function is provided to perform *one step* of a given computation:

val one_step: (α, γ) computation $\to$ unit

Calling this function results in one exchange of messages between master and workers: task assignments to workers, results returned to the master, etc. A few other functions are provided, such as status to query the status of a computation, clear to remove all tasks, etc.

Using these low-level primitives, it is straightforward to implement the compute function. Basically, it is as simple as the following:

```
let compute ~worker ~master tasks =
  let c = create worker master in
  List.iter (add_task c) tasks;
  while status c = Running do one_step c done
```

2.3 High-Level API

In most cases, the easiest way to parallelize an execution is to make use of operations over lists, where processing of the list elements are done in parallel. To facilitate such a processing, our library provides most commonly used list operations, all implemented using our generic compute function.

The most obvious operation is the traditional map operation over lists, that is **val** map: f:$(\alpha \to \beta) \to \alpha$ list $\to \beta$ list. Each task consists of the application of function f to a list element. More interesting is a combination of map and fold operations. For instance, we provide different flavors of function

val map_fold: f:$(\alpha \to \beta) \to$ fold:$(\gamma \to \beta \to \gamma) \to \gamma \to \alpha$ list $\to \gamma$

which, given two functions, an accumulator a and a list l, computes

$$\text{fold}...(\text{fold}(\text{fold } a \ (\text{f } x_1))(\text{f } x_2))...(\text{f } x_n) \tag{1}$$

for some permutation $[x_1, x_2, ..., x_n]$ of the list l. We assume that the f operations are always performed in parallel. Regarding fold operations, we distinguish two cases: either fold operations are computationally less expensive than f and we perform them locally; or fold operations are computationally expensive and we perform them in parallel. Thus we provide two functions map_local_fold and map_remote_fold.

In the case of map_remote_fold, only one fold operation can be performed at a time (possibly in parallel with f operations), as obvious from (1). However, there are cases where several fold operations can be performed in parallel, as early as intermediate results of fold operations are available. This is the case when fold is an associative operation (which implies that types β and γ are the same). Whenever fold is also commutative, we can perform even more fold operations in parallel. Thus our API provides two functions map_fold_a and map_fold_ac for these two particular cases, with types

val map_fold_ac, map_fold_a:
  f:$(\alpha \to \beta) \to$ fold:$(\beta \to \beta \to \beta) \to \beta \to \alpha$ list $\to \beta$

It is rather straightforward to derive these five functions from the generic compute function; we invite readers interested in details to refer to the source code.

2.4 Deployment Scenarios

Actually, our library provides not just one implementation for the API above, but instead five different implementations depending on the deployment scenario. The first two scenarios are the following:

1. **Purely sequential execution:** this is mostly intended to be a reference implementation for performance comparisons, as well as for debugging;
2. **Several cores on the same machine:** this implementation is intended to distribute the computation over a single machine and it makes use of UNIX processes;

The next three scenarios are intended for distributing the computation over a network of machines.

3. **Same executable run on master and worker machines:** this implementation makes use of the ability to marshal OCaml closures and polymorphic values.
4. **Master and workers are different programs, compiled with the same version of OCaml:** we can no longer marshal closures but we can still marshal polymorphic values. API functions are split into two sets, used to implement master and workers respectively.
5. **Master and workers are different programs, not even compiled with the same version of OCaml:** we can no longer use marshaling, so API functions are restricted to work on strings instead of polymorphic values.

Our library is organized into three modules: Sequential for the pure sequential implementation, Cores for multiple cores on the same machine and Network for a network of machines, respectively. The Network module itself is organized into three sub-modules, called Same, Poly and Mono, corresponding to contexts 3, 4 and 5 above.

2.5 Several Libraries in One

From the description above, it is clear that our library provides several APIs of different granularities, as well as several implementations for various deployment scenarios. Most combinations are meaningful, resulting in thirteen possible different ways of using our library. For instance, one may use the low-level API on a single multi-core machine, or use the high-level API on a network of machines all running the same executable, etc. From the implementation point of view, there is almost no code duplication. We are using OCaml functors to derive specific implementations from generic ones.

3   Implementation Details

The implementation of the Sequential module is straightforward and does not require any explanation. The Cores module is implemented with UNIX processes, using the fork and wait system calls provided by the Unix library of OCaml. We do not describe this implementation but rather focus on the more interesting module Network.

3.1   Marshaling

As mentioned in Section 2, the Network module actually provides three different implementations as sub-modules, according to three different execution scenarios, the details of which are presented below:

Same. This module is used when master and workers are running the same executable. The master and workers have to be differentiated in some manner. We use an environment variable WORKER for this purpose. When set, it indicates that the executable acts as a worker. At runtime, a worker immediately enters a loop waiting for tasks from the master, without even getting into the user code. As explained in Section 2, the master function has the following signature.

```
val compute: worker:(α → β) →
   master:(α × γ → β → (α × γ) list) → (α × γ) list → unit
```

The master uses marshaling to send both a closure of type $\alpha \to \beta$ and a task of type α to the worker. The resulting strings are passed as argument f and x in message Assign. Similarly, the worker uses marshaling to send back the result of the computation of type β, which is the argument s in message Completed. These messages are described in detail in Section 3.2.

Though the ability to run the same executable helps a lot in deploying the program in different machines, it comes at a small price. Since the worker is not getting into the user code, closures which are transmitted from the master cannot refer to global variables in the user code. Indeed, the initialization code for these global variables is never reached on the worker side. For instance, some code for drawing Mandelbrot's set could be written as follows:

```
let max_iterations = 200
let worker si = ... draw sub-image si using max_iterations ...
```

That is, the global function worker makes use of the global variable max_iterations. The worker gets the function to compute from the master, namely the closure corresponding to function worker in that case, but on the worker side the initialization of max_iterations is never executed.

One obvious solution is not to use global variables in the worker code. This is not always possible, though. To overcome this, the Same sub-module also provides a Worker.compute function to start the worker loop manually from the user code. This way, it can be started at any point, in particular after the initialization of the required global variables. Master and worker are still running the same executable, but are distinguished using a user-defined way (command-line argument, environment variable, etc.).

There are situations where it is not possible to run the same executable for master and workers. For instance, architectures or operating systems could be different across the network. For that reason, the Network module provides two other implementations.

Poly. When master and workers are compiled with the same version of OCaml, we can no longer marshal closures but we can still marshal polymorphic values. Indeed, an interesting property of marshaling in OCaml is to be fully architecture-independent, as long as a single version of OCaml is used. It is worth pointing out that absence of marshaled closures now enables the use of two different programs for master and workers. This is not mandatory, though, since master and workers could still be distinguished at runtime as in the previous case.

On the worker side, the main loop is started manually using Worker.compute. The computation to be performed on each task is given as an argument to this function. It thus looks as follows:

Worker.compute: $(\alpha \to \beta) \to$ unit $\to$ unit

On the master side, the compute function is simpler than in the previous case, as it has one argument less, and thus has the following signature.

Master.compute:
    master:$(\alpha \times \gamma \to \beta \to (\alpha \times \gamma)$ list$) \to (\alpha \times \gamma)$ list $\to$ unit

For realistic applications, where master and workers are completely different programs, possibly written by different teams, this is the module of choice in our library, since it can still pass polymorphic values over the network. The issues of marshaling are automatically taken care of by the OCaml runtime.

The derived API presented in Section 2.3 is adapted to deal with the absence of closures. Exactly as the compute function, each API now takes two forms, one for the master and another for the workers. For example, map_fold_ac takes the following forms.

Worker.map_fold_ac: f:$(\alpha \to \beta) \to$ fold:$(\beta \to \beta \to \beta) \to$ unit
Master.map_fold_ac: $\beta \to \alpha$ list $\to \beta$

It is the responsibility of the user to ensure consistency between master and workers.

Mono. When master and workers are compiled using different versions of OCaml, we can no longer use marshaling. As in the previous case, we split compute into two functions, one for master and one for workers. In addition, values transmitted over the network can only be strings. The signature thus takes the following form.

Worker.compute: (string $\to$ string) $\to$ unit
Master.compute: master:(string $\times \gamma \to$ string $\to$ (string $\times \gamma)$ list) $\to$
    (string $\times \gamma)$ list $\to$ unit

Any other datatype for tasks should be encoded to/from strings. This conversion is left to the user. Note that the second component of each task is still polymorphic (of type γ here), since it is local to the master.

3.2 Protocol

The Network module implements the distributed computing library for a network of machines. It provides a function declare_workers: n:int $\rightarrow$ string $\rightarrow$ unit to fill a table of worker machines.

The Network module is based on a traditional TCP-based client/server architecture, where each worker is a server and the master is the client of each worker. The main execution loop is similar to the one in the Cores module, where distant processes on remote machines correspond to sub-processes and idle cores are the idle cores of remote workers. The master is purely sequential. In particular, when running the user master function, it is not capable of performing any task-related computation. This is not an issue, as we assume the master function not to be time-consuming. The worker, on the other hand, forks a new process to execute the task and hence can communicate with the master during its computation. We subsequently describe issues of message transfer and fault-tolerance.

Messages sent from master to workers could be any of the following kinds:

Assign(id:int, f:string, x:string). This message assigns a new task to the worker, the task being identified by the unique integer id. The task to be performed is given by strings f and x, which are interpreted depending on the context.

Kill(id:int). This message tells the worker to kill the task identified by id.

Stop. This message informs the worker about completion of the computation, so that it may choose to exit.

Ping. This message is used to check if the worker is still alive, expecting a Pong message from the worker in return.

Messages sent by workers could be any of the following kinds:

Pong. This message is an acknowledgment for a Ping message from the master.

Completed(id:int, s:string). This message indicates the completion of a task identified by id, with result s.

Aborted(id:int). This message informs the master that the task identified by id is aborted, either as a response to a Kill message or because of a worker malfunction.

Our implementation of the protocol works across different architectures, so that master and workers could be run on completely different platforms w.r.t. endianness, version of OCaml and operating system.

3.3 Fault-Tolerance

The main issue in any distributed computing environment is the ability to handle faults, which is also a distinguishing feature of our library. The fault-tolerance mechanism of Functory is limited to workers; handling master failures is the responsibility of the user, for instance by periodically logging the master's state. Worker faults are mainly of two kinds: either a worker is stopped, and possibly later restarted; or a worker is temporarily or permanently unreachable on the network. To provide fault-tolerance, our master implementation is keeping track of the status of each worker. This status is controlled by two timeout parameters T_1 and T_2 and Ping and Pong messages sent by master and workers, respectively. There are four possible statuses for a worker:

not connected: there is no ongoing TCP connection between the master and the worker;

alive: the worker has sent some message within T_1 seconds;

pinged: the worker has not sent any message within T_1 seconds and the master has sent the worker a Ping message within T_2 seconds;

unreachable: the worker has not yet responded to the Ping message (for more than T_2 seconds).

Whenever we receive a message from a worker, its status changes to alive and its timeout value is reset.

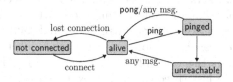

Fault tolerance is achieved by exploiting the status of workers as follows. First, tasks are only assigned to workers with either alive or pinged status. Second, whenever a worker executing a task t moves to status not connected or unreachable, the task t is rescheduled, which means it is put back in the set of pending tasks. Whenever a task is completed, any rescheduled copy of this task is either removed from the set of pending tasks or killed if it was already assigned to another worker.

It is worth noticing that our library is also robust w.r.t. exceptions raised by the user-provided worker function. In that case, an Aborted message is sent to the master and the task is rescheduled. It is the responsibility of the user to handle such exceptions if necessary.

4   Experiments

In this section, we demonstrate the potential of using Functory on several case studies. The source code for all these case studies is contained in the distribution, in sub-directory tests/.

The purpose of the following experiments is to compare the various deployments, namely sequential, cores and network. For this comparison to be fair, all computations are performed on the same machine, an 8 core Intel Xeon 3.2 GHz running Debian Linux. The sequential implementation uses a single core. The multi-core implementation uses up to 8 cores of the machine. The network implementation uses 8 workers running locally and a master running on a remote machine over a LAN (which incurs communication cost).

4.1 N-Queens

The first example is the classical N-queens problem, where we compute the total number of ways to place N queens on a $N \times N$ chessboard in such a way no two queens attack each other. We use a standard backtracking algorithm for this problem, which places the queens one by one starting from the first row. Distributing the computation is thus quite easy: we consider all possible ways to place queens on the first D rows and then perform the subsequent search in parallel. Choosing $D = 1$ will result in exactly N tasks; choosing $D = 2$ will result in $N^2 - 3N + 2$ tasks; greater values for D would result in too many tasks.

Each task only consists of three integers and its result is one integer, which is the total number of solutions for this task. We make use of function map_local_fold from the derived API, where f is performing the search and fold simply adds the intermediate results. In the network configuration, we make use of the Network.Same module, workers and master being the same executable.

The following table shows execution times for various values of N and our three different implementations: Sequential, Cores, and Network. The purpose of this experiment is to measure the speedup w.r.t. the sequential implementation. The first column shows the value of N. The number of tasks is shown in second column. Then the last three columns show execution times in seconds for the three implementations. The figures within brackets show the speedup w.r.t. sequential implementation. Speedup ratios are also displayed in Fig. 1 (note the logarithmic scale).

N	D	#tasks	Sequential	Cores	Network
16	1	16	15.2	2.04 (7.45×)	2.35 (6.47×)
	2	210	15.2	2.01 (7.56×)	21.80 (0.69×)
17	1	17	107.0	17.20 (6.22×)	16.20 (6.60×)
	2	240	107.0	14.00 (7.64×)	24.90 (4.30×)
18	1	18	787.0	123.00 (6.40×)	125.00 (6.30×)
	2	272	787.0	103.00 (7.64×)	124.00 (6.34×)
19	1	19	6120.0	937.00 (6.53×)	940.00 (6.51×)
	2	306	6130.0	796.00 (7.70×)	819.00 (7.48×)

From the table above and Fig. 1, it is clear that the Cores and Network implementations provide a significant speedup. As evident from the last row, the speedup is almost 8, which is also the number of cores we use. It is also evident from the last column that the Network implementation performs significantly better when the computation time dominates in the total execution time. The two extreme cases correspond to the second and the last row: in the second row, the communication time dominates and is in fact more than 91% of the total execution time; on the other hand, for the last row communication time amounts to just

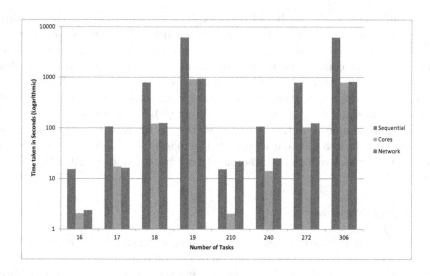

Fig. 1. Speedup ratios for the N-queens experiment

4.6% of the total execution time. As expected, the network implementation is only beneficial when the computation time for each individual task is significant, which is the case in realistic examples.

4.2   Matrix Multiplication

This benchmark was inspired by the PASCO'10 programming contest [5]. It consists of multiplication of two square matrices of dimension 100 with integer coefficients. Coefficients have several thousands of digits, hence we use GMP [4] to handle operations over coefficients.

We compare the performances of two different implementations. In the first one, called mm1, each task consists of the computation of a single coefficient of the resultant matrix. In the second one, called mm2, each task consists of the computation of a whole row of the resultant matrix. As a consequence, the total number of tasks is 10,000 for mm1 and only 100 for mm2. On the contrary, each task result for mm1 is a single integer, while for mm2 it is a row of 100 integers. The experimental results (in seconds) are tabulated below.

	mm1 (10,000 tasks)	mm2 (100 tasks)
Sequential	20.3	20.2
Cores (2 cores)	22.7 (0.89×)	11.3 (1.79×)
(4 cores)	12.3 (1.65×)	6.1 (3.31×)
(6 cores)	8.6 (2.36×)	4.3 (4.70×)
(8 cores)	8.0 (2.54×)	3.5 (5.77×)

The difference in the number of tasks explains the differences in the speedup ratios above. We do not include results for the network configuration, as they do not achieve any benefit with respect to the sequential implementation. The reason is that the communication cost dominates the computation cost in such a way that the total execution time is always greater than 30 seconds. Indeed, irrespective of the implementation (mm1 or mm2), the total size of the transmitted data is 10^6 integers, which in our case amounts to billions of bytes.

A less naive implementation would have the worker read the input matrices only once, *e.g.* from a file, and then have the master send only row and column indices. This would reduce the amount of transmitted data to 10,000 integers only.

4.3   Mandelbrot Set

Drawing the Mandelbrot set is another classical example that could be distributed easily, since the color of each point can be computed independently of the others. This benchmark consists in drawing the fragment of the Mandelbrot set with lower left corner $(-1.1, 0.2)$ and upper right corner $(-0.8, 0.4)$, as a $9,000 \times 6,000$ image. If the total number of tasks $t \geq 1$ is given as a parameter, it is straight forward to split the image into t sub-images, each of which is computed in parallel with and independently of the others. In our case, the image is split into horizontal slices. Each task is thus four floating-point numbers denoting the region coordinates, together with two integers denoting the dimensions of the sub-image to be drawn. The result of the task is a matrix of pixels, of size $54,000,000/t$. For instance, using $t = 20$ tasks will result in 20 sub-images of size 10.3 Mb each, assuming each pixel is encoded in four bytes.

The sequential computation of this image consumes 29.4 seconds. For Cores and Network implementations, the computation times in seconds are tabulated below.

#cores	#tasks	Cores	Network
2	10	15.8 (1.86×)	20.3 (1.45×)
	30	15.7 (_1.87_×)	18.7 (1.57×)
	100	16.1 (1.83×)	19.8 (1.48×)
	1000	19.6 (1.50×)	38.6 (0.76×)
4	10	9.50 (3.09×)	14.4 (2.04×)
	30	8.26 (_3.56_×)	11.4 (2.58×)
	100	8.37 (3.51×)	11.4 (2.58×)
	1000	10.6 (2.77×)	20.5 (1.43×)
8	10	9.40 (3.13×)	12.6 (2.33×)
	30	4.24 (_6.93_×)	7.6 (3.87×)
	100	4.38 (6.71×)	7.5 (3.92×)
	1000	6.86 (4.29×)	11.3 (2.60×)

The best timings are achieved for the Cores configuration, where communications happen within the same machine and are thus cheaper. There are two significant differences with respect to the n-queens benchmark. On one hand, the number of tasks can be controlled more easily than in the case of n-queens. We experimentally figured out the optimal number of tasks to be 30. On the other hand, each computation result is an image, rather than just an integer as in the case of n-queens. Consequently, communication costs are much greater. In this particular experiment, the total size of the results transmitted is more than 200 Mb.

4.4 SMT Solvers

Here we demonstrate the potential of our library for our application needs as mentioned in the introduction. We consider 80 challenging verification conditions (VC) obtained from the Why platform [7]. Each VC is stored in a file, which is accessible over NFS. The purpose of the experiment is to check the validity of each VC using several automated provers (namely Alt-Ergo, Simplify, Z3 and CVC3).

The master program proceeds by reading the file names, turning them into tasks by multiplying them by the number of provers, resulting in 320 tasks in total. Each worker in turn invokes the given prover on the given file, within a timeout limit of 1 minute. Each task completes with one of the four possible outcomes: *valid, unknown* (depending on whether the VC is valid or undecided by the prover), *timeout* and *failure*. The result of each computation is a pair denoting the status and the time spent in the prover call. The master collects these results and sums up the timings for each prover and each possible status.

Our computing infrastructure for this experiment consists of 3 machines with 4, 8 and 8 cores respectively, the master being run on a fourth machine. The figure below shows the total time in minutes spent by each prover for each possible outcome.

prover	valid	unknown	timeout	failure
Alt-ergo	406.0	3.0	11400.0	0.0
Simplify	0.5	0.4	1200.0	222.0
Z3	80.7	0.0	1800.0	1695.0
CVC3	303.0	82.7	4200.0	659.0

These figures sum up to more than 6 hours if provers were executed sequentially. However, using our library and our 3-machine infrastructure, it completes in 22 minutes and 37 seconds, giving us a speedup of more than 16×. We are still far away from the ideal ratio of 20× (we are using 20 cores), since some provers are allocating a lot of memory and time spent in system calls is not accounted for in the total observed time. However, a ratio of 16× is already a significant improvement for our day-to-day experiments. Further a large parallelizable computation could be distributed by just adding 3-4 lines of code (to just specify the module to be used and the tasks) which is an important user-friendly feature of the library. Further we assume files available over NFS. Intelligent distribution of data over a network is in itself an area of research which is beyond the scope of our work.

5 Conclusions and Future Work

In this paper, we presented a distributed programming library for OCaml. The main features are the genericity of the interface, which makes use of polymorphic higher-order functions, and the ability to easily switch between sequential, multi-core, and network implementations. In particular, Functory allows to use the same executable for master and workers, which makes the deployment of small programs immediate — master and workers being only distinguished by an environment variable. Functory also allows master and workers to be completely different programs, which is ideal for large scale deployment. Another distinguishing feature of our library is a robust fault-tolerance mechanism which relieves the user of cumbersome implementation details. Yet another interesting feature of the library is the ability to add workers dynamically. Functory also allows to cascade several distributed computations inside the same program. Finally, the low-level API of Functory can be used to write interactive programs where one can adjust certain parameters in a GUI, like increasing or decreasing the number of workers, to observe the progress in computation, resource consumption, etc.

Future Work. There are still some interesting features that could be added to our library.

- One is the ability to efficiently assign tasks to workers depending on resource parameters, such as data locality, CPU power, memory, etc. This could be achieved by providing the user with the means to control task scheduling. This would enable Functory to scale up to MapReduce-like applications.
  Currently, without any information about the tasks, the scheduling is completely arbitrary. In both Cores and Network modules, we use traditional queues for the pending tasks; in particular, new tasks produced by the master are appended to the end of the queue.
- Our library provides limited support for retrieving real-time information about computations and communications. Processing and storing information about workers and tasks locally in the master is straightforward.
- One very nice feature of Google's MapReduce is the possibility to use redundantly several idle workers on the same tasks for speedup when reaching the end of computation. Since we already have the fault-tolerance implemented, this optimization should be straightforward to add to our library.

We intend to enrich our library with all above features.

Acknowledgments. We are grateful to the ProVal team for support and comments on early versions of the library and of this paper. We thank the anonymous reviewers for their helpful comments and suggestions.

References

1. CamlP3l, http://camlp3l.inria.fr/
2. Plasma, http://plasma.camlcity.org/plasma
3. The Erlang Programming Language, http://www.erlang.org/
4. The GNU Multiple Precision Arithmetic Library, http://gmplib.org/
5. Parallel Symbolic Computation 2010 (PASCO) (2010),
   http://pasco2010.imag.fr/
6. Dean, J., Ghemawat, S.: MapReduce: Simplified Data Processing on Large Clusters. In: OSDI, pp. 137–150 (2004)
7. Filliâtre, J.-C., Marché, C.: The Why/Krakatoa/Caduceus Platform for Deductive Program Verification. In: Damm, W., Hermanns, H. (eds.) CAV 2007. LNCS, vol. 4590, pp. 173–177. Springer, Heidelberg (2007)
8. Jansen, J.M., Plasmeijer, R., Koopman, P., Achten, P.: Embedding a Web-based Workflow Management System in a Functional Language. In: Proceedings of the Tenth Workshop on Language Descriptions, Tools and Applications, LDTA 2010, pp. 7:1–7:8. ACM, New York (2010)
9. Leroy, X.: OCamlMPI: Interface with the MPI Message-passing Interface,
   http://pauillac.inria.fr/~xleroy/software.html
10. Mandel, L., Maranget, L.: Programming in JoCaml (Tool Demonstration). In: Gairing, M. (ed.) ESOP 2008. LNCS, vol. 4960, pp. 108–111. Springer, Heidelberg (2008)
11. Murphy VII., T., Crary, K., Harper, R.: Type-Safe Distributed Programming with ML5. In: Barthe, G., Fournet, C. (eds.) TGC 2007. LNCS, vol. 4912, pp. 108–123. Springer, Heidelberg (2008)
12. Padioleau, Y.: A Poor Man's MapReduce for OCaml (2009),
    http://www.padator.org/ocaml/mapreduce.pdf
13. Pointon, R.F., Trinder, P.W., Loidl, H.-W.: The Design and Implementation of Glasgow Distributed Haskell. In: Mohnen, M., Koopman, P. (eds.) IFL 2000. LNCS, vol. 2011, pp. 53–70. Springer, Heidelberg (2001)

ParaForming: Forming Parallel Haskell Programs Using Novel Refactoring Techniques

Christopher Brown[1], Hans-Wolfgang Loidl[2], and Kevin Hammond[1]

[1] School of Computer Science, University of St. Andrews, UK
{chrisb,kh}@cs.st-andrews.ac.uk
[2] School of Mathematical and Computer Sciences, Heriot-Watt University, UK
hwloidl@macs.hw.ac.uk

Abstract. Enabling programmers to "think parallel" is critical if we are to be able to effectively exploit future multicore/manycore architectures. This paper introduces *paraforming*: a new approach to constructing parallel functional programs using formally-defined refactoring transformations. We introduce a number of new refactorings for Parallel Haskell that capture common parallel abstractions, such as *divide-and-conquer* and *data parallelism*, and show how these can be used by HaRe, the Haskell Refactorer. Using a paraforming approach, we are able to easily obtain significant and scalable speedups (up to 7.8 on an 8-core machine).

1 Introduction

Despite Moore's "law" [1], uniprocessor clock speeds have now stalled. Rather than using single processors running at ever-higher clock speeds, even consumer laptops and desktops now have dual-, quad- or hexa-core processors. **Haswell**, Intel's next multicore architecture, will have eight cores by default. Future hardware will not be *slightly parallel*, however, as with today's multicore systems, but will be *massively* parallel, with *manycore* and perhaps even *megacore* systems becoming mainstream. This means that programmers need to start *thinking parallel*, moving away from traditional programming models where parallelism is a bolted-on afterthought. *Rather, programmers must use languages where parallelism is deeply embedded into the programming model from the outset.* This is a golden opportunity for purely functional languages, such as Haskell [2], which naturally supports parallelism, and avoids many of the classical difficulties with parallel programming. However, transforming parallel thoughts into parallel functional code can still require substantial effort.

This paper introduces *paraforming*: using software refactoring [3] to assist the programmer in writing efficient parallel functional programs. Refactoring tool support gives many advantages over unaided parallel programming: it guides the programmers through the process of writing a parallel program, without them having to understand the exact syntax of the underlying parallel language; it identifies general patterns of parallelism for their algorithms; it enforces separation of concerns between *application programmers* (those coding the business

R. Peña and R. Page (Eds.): TFP 2011, LNCS 7193, pp. 82–97, 2012.
© Springer-Verlag Berlin Heidelberg 2012

logic of the application) and *system programmers* (those taking care of the refactoring tools); it reduces *time-to-deploy*; it can incorporate information on extra-functional properties such as computational costs; it can automatically warn the programmer of drastic changes in the estimated balance of parallelism; and it helps tune existing parallel programs. All of these advantages (and more) help programmers understand how to write parallel functional programs.

1.1 Contributions

In this paper, we show and demonstrate a number of new refactorings for Haskell that allow programmers to refactor their original source programs into parallel ones, choosing from a well-defined set of high-level parallel source-code transformations that will gradually refine an idea into an effective parallel program. Rather than programming blindly, the refactoring tool guides the user through the process of making their program parallel. In this way, they will be able to *form* sensible parallel programs from their initial ideas.

The main technical contributions made by this paper are:

1. we present a number of new refactorings for the HaRe [4] refactoring system for Haskell, that help to introduce and tune Parallel Haskell programs;
2. we *formally define rewrite rules for the refactorings* presented in the paper;
3. we demonstrate the effectiveness of the refactorings on two worked examples, showing good performance speedups;
4. we show how it is possible to implement common task- and data-parallelism using the refactorings.

2   The HaRe Refactoring System for Haskell

The refactorings presented here are built on the framework of HaRe, the Haskell Refactorer, that provides refactoring support for the full Haskell 98 standard. Figure 1 shows a screenshot of HaRe in Emacs[1] with a menu of possible refactorings that could be applied to the source program. HaRe currently provides a substantial number of structural and data-type based refactorings, aimed at refactoring pure sequential Haskell 98 programs. HaRe is built on the Programatica [5] front-end for parsing, and the Strafunski library [6] for generic tree traversals, together abstracted into a low-level refactoring API [4] for designing and developing refactorings. This API provides the user with an Abstract Syntax Tree (AST) for the source program together with utility functions (tree traversal and tree transformations) to assist in the implementation of refactorings. HaRe is itself written in Haskell, and the refactorings it supports can be applied to both single and multi module projects. Application programmers use these refactorings to "enrich" their original programs. Unlike automatic parallelisation, the application programmer chooses from a well-defined set of refactorings, contributing to the development of a "parallel programming" attitude in application programmers.

---

[1] A vi version is also available.

Fig. 1. HaRe embedded in Emacs, showing some refactorings for parallelisation

3   GpH and Evaluation Strategies

The refactorings in this paper target Glasgow parallel Haskell (GpH) [7,8], a conservative extension to Haskell. However, they could easily be applied to other parallel variants of Haskell, such as Eden [9], and should generalise to other parallel functional notations. In GpH, parallelism is introduced by applying the rpar *strategy* (called *sparking*) and evaluation order is specified by applying the rseq strategy.

```
rpar :: Strategy a
rseq :: Strategy a
```

These strategies are always applied in the context of the Eval monad: a specific monad for specifying evaluation order, evaluation degree and parallelism. A lifting function runEval :: Eval a -> a allows the monad to be integrated into other computations. Finally, using :: a -> Eval a -> a applies the specified strategy to its first argument, for example, f x `using` rpar x sparks x in parallel with f x. A full discussion of GpH and evaluation strategies is given in [8].

4   Refactorings for Forming Parallel Programs

This section gives a set of rewrite rules that define the new parallel refactorings for HaRe. The refactorings fall into two categories: *data* parallelism (Section 4.2), including the *Introduce Data Parallelism* and *Introduce Clustering* refactorings; and *task* parallelism (Section 4.3), including the *Introduce Task Parallelism*, *Introduce Thresholding* and *Modify Evaluation Degree* refactorings. The main refactorings are *Introduce Task/Data Parallelism*. The other refactorings can subsequently be used to improve parallel performance, by increasing the granularity of the parallelism (*Introduce Thresholding* and *Introduce Clustering*) and by modifying the order or degree of evaluation (*Modify Evaluation Degree*). In some cases it is also useful to modify the structure of the code beforehand, enabling a refactoring that introduces or improves parallelism.

4.1   Rewrite Rules

Each refactoring is a function taking a list of possible rewrite rules to apply to nodes of the Abstract Syntax Tree (AST). Each rewrite rule has its own set of conditions that state which nodes the rewrite rules can be applied to. If the condition fails, then the AST is traversed to the next applicable node (the traversal is top-down, which exactly corresponds with the corresponding implementation in HaRe, using Strafunski) where the rule and conditions are applied again. Futhermore, a transformation is applied to a node only once, so that a transformed node is not traversed further. This prevents nodes that were originally of the form f, being transformed into f v and then *further* being transformed into f f v. If a condition fails for a rewrite rule, then subsequent rules will also fail automatically, unless the rule is part of a *choice* construct, where the failing would result in the alternative rule being attempted instead. We define our refactoring function as follows:

$$Refactoring(x_0, ..., x_n) = \{Rule \times \{Condition\}\}$$

where $x_0, .., x_n$ are the arguments to the refactoring. The rewrite rules are defined as functions over types of nodes in the AST:

$$\mathcal{D}[\![.]\!] :: Declaration \rightarrow Declaration$$
$$\mathcal{E}[\![.]\!] :: Expr \rightarrow Expr$$
$$\mathcal{T}[\![.]\!] :: Type \rightarrow Type$$

The above functions work over nodes of an AST. In addition, some refactorings need to choose which rewrite rules to apply. Choice is denoted by $a \oplus b$ where rule a is applied first, and if that fails then b is applied instead. Sequencing, on the other hand, states that the rules should be applied in a strict sequence. It is denoted by $a \triangleright b$ where rule a is applied first and then rule b.

Code syntax is separated from the rule semantics by quasi quotes, so that $[\![f = e]\!]$ denotes a function in the AST of the form f = e. We denote substitution as $[\![f = e[x'/x]]\!]$, where we mean that all occurrences of x are substituted with x' in the expression e; here, x may either be free or bound in e, however we do not perform substitutions within bindings in e.

$$IntroDataParallelism(\rho, \mathbf{e}) =$$
$$\mathcal{E}[\![\ \mathbf{e}\ ]\!]\ \Rightarrow\ [\![\ \mathbf{e}\ \text{'using'}\ \text{parList rdeepseq}\ ]\!] \qquad (1)$$
$$\{typeof(\mathbf{e}) = instanceof([\mathbf{a}]), \text{parList} \in \rho, \text{using} \in \rho, \text{rdeepseq} \in \rho\}$$

Fig. 2. Rewrite rules for the *Introduce Data Parallelism* refactoring

$$IntroClustering(\rho, \mathbf{e}, \mathbf{v}) =$$
$$(\mathcal{D}[\![\ \mathbf{f}\ \overrightarrow{p}\ =\ \text{let decls in e}\ ]\!]$$
$$\Rightarrow\ [\![\ \mathbf{f}\ \mathbf{c}\ \overrightarrow{p}\ =\ \text{let decls in e 'using' parListChunk c rdeepseq}\ ]\!]$$
$$\{\mathbf{c}\ fresh, typeof(\mathbf{e}) = instanceof([\mathbf{a}]), \text{parListChunk} \in \rho, \text{using} \in \rho, \text{rdeepseq} \in \rho\}$$
$$\oplus$$
$$\mathcal{D}[\![\ \mathbf{f}\ \overrightarrow{p}\ =\ \text{let decls in e 'using' parList strat}\ ]\!]$$
$$\Rightarrow\ [\![\ \mathbf{f}\ \mathbf{c}\ \overrightarrow{p}\ =\ \text{let decls in e 'using' parListChunk c strat}\ ]\!]$$
$$\{\mathbf{c}\ fresh, \text{parListChunk} \in \rho, \text{using} \in \rho\})$$
$$\triangleright$$
$$\mathcal{T}[\![\ \mathbf{f}\ ::\ \tau\ ]\!]\ \Rightarrow\ [\![\ \mathbf{f}\ ::\ \text{Int} \to \tau\ ]\!]\ \{\}$$
$$\triangleright$$
$$\mathcal{E}[\![\mathbf{e}]\!]\ \Rightarrow\ \mathbf{e}[(\mathbf{f}\ \mathbf{v})/\mathbf{f}]\ \{\}$$
$$\qquad (2)$$

Fig. 3. Rewrite rules for the *Introduce Clustering* refactoring

These refactorings are implemented in HaRe, covering the full Haskell 98 standard. However, for brevity we define our transformation rules over a subset of Haskell 98, where we omit guards and where clauses.

4.2   Data Parallelism

Introduce Data Parallelism. This refactoring attaches a (parallel) strategy to an expression in the code, so introducing data parallelism on the result generated by the expression. The choice of the concrete strategy is left to the programmer. Usually, a maximally parallel strategy is the best choice, in the sense that it generates the highest degree of parallelism or a better granularity of parallelism (by using **rdeepseq** instead of **rseq**). Currently HaRe will issue a warning if **rdeepseq** is not being applied (see Section 4.3).

The refactoring *Introduce Data Parallelism* is shown in Figure 2 (Rule 1). The refactoring simply takes an expression and then transforms the expression into a **parList** strategy, providing the selected expression is a list.

Introduce Clustering. This refactoring refines an already existing **parList** strategy, by improving the granularity of the data parallelism. This involves using a **parListChunk** strategy instead of the original **parList**. The new strategy takes a cluster (or chunk) size as an argument, allowing user-defined control over the granularity. This can be very effective in increasing parallel performance.

The refactoring is shown in Figure 3 (Rule 2) and is defined to take two arguments: e, the expression to convert to a **parListChunk**; and v, the specified

$$Introduce\,TaskPar\,(\rho, \mathtt{x}) =$$
$$\mathcal{D}[\![\ \mathtt{f}\ \overrightarrow{p}\ =\ \mathtt{let\ decls\ in\ e}\ ]\!]$$
$$\Rightarrow\ [\![\mathtt{f}\ \overrightarrow{p}\ =\ \mathtt{let\ decls\ in}\ (\mathtt{let}\ \mathtt{x'}\ =\ \mathtt{runEval}\ \$\ \mathtt{do}\ \{\mathtt{x'} \leftarrow \mathtt{rpar}\ \mathtt{x};\ \quad (3)$$
$$\mathtt{return\ x'}\}\ \mathtt{in}\ \mathtt{e}[\mathtt{x'}/\mathtt{x}])]\!]$$
$$\{\mathtt{x} \in \rho \vee \mathtt{x} \in \mathtt{decls} \vee \mathtt{x} \in \overrightarrow{p}, \mathtt{x'}\,fresh\}$$

$$Introduce\,TaskPar'\,(\rho, \mathtt{x}, \mathtt{d}) =$$
$$\mathcal{D}[\![\ \mathtt{f}\ \overrightarrow{p}\ =\ \mathtt{let\ decls\ in\ e}\ ]\!]$$
$$\Rightarrow\ [\![\ \mathtt{f}\ \overrightarrow{p}\ =\ \mathtt{let\ decls}[\mathtt{d'}/\mathtt{d}]\ \mathtt{in}\ \mathtt{e}[\mathtt{x'_{n+1}}/\mathtt{x}]\ ]\!]$$
$$\{\mathtt{x} \in \rho \vee \mathtt{x} \in \mathtt{decls} \vee \mathtt{x} \in \overrightarrow{p}, \mathtt{d} \in \mathtt{decls}, \mathtt{x} \notin bound(\mathtt{d}), \mathtt{x'}\,fresh\}$$
where
$$\mathtt{d'} = [\![\ (\mathtt{x'_0}, ..., \mathtt{x'_n}, \mathtt{x'_{n+1}}) = \mathtt{runEval}\ \$\ \mathtt{do}\{\mathtt{x'_0} \leftarrow \mathtt{rpar}\ \mathtt{x_0}; ...; \mathtt{x'_n} \leftarrow \mathtt{rpar}\ \mathtt{x_n};$$
$$\mathtt{x'_{n+1}} \leftarrow \mathtt{rpar}\ \mathtt{x_{n+1}}; \mathtt{return}\ (\mathtt{x'_0}, ..., \mathtt{x'_n}, \mathtt{x'_{n+1}})\}\ ]\!]$$
$$\mathtt{d} = [\![\ (\mathtt{x'_0}, ..., \mathtt{x'_n}) = \mathtt{runEval}\ \$\ \mathtt{do}\{\mathtt{x'_0} \leftarrow \mathtt{rpar}\ \mathtt{x_0}; ...; \mathtt{x'_n} \leftarrow \mathtt{rpar}\ \mathtt{x_n}; \mathtt{return}\ (\mathtt{x'_0}, ..., \mathtt{x'_n})\}\ ]\!]$$
$$(4)$$

Fig. 4. Rewrite rules for the *Introduce Task Parallelism* refactorings

cluster size. The refactoring then either attaches a `parListChunk` strategy to a selected expression, or it refines a selected expression that already has an attached `parList` strategy by converting it into a `parListChunk`. In addition to this, the user-defined argument v is added as an argument to the `parListChunk` and also as an argument to the function that defines the expression. The type of the function is changed to reflect the new argument, and all calls to the function are changed, so that the user-defined value is passed in as an argument.

4.3   Task Parallelism

Introduce Task Parallelism. This refactoring sparks a selected computation by adding an `Eval` monad within a `let` expression bound on the right-hand-side of the selected computation. The refactoring also allows for addition computations to be added as further sparks within the `Eval` monad. This refactoring has two variants. The first variant, *Introduce TaskPar* (defined by Rule 3 in Figure 4) simply takes a selected computation as an argument (x). The refactoring locates the definition, say f, that defines x and then transforms f to introduce a `let` expression at the deepest point on the right-hand-side (this is to retain the scope of any bindings introduced in the `Eval` monad). This new `let` expression sparks x, returning a handle to the sparked computation. The refactoring then substitutes all occurrences of x for the newly sparked computation, x'. Notice that if there was a `where` clause attached to the definition of f, then the introduced x' would not be in scope within the `where` clause. In this case, it would be possible to *lift* the x' `let` clause to the `where` using the *Convert Let to Where* refactoring [10], and then *fold* occurrences of x (using *Function Folding* [10]) against the lifted x' to perform substitution in the `where` clause.

$Introduce\,Threshold\,(\rho, \mathtt{d}, \mathtt{x}, \mathtt{t}, \mathtt{v}) =$

$\quad \mathcal{D}[\![\ \mathtt{f}\ \overrightarrow{p}\ =\ \mathtt{let\ decls\ in\ e}]\!] \Rightarrow [\![\ \mathtt{f}\ \mathtt{x}\,\overrightarrow{p}\ =\ \mathtt{let\ decls}[\{\mathtt{d'};\mathtt{abs}\}/\mathtt{d}]\ \mathtt{in\ e}\ ]\!]$

$\quad \{\mathtt{t} \in \rho \vee \mathtt{t} \in \mathtt{decls} \vee \mathtt{t} \in \overrightarrow{p}, \mathtt{d} \in \mathtt{decls}, \mathtt{t} \in \mathit{free}(\mathtt{d}), \mathtt{abs}\ \mathit{fresh}, \mathtt{x}\ \mathit{fresh},$

$\quad\quad \mathit{typeof}(\mathtt{t}) = \mathit{instanceof}(\mathtt{Ord\ a} \Rightarrow \mathtt{a}),\ \mathit{typeof}(\mathtt{x}) = \mathit{instanceof}(\mathtt{Ord\ a} \Rightarrow \mathtt{a})\}$

$\triangleright$

$\quad \mathcal{T}[\![\ \mathtt{f}\ ::\ \tau_2]\!] \Rightarrow [\![\ \mathtt{f}\ ::\ \tau_1 \rightarrow \tau_2\ ]\!]\ \{\tau_1 = \mathit{typeof}(\mathtt{x})\}$

$\triangleright$

$\quad \mathcal{E}[\![\ \mathtt{exp}\ ]\!] \Rightarrow [\![\ \mathtt{exp}[(\mathtt{f}\ \mathtt{v})/\mathtt{f}]\ ]\!]\ \{\}$

$\triangleright$

$\quad \mathcal{T}[\![\ \mathtt{t}\ ::\ \tau]\!] \Rightarrow [\![\ \mathtt{t}\ ::\ \mathtt{Ord}\ \tau \Rightarrow \tau\ ]\!]\ \{\}$

$where$

$\mathtt{d'} = [\![\ (\mathtt{x'_0}, ..., \mathtt{x'_n}) = \mathtt{runEval}\ \$\ \mathtt{do}\{\mathtt{x'_0} \leftarrow \mathtt{rabs}\ \mathtt{x_0}; ...; \mathtt{x'_n} \leftarrow \mathtt{rabs}\ \mathtt{x_n}; \mathtt{return}\ (\mathtt{x'_0}, ..., \mathtt{x'_n})\}]\!]$

$\mathtt{abs} = [\![\ \mathtt{rabs}\ =\ \mathtt{if}\ \mathtt{t} > \mathtt{x}\ \mathtt{then}\ \mathtt{rpar}\ \mathtt{else}\ \mathtt{rseq}\ ]\!]$

$\mathtt{d} = [\![\ (\mathtt{x'_0}, ..., \mathtt{x'_n}) = \mathtt{runEval}\ \$\ \mathtt{do}\{\mathtt{x'_0} \leftarrow \mathtt{rpar}\ \mathtt{x_0}; ...; \mathtt{x'_n} \leftarrow \mathtt{rpar}\ \mathtt{x_n}; \mathtt{return}\ (\mathtt{x'_0}, ..., \mathtt{x'_n})\}\ ]\!]$

$$(5)$$

Fig. 5. Rewrite rules for the *Introduce Threshold* refactoring

The second version, *Introduce TaskPar'* (defined by Rule 4 in Figure 4) also takes an activated `Eval` monad as a second argument. Here we already have an `Eval` monad in the program and we simply want to add further sparks as additional bindings in the monad. In this case, we modify the activated `Eval` monad so that it returns an additional binding in its result. This new binding then substitutes the previous definition of `x` in the scope in which `x` is bound. It is important to note that the introduced (and modified) `Eval` monad is *identity safe*, in the sense that `rpar` simply returns a handle to a sparked computation. Substituting occurrences of the non-sparked computation `x` for the new sparked version, `x'` is semantics-preserving. At both steps of this refactoring, HaRe *warns* the user that the `rpar` annotation uses a default *weak head normal form* evaluation strategy. This is very useful, because inexperienced users of GpH often fail to enforce a deeper evaluation degree on data structures that should be processed in parallel, so producing code that contains less parallelism than expected.

The case study in Section 5.2 shows an example of both steps of this refactoring in practice.

Introduce Thresholding. Having introduced parallelism, the programmer often needs to tune the parallel performance. In this section we discuss one common refactoring that can be used to increase the granularity of the parallelism, i.e. to generate larger units of parallelism. The *Introduce Threshold* refactoring (defined by Rule 5 in Figure 5) allows the programmer to control the parallelism by disabling it if a selected value is below a threshold limit. This limit is supplied as a parameter to the refactoring, that is compared against the current value.

The *Introduce Threshold* refactoring takes a number of arguments. Here argument `d` is the activated evaluation monad; `t` is the variable that the threshold is compared against; `v` is the value for the threshold; and finally `x` is the name of

$$ModifyEvalDegree(\rho, \mathbf{x}) =$$
$$\mathcal{E}[\![\; \mathtt{f \; x} \;]\!] \Rightarrow [\![\; (\mathtt{f \; `dot`\; rdeepseq) \; x} \;]\!]$$
$$\{typeof(\mathtt{f}) = \mathtt{Strategy \; a}, \mathtt{rdeepseq} \in \rho, \mathtt{dot} \in \rho\} \qquad (6)$$
$$\rhd$$
$$\mathcal{T}[\![\; \mathtt{x} :: \tau \;]\!] \Rightarrow [\![\; \mathtt{x} :: \mathtt{NFData} \; \tau \Rightarrow \tau \;]\!] \; \{\}$$

Fig. 6. Rewrite rules for the *Modify Evaluation Degree* refactoring

the threshold value. The refactoring first locates the activated evaluation monad in the Abstract Syntax Tree, and replaces it with **d'**, a generalised version which replaces all occurrences of `rpar` and `rseq` to `rabs` instead. The definition of `rabs` is also added to the same scope as the activated evaluation monad, and its body simply returns either `rpar` or `rseq` depending on the value of a *threshold* guard. The threshold name is added as an argument to the function definition that declares the active eval monad. The argument is added in the first position of the function, which simplifies the process of partial application. The next step is then to change the type of the function so that it takes an extra argument for the new threshold value. All calls to this function in the scope in which it is defined are then replaced with calls to the new function, passing in the user-defined threshold value. It is worth noting that a performance conscious programmer may want to extract the parameter into a call-site specific threshold value. This would be perfectly possible using the *Introduce New Definition* refactoring from HaRe. In the final step, the type signature for the variable defining the threshold value is modified to take an `Ord` constraint.

Modify Evaluation Degree. Often simply sparking computations using the `rpar` strategy is not enough to obtain good parallelism. This is because `rpar` uses the default Haskell reduction to *weak head normal form*. For example, if we sparked two lists in a divide-and-conquer program using `rpar`, we would simply obtain a handle to the *spine* of the lists. This would be almost useless in a parallel program involving lists, as it would still require the lists to be evaluated sequentially *on demand*. Instead, we allow the option of using the `rdeepseq` evaluation strategy, that evaluates its argument to full normal form. The refactoring *Modify Evaluation Degree* is shown in Figure 6 (Rule 6).

5   Refactoring Case Studies

We present two worked examples, showing how the rules presented in Section 4 can be applied to introduce task-parallelism or data-parallelism to the same sequential source program. Our source program is a simple symbolic computation, `sumEuler`, which computes the sum over the Euler totient function, applied to a list of integer numbers. We initially develop a data-parallel version of `sumEuler` using our refactoring, and then refine this using clustering. We subsequently develop a divide-and-conquer version using thresholding and give performance results for both examples.

5.1   Data Parallelism

We start with the following top-level, sequential code for `sumEuler`. Our performance results are summarised in Figure 7 and discussed in Section 5.3.

```
sumEulerSeq :: Int -> Int
sumEulerSeq = sum . map euler . mkList
```

We first need to eta-expand this definition, so that the function applications become explicit in the code. We use the existing *introduce parameter* refactoring to transform the definition to one that applies all the functions to a newly introduced parameter. The refactored code is:

```
sumEulerSeq :: Int -> Int
sumEulerSeq n = sum (map euler (mkList n))
```

Stage 1: Introducing Data Parallelism: Introducing data parallelism envolves identifying a sub-expression in the program that generates a compound data structure, such as a list, and whose components should be evaluated in parallel. For basic data structures, such as lists, the Strategies library provides predefined data parallel strategies, which can be directly used. To introduce data parallelism, we first select the expression `map euler (mkList n)` and then apply the *Introduce Data Parallelism* refactoring from HaRe, where Rule 1 from Figure 2 is applied:

```
sumEulerPar1 :: Int -> Int
sumEulerPar1 n = sum ( map euler (mkList n)
                        'using' parList rdeepseq )
```

Stage 2: Clustering: While this version of the program creates an ample amount of parallelism, the parallelism is very fine grained and the program is therefore not very efficient, as shown in Figure 7. This is a common problem in early stages of exploiting data parallelism. To tune the performance of this data parallel program, we use a general technique of clustering, encoded in a separate refactoring. This restructures the code so that computations on a "cluster" (or chunk) of elements in the data structure are combined to one parallel task. In our example, we want to use one parallel thread to process an entire sub-list, rather than just one element. By increasing the size of the computation for each task in this way, we reduce the overhead of the parallel execution and thus improve performance. Such clustering can be achieved in various ways. The simplest is to replace a data parallel strategy with its clustered equivalent, that is additionally parameterised by the cluster size. For example, on lists we can use the existing strategy `parListChunk` by selecting the `parList` expression and performing the *Introduce Clustering* refactoring. This applies Rule 2 from Figure 3 to produce:

```
sumEulerParListChunk :: Int -> Int -> Int
sumEulerParListChunk c n = sum (map euler (mkList n)
                                  'using'
                                  parListChunk c rdeepseq )
```

5.2   Task Parallelism

The second example is a divide-and-conquer version of `sumEuler`, which we use to illustrate how our refactorings apply to divide-and-conquer programs in general. The program divides the input list into two halves, applies the Euler totient function in the base case, and combines the results by summing them. Our performance results are summarised in Figure 7 and discussed in Section 5.3.

```
sumEulerDnc :: [Int] -> Int
sumEulerDnc [] = 0
sumEulerDnc [x] = euler x
sumEulerDnc xs  = s1+s2
            where (left, right) = splitAt (length xs 'div' 2) xs
                  s1 = sumEulerDnc left
                  s2 = sumEulerDnc right
```

Stage 1: Introduce Task Parallelism: The first stage in parallelising this program is to identify which components in `sumEulerDnc` we would like to parallelise. Using the standard *divide-and-conquer* approach, we need to separate out the recursive calls to `sumEulerDnc` in the bindings of `s1` and `s2`, so that `s1` is sparked in parallel to the evaluation of `s2`. In order to do this, we need to use the `Eval` monad. The first step is therefore to apply Rule 3 from Figure 4, by selecting `s1` and choosing the *Introduce Task Parallelism* refactoring. The refactoring introduces a new pattern-match in the `where` clause of `sumEulerDnc`:

```
sumEulerDnc :: [Int] -> Int
...
sumEulerDnc xs   = let s1_2 = runEval $ do
                                    s1_2 <- rpar s1
                                    return (s1_2)
                                in s1_2+s2
            where (left, right) = splitAt (length xs 'div' 2) xs
                  s1 = sumEulerDnc left
                  s2 = sumEulerDnc right
```

It is important to observe that in this step the refactoring also substitutes occurrences of `s1` within the body of `sumEulerDnc` so that it uses the new `s1_2` binding instead. This is crucial for performance, since using `s1` would ignore the parallelism in the program. This is a common pitfall, which is circumvented by using a refactoring-based approach. The next step is to add `s2` as a binding within the same monad, by applying Rule 4 from Figure 4. The refactoring *Introduce Task Parallelism* will let us do this using the *IntroduceTaskPar'* variant instead (Rule 4 from Figure 4); the user selects `s2` within the `where` clause of `sumEulerDnc` and selects *Introduce Task Parallelism* from the HaRe menu. This time HaRe *augments* the existing `Eval` monad by adding an additional binding, `s2_2 <- rpar s2`, after the original binding of `s1_2 <- rpar s1`. Finally, the `return` statement is changed to return a tuple, where each component returns a binding within the monad. The pattern-match is also changed to reflect this, as is the substitution of `s2` for `s2_2` within the body of `sumEulerDnc`. The modified code is now as follows:

```
sumEulerDnc :: [Int] -> Int
...
sumEulerDnc xs    = let (s1_2, s2_2) = runEval $ do
                                s1_2 <- rpar s1
                                s2_2 <- rpar s2
                                return (s1_2, s2_2)
                        in s1_2+s2_2
            where ...
```

At each of the steps above, HaRe warns us that the evaluation degree used with `rpar` is Haskell's default reduce to weak-head-normal-form strategy. In this example such evaluation is sufficient, because for the unstructured `Int` type this amounts to a full evaluation. However, in general it is desirable to combine the generation of parallelism with explicit specification of the evaluation degree. This often involves full normal form evaluation using `rdeepseq`. Although not strictly necessary here, we perform the corresponding refactoring (Rule 6 from Figure 6) to demonstrate this step in the parallelisation and to future-proof `sumEulerDnc`.

```
sumEulerDnc :: [Int] -> Int
...
sumEulerDnc xs = let (s1_2, s2_2) = runEval $ do
                            s1_2 <- (rpar 'dot' rdeepseq) s1
                            s2_2 <- (rpar 'dot' rdeepseq) s2
                            return (s1_2, s2_2)
                    in s1_2+s2_2
        where (left, right) = splitAt (length xs 'div' 2) xs
              s1 = sumEulerDnc left
              s2 = sumEulerDnc right
```

Stage 2: Introduce Thresholding: Unrestricted parallelism in divide-and-conquer programs often generates an excessive amount of fine-grained parallelism, which imposes high parallelism overhead. Therefore, the programmer tunes this initial version by introducing a threshold on the length of the input list `xs`, below which no parallelism will be generated. In order to perform this transformation, the programmer need only call the *Introduce Threshold* refactoring from HaRe, rather than manually introducing this threshold. First the programmer makes the expression `length xs` a new definition, by using the *Introduce New Definition* refactoring that is already defined in HaRe [11]. This introduces the new definition `lenXs = length xs`. The programmer then selects `lenXs` in the `where` clause of `sumEulerDnc`. After choosing the *Introduce Threshold* refactoring from the HaRe drop down menu, HaRe prompts for a threshold value, where the programmer enters the value 100 and applies Rule 5 from Figure 5:

```
sumEulerDnc :: Int -> [Int] -> Int
...
sumEulerDnc t xs = let (s1_2, s2_2) = runEval $ do
                            s1_2 <- (rabs 'dot' rdeepseq) s1
                            s2_2 <- (rabs 'dot' rdeepseq) s2
                            return (s1_2, s2_2)
```

```
                       rabs = if (lenXs > t)
                              then rpar
                              else rseq
                  in s1_2+s2_2
      where (left, right) = splitAt (length xs 'div' 2) xs
            s1 = sumEulerDnc t left
            s2 = sumEulerDnc t right
            lenXs = length xs
```

The refactoring introduces the threshold as an argument to sumEulerDnc, replacing all calls to sumEulerDnc in the scope that it is defined with sumEulerDnc
100. The argument is added in the first position so as not to interfere with partial
applications. A new abstraction, rabs, controls the parallelism threshold.

5.3   Performance Results

All our measurements have been made on an eight-core, 8GB RAM, 6MB L2
cache, HP XW6600 Workstation comprising two Intel Xeon 5410 quad-core processors, each running at 2.33GHz. The benchmarks run under Linux Fedora 7
using GHC 7.0.1, and parallel package 3.1.0.1 for evaluation strategies.

For both programs we measured parallelism overhead by comparing the sequential runtime with the runtime of a one processor parallel version. For the
data-parallel version sequential runtime is $104.63s$ and one processor runtime is
$104.73s$. For the divide-and-conquer version sequential runtime is $198.49s$ and
one processor runtime is $198.71s$. Thus, parallelism overhead is less than 0.2%
in all cases, as expected from a highly-tuned parallel runtime-system.

The results for the *data-parallel* sumEuler implementation are shown in the
first two plots (from top to bottom) in Figure 7. The naive implementation
generates one task for every list element, in this example 40,000 tasks in total.
As a result, the parallelism is extremely fine-grained, i.e. each task performs only
a small amount of computation, something that can be ascertained by using
GHC's profiling tools. The overhead of thread creation and synchronisation has
a significant impact on parallel performance, resulting in almost no speedup at
all: 1.4 on 8 cores. Based on this profiling information, some form of clustering
is essential to increase performance. Indeed, the second plot in Figure 7 exhibits
much improved speedup of 7.8 on 8 cores.

The results for the *divide-and-conquer* implementation of sumEuler are shown
in Figure 7. In this simple example already the initial parallel version achieves a
good speedup of 6.2 on 8 cores, although performance tails off for higher numbers of cores, indicating limited scalability of this version. We have observed the
importance of thresholding, in particular for massively parallel architectures,
in several larger applications [12], and this motivated our initial choice of performance tuning refactorings. The reason for the good speedups with smaller
numbers of cores is that the parallel runtime-system allows for the subsump-
tion of potential parallelism by parent tasks, where the application contains an
abundance of hierarchical parallelism. This is the case in a divide-and-conquer

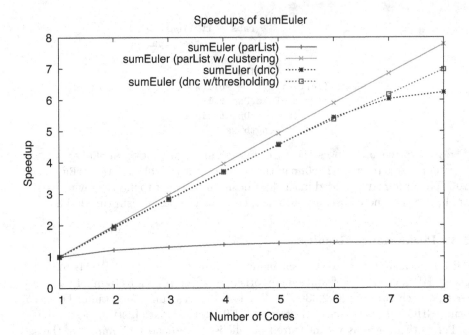

Fig. 7. Speedups showing *data-parallel* `sumEuler` and *divide-and-conquer* `sumEuler` on an 8-core machine

structure and works very well in this example, reducing the number of generated tasks to 257 out of 85,018 sparks that are generated in total. Adding a threshold of 100 improves speedup slightly, achieving 6.9 on 8 cores, but guaranteeing, through user code, that no more than 80 tasks are generated.

6   Related Work

Despite the obvious advantages, there has so far been little work in the field of applying software refactoring technology to assist parallel programming. The earliest work on interactive tools for parallelisation stemmed from the Fortran community, targeting loop parallelisation [13]. These interactive tools were early transformation engines allowing users to manipulate loops in their Fortran programs by specifying what loops to interchange, align, replicate or expand. The interactive tools typically reported to the programmer various information such as dependence graphs, and were mainly applied to the field of numerical computation. More recent work includes Reentrancer [14]: a refactoring tool developed by IBM for making code reentrant, which targets global data by making them thread-safe; and Dig [15], which introduces concurrency in Java programs by making them more thread safe, increasing throughput and improving scalability. Software refactoring techniques have therefore only previously been applied in a very limited parallel setting: by applying simple transformations to introduce parallel loops and thread safety in object-oriented programs. Currently, these approaches are limited to object-oriented languages.

While there has been some work on transformational approaches, to the best of our knowledge, there has been no previous work on applying refactoring technology to parallel functional programs. For example, Hammond et. al. [16] used Template Haskell to apply Eden [9] skeletons to Haskell programs, using an integrated cost model for selecting the transformations to apply. A similar approach is taken by SkelML [17], which uses an *automatic program synthesis* for identifying specific program patterns to apply to ML programs at compile time. However, unlike refactoring, which is designed to guide the user through the structured steps of forming (and tuning) parallel programs on a source code level, these approaches are deployed at compile time, and so do not expose the transformed source code to the user. This is valuable in providing the opportunity for the programmer to further tune their parallel Haskell programs. Our approach also differs in providing building blocks for building generalised skeletons rather than the skeletons themselves.

The renewed interest in parallel programming has spawned several parallel language extensions for Haskell that vary in the level of control they give to the application programmer. For example the `Par` monad presented in [18] uses explicit parallelism together with M-Vars for synchronisation, and demonstrates the expressive power by implementing a Haskell level scheduler. Cloud Haskell [19] takes an even more drastic step of lifting the entire machinery of co-ordinating parallelism to the Haskell level. By exposing more detailed control to the programmer, classic challenges of parallel programming also reappear. Therefore, these models would profit even more from a refactoring-based approach to avoid common pitfalls, or at least to warn the programmer of potential dangers.

7   Conclusions and Future Work

In principle, parallelising a Haskell program is simple: all the programmer has to do is to introduce evaluation strategies to describe which expression could be evaluated in parallel. In practice, however, identifying the *most useful* sources of parallelism and then *tuning* the performance of the initial parallel code can be tricky and often requires expertise in the parallel programming as well as an understanding of evaluation order and degree in Haskell. The *paraforming* approach described here, allows this expertise to be encoded in a way that can assist the programmer *without being prescriptive*. The refactoring tool warns the programmer to avoid common pitfalls, such as under-defining the degree of evaluation, and gives a structured way to perform common optimisations such as introducing thresholding in a parallel program. We have shown that this approach can be effective for both task- and data-parallelism, giving real and scalable speedup.

This work is still in a fairly early stage of development and there are several directions for further work. We have described only a few simple refactorings:

there are many more common patterns of parallelism that could be added, such as pipelining, branch-and-bound, or dynamic workpools. We also need to investigate *enabling refactorings* that may modify the code structure to expose parallel refactorings. We then plan to apply the refactorings both to some of the larger examples that we have studied in the past [8] and also to new applications so that we can assess their usefulness in the complete process of parallelisation. In addition to the refactorings presented in this paper, we also intend on implementing their *inverses*; so, for example, it is possible to *un-spark* a computation that is bound in an `Eval` monad, if it later shows to be too fine grained. We also aim to provide soundness proofs both for the refactorings described here, and possibly for other refactorings already implemented in HaRe. Finally, although we have expressed our ideas in terms of GpH, they are, of course, much more widely applicable. In the long term, we hope to apply the ideas described here to other parallel dialects of Haskell, and to other language settings. Parallel refactoring technology combined with programming at a high level of abstraction provides a key to helping programmers *think in parallel*.

Acknowledgements. This work has been supported by the European Union grants RII3-CT-2005-026133 "SCIEnce: Symbolic Computing Infrastructure in Europe", IST-2010-248828 "ADVANCE: Asynchronous and Dynamic Virtualisation through performance ANalysis to support Concurrency Engineering ", and IST-2011-288570 "ParaPhrase: Parallel Patterns for Adaptive Heterogeneous Multicore Systems", and by the UK's Engineering and Physical Sciences Research Council grant EP/G055181/1 "HPC-GAP: High Performance Computational Algebra. We also acknowledge the anonymous referees for their helpful suggestions.

References

1. Moore, G.E.: Readings in Computer Architecture, pp. 56–59. Morgan Kaufmann Publishers Inc., San Francisco (2000)
2. Peyton Jones, S., Hammond, K.: Haskell 98 Language and Libraries, the Revised Report. Cambridge University Press (2003)
3. Opdyke, W.F.: Refactoring Object-Oriented Frameworks. PhD thesis, Department of Computer Science, University of Illinois at Urbana-Champaign, Champaign, IL, USA (1992)
4. Li, H., Thompson, S., Reinke, C.: The Haskell Refactorer: HaRe, and its API. In: Proc. of the 5th Workshop on Language Descriptions, Tools and Applications (LDTA 2005). Electronic Notes in Theoretical Computer Science, vol. 141(4) (April 2005)
5. Hallgren, T.: Haskell Tools from the Programatica Project. In: ACM SIGPLAN Workshop on Haskell, pp. 103–106. ACM Press, Uppsala (2003)
6. Lämmel, R., Visser, J.: A **Strafunski** Application Letter. In: Dahl, V. (ed.) PADL 2003. LNCS, vol. 2562, pp. 357–375. Springer, Heidelberg (2002)
7. Trinder, P.W., Hammond, K., Loidl, H.W., Peyton Jones, S.L.: Algorithm + Strategy = Parallelism. J. of Functional Programming 8(1), 23–60 (1998)

8. Marlow, S., Maier, P., Loidl, H.W., Aswad, M.K., Trinder, P.: Seq no more: Better Strategies for Parallel Haskell. In: 3rd ACM SIGPLAN Symposium on Haskell, pp. 91–102. ACM Press, Baltimore (2010)
9. Loogen, R., Ortega-Mallén, Y., Peña-Marí, R.: Parallel Functional Programming in Eden. J. of Functional Programming 15(3), 431–475 (2005)
10. Brown, C.: Tool Support for Refactoring Haskell Programs. PhD thesis, Computing Laboratory, University of Kent, Canterbury, Kent, UK (September 2008)
11. Li, H.: Refactoring Haskell Programs. PhD thesis, School of Computing, University of Kent, Canterbury, Kent, UK (September 2006)
12. Loidl, H.W., Trinder, P., Hammond, K., Junaidu, S., Morgan, R., Peyton Jones, S.: Engineering Parallel Symbolic Programs in GpH. Concurrency — Practice and Experience 11(12), 701–752 (1999)
13. Kennedy, K., McKinley, K.S., Tseng, C.W.: Interactive Parallel Programming using the ParaScope Editor. IEEE Trans. Parallel Distrib. Syst. 2, 329–341 (1991)
14. Wloka, J., Sridharan, M., Tip, F.: Refactoring for Reentrancy. In: ESEC/FSE 2009, pp. 173–182. ACM, Amsterdam (2009)
15. Dig, D.: A Refactoring Approach to Parallelism. IEEE Softw. 28, 17–22 (2011)
16. Hammond, K., Berthold, J., Loogen, R.: Automatic Skeletons in Template Haskell. Parallel Processing Letters 13(3), 413–424 (2003)
17. Scaife, N., Horiguchi, S., Michaelson, G., Bristow, P.: A Parallel SML Compiler Based on Algorithmic Skeletons. J. Funct. Program. 15, 615–650 (2005)
18. Marlow, S., Newton, R., Peyton Jones, S.: A Monad for Deterministic Parallelism. In: Intl. Conference on Functional Programming (ICFP 2011) (2011) (submitted)
19. Epstein, J., Black, A., Peyton Jones, S.: Towards Haskell in the Cloud. In: 4th ACM SIGPLAN Symposium on Haskell. ACM Press, Tokyo (2011)

Functional High Performance Financial IT
The HIPERFIT* Research Center in Copenhagen

Jost Berthold[1], Andrzej Filinski[1], Fritz Henglein[1], Ken Friis Larsen[1],
Mogens Steffensen[2], and Brian Vinter[3]

[1] Department of Computer Science (DIKU), University of Copenhagen, Denmark
{berthold,kflarsen,andrzej,henglein}@diku.dk
[2] Department of Mathematical Sciences (IMF), University of Copenhagen, Denmark
mogens@math.ku.dk
[3] eScience Center, Niels Bohr Institute (NBI), University of Copenhagen, Denmark
brian.vinter@nbi.dk

Abstract. The world of finance faces the computational performance challenge of massively expanding data volumes, extreme response time requirements, and compute-intensive complex (risk) analyses. Simultaneously, new international regulatory rules require considerably more transparency and external auditability of financial institutions, including their software systems. To top it off, increased product variety and customisation necessitates shorter software development cycles and higher development productivity. In this paper, we report about HIPERFIT, a recently etablished strategic research center at the University of Copenhagen that attacks this triple challenge of increased performance, transparency and productivity in the financial sector by a novel integration of financial mathematics, domain-specific language technology, parallel functional programming, and emerging massively parallel hardware.

HIPERFIT seeks to contribute to effective high-performance modelling by domain specialists, and to functional programming on highly parallel computer architectures in particular, by pursuing a research trajectory informed by the application domain of finance, but without limiting its research scope, generality, or applicablity, to finance. Research in HIPERFIT draws on and aims at producing new research in its different scientific fields, and it fosters synergies between them to deliver showcases of modern language technology and advanced functional methods with the potential for disruptive impact on an area of increasing societal importance.

1   Introduction

Today, the financial sector is confronted with fundamental computational challenges: Data volumes to be handled are growing at an exponential rate; stochastic

---

* HIPERFIT (http://hiperfit.dk) is a strategic research center funded by the Danish Council for Strategic Research (DSF) under grant no. 10-092299, founded in cooperation with the following partners from the financial industry: Danske Bank, Jyske Bank, LexiFi, Nordea, Nykredit Bank, and SimCorp.

simulations consume in principle limitless numbers of compute cycles; quantitative and auditable risk management is becoming mandatory; real-time requirements hit speed-of-light limitations. At the same time, it becomes more and more common to negotiate non-standardised financial contracts, so-called over-the-counter (OTC) contracts. These are complex to model, manage and analyse, and yet product development cycles have become shorter than imagined even five years ago. This requires complex computational models, specifications and systems that are guaranteed to be correct, transparent, rapidly developed, and scalable on today's and tomorrow's hardware. What makes this a fundamentally new and interesting *scientific* challenge is that the problems need to be solved *simultaneously,* and thus trade-offs between the underlying financial mathematics, problem modelling, programming language technology, high-performance systems, and practical applicability must be explicitly accounted for.

To address these problems, we have recently established the *Research Center for Functional High-Performance Computing for Financial Information Technology* (HIPERFIT) at the University of Copenhagen, which brings together key researchers in the required scientific fields – programming languages, parallel systems, and mathematical finance – with the relevant industrial partners. Our fundamental hypothesis is that the above-mentioned simultaneous challenges of high transparency, high computational performance and high productivity can be solved more easily by an integrated approach using declarative domain-specific and high-level functional programming languages rather than by an incremental approach building on top of historically evolved software architectures and code bases that have originally been developed for sequential computer architectures. The approach taken by HIPERFIT is to eliminate low-level imperative programming by exploiting natural parallelism in declaratively expressed solutions and mapping it directly to emerging massively parallel commodity hardware.

1.1   Overview

In the present paper we first describe the research paradigm, strategy and organisation of HIPERFIT. We then explain the integrated approach taken, and the particular research themes we will work on (Section 3). Section 4 focuses on the functional programming aspects: We summarise the state of the art in language support for financial applications (Section 4.1) and give an overview of parallel functional programming paradigms and trends (Sections 4.2 and 4.3). In Section 5, we outline the two first project activities within HIPERFIT related to functional programming. Section 6 concludes.

2   Motivation and Background

In the year 2008, we saw one of the most severe worldwide financial crises ever. Induced by defaults in the American real-estate market (sub-prime loans), some investment banks collapsed and a large numbers of others were affected – taking down many other industries and ultimately leading to a general economic crisis of global scale [19]. The crisis in 2008 demonstrates how complex dependencies are built up in the financial industry and that experts can vastly misjudge the impact of a local crash on other sectors.

2.1 Need for More Accurate Modelling in Mathematical Finance

To help avoid a repeat of the 2008 crash, financial institutions have initiated internal activities at a massive scale. Huge sums are invested in computational methods to improve modelling financial phenomena with all concerned parties. While the banks already have extensive modelling and pricing activities, the new problems establish a modelling and simulation paradigm vastly different from the existing system. Existing systems are based on macroscopic models and only model individual contracts in parameterised representations. The new requirement will be a detailed system of microeconomic models of the individual businesses and the combination of these into a global economic barometer that identifies the value and risk in a given bank.

2.2 Need for More Financial System and Software Transparency

The financial crisis that hit the world economy in 2008 has also triggered several new legislative initiatives that seek to govern the financial sector more carefully. The Basel-II agreement, its successor Basel-III under preparation (as CRD II-IV), and recently proposed SEC rules for computational models of securities [40], impose new capital adequacy and transparency requirements on the financial sector. These new rules have impact on banks' IT systems at all levels, ranging from high-level modelling of financial instruments to auditable internal risk models and their reliable implementation.

2.3 Need for More Computational Performance

Quantitative analyses in the financial industry have always called on great computing power. Such analyses have usually been devised by so-called "quants", having a background in mathematical finance, financial engineering, mathematics and physics. Their expertise is in the fields of option pricing, calibration, simulation, stochastic differential equations, partial differential equations, and statistics. Only recently have we seen increased focus on the efficiency and transparency of numerical and computational methods used in the analyses, which increasingly use Monte-Carlo and other simulation techniques [21]. Reasons for this trend lie both inside the industry, through an ever-growing competition for achieving more and more marginal benefits, and outside, by imposing new auditing and solvency procedures from international regulation (c.f. Section 2.2).

Recently, domain experts have started using the potentially tremendous parallel computing power of modern General-Purpose Graphics Processing Units (GPGPUs), encoding their algorithms in highly platform-dependent low-level languages. Low-level code written by a domain expert may perform well in the

short term, but is bound to lead to over-specialised, unmaintainable systems
that do not satisfy auditing and transparency requirements. In consequence,
there is an increasing demand for high-level programming language and high-
performance systems expertise, complementing the requisite principal financial
expertise.

3 The HIPERFIT Center

Funded by the Danish Council for Strategic Research, HIPERFIT started its work
in January 2011. The center comprises four main research areas involving three
departments of the University of Copenhagen, five partners from the Danish
financial industry, and a French functional-programming based finance IT company. The center has been made possible by a grant by the Danish Strategic
Research Council under its Programme for Strategic Growth Technologies. The
grant provides funding for 1 permanent faculty, 3 post-doctoral and 6 PhD schol-
arship positions, totalling 33 person years spread over the different scientific
disciplines. The first HIPERFIT appointments will be in place by the end of 2011.

3.1 Research Goals, Organisation, and Methodology

Research in HIPERFIT aims at solving problems of today's computing in finance in a holistic, integrated approach. HIPERFIT therefore joins researchers
with state-of-the-science expertise in four *research areas* relevant for high-
performance financial applications: Theory and practice of mathematical finance (MF), domain-specific languages (DSL), functional programming (FP),
and high-performance systems (HPS).

A major goal of HIPERFIT is to present alternatives to the above-mentioned
low-level code with platform-dependent optimisations so as to facilitate a more

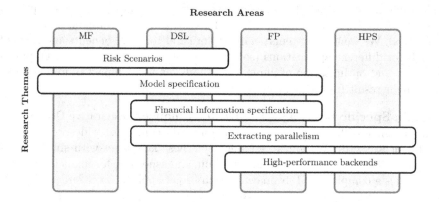

Fig. 1. Relationship between research areas and research themes

enduring development process of efficient maintainable systems. Essential ingredients to achieving this are declarative languages and advanced compilation of domain-specific abstractions. We believe that side-stepping imperative programming bears the elements of a *disruptive technology* with drastic productivity and performance improvement potential.

The work in HIPERFIT is organised in general *research themes*, which cut across research areas and are driven by *cases*. Figure 1 depicts the research areas and their relationship to our initial research themes. *Cases* are concrete projects for exploration and development, either motivated by practical needs of industry partners (problem-driven), or by the intent to evaluate novel technologies and gather know-how for later use (technology driven). Cases may or may not contain information protected by industry partners. They usually have focused objectives adequate for Master's thesis projects, and they realise useful and timely short-term goals. The overarching research themes, on the other hand, are more open-ended to foster exploratory thinking that is not entrenched in and tied to incremental evolution of current practice. Research theme work is carried out primarily by faculty, postdocs and Ph.D. students researchers.

3.2   Research Themes in HIPERFIT

Initial discussions with our industry partners have led to identifying several cross-cutting research themes for the start of HIPERFIT, depicted in Figure 1. Each research theme will be supported by cases, part of which are provided by the industry partners.

Risk Scenarios. We try to describe the transition from observables (like current prices and historical data) to scenario generation and from scenario generation to reporting and management. Adequate risk scenarios have immediate relevance for management decisions, including deriving capital requirements to ensure stability in unlikely and extreme situations.

Model Specification. Financial models in practical use today vary from so-called "model-free" evaluation (prices given completely in terms of other prices) to sophisticated stochastic processes (such as advanced multi-dimensional jump-diffusions). We want to systematically explore and compare benefits and costs of models for different applications (solvency, accounting, or management), parallelisation and optimisation of numeric methods, and the impact of imprecisions that might result from the latter.

Domain-Specific Languages (DSLs) for Finance. Declarative DSLs to describe a range of financial products have already come into widespread use in the financial sector. We aim to complement these languages with similarly expressive DSLs for other financial information, and especially for financial models. Our goal is a complete DSL framework with broad application coverage, suitable both for internal reporting and statistics, external auditing, and computation in large risk scenarios. We will describe the DSL approach in the financial domain, and our goals, in more detail in Section 4.1.

Extracting Parallelism from Declarative Specifications. The core goal of this research theme is to analyse and transform large-scale financial computations to expose their inherent computational parallelism. Departing from work on existing applications and domain-specific abstractions, we plan to derive a tailor-made language for large-scale numeric computations which suits the needs of mathematical finance, while efficiently executable on modern parallel hardware. Thanks to their high-level nature, parallel functional languages appear to be an excellent platform for this. We expect vector and matrix operations and accumulating reductions to be the major source of parallelism at this stage, but aim to identify more domain-specific parallelisation schemes. The DSL development for financial models will lead to additional or modified requirements. Typical operations for *valuation (pricing)* of stochastic financial models need to be translated into the parallel operations provided. The functional approach we take gives us a good position to formally assess correctness and precision of the obtained results, and – to some extent – to statically estimate the translated programs' performance. Sections 4.2 and 4.3 expand on previous and related work in the area of parallel functional programming and parallel hardware support.

High-Performance Backends for Novel Hardware. Embracing novel parallel hardware like GPGPUs is an integral part of HIPERFIT. Models and language framework will be designed with execution on next-generation processors in mind from the start, mapping the parallelism that is expressed by the functional programming activities onto a number of parallel computer architectures. In this research theme, activities will start by optimising existing algorithms and implementations, and profit from synergies with other scientific computing activities on parallel hardware. We expect to follow a byte-code based approach and just-in-time compilation, and ultimately intend to deliver a full high-performance backend tailored for financial and scientific applications.

4   Functional Programming and HIPERFIT

4.1   Domain-Specific Languages for Financial Applications

Pervasive Trend to Domain-Specific Languages. Domain-specific languages (DSLs) capture knowledge of application experts in tailor-made constructs and thereby offer great programing comfort. DSLs are so widespread and successful in practice that it is easy to overlook them: Logical data modelling and declarative querying, with high-level support for physical storage layout (particular index data structures) and automatic query optimisation, as embodied in Relational Database Systems (RDBMSs); functional dependencies between atomic, vector- and matrix-based data, with automatic incremental recomputation, as embodied in spreadsheets; structural specification of strings, with automatic generation of provably efficient streaming processors, as embodied in regular expression ("lexing") and context-free grammar ("parsing") tools.

Programming language research has only recently discovered DSLs as a research area and capitalised on the notion, though [32]. Simultaneously with the rise of the term in research, one could observe DSL technology invading profitable commercial domains. For example, the Cryptol language [26] enables constructing reliable cryptographic software and hardware implementations with ease and high assurance. Recently, we also see some proposals for "DSLs" for parallel programming [42], or specifically for next-generation parallel hardware, GPGPUs or FPGAs. However, whether to really label these "DSL" is a debatable subject: A particular target platform definitely does not constitute an *application* domain, and the particular field hardly exposes characteristics which would justify DSL development (special notation, automation, data structures [32]). We are not aware of many scientific projects combining a proper DSL approach with novel parallel hardware. Notable exception are a relatively new project Diderot [45] (a "parallel DSL" for image analysis), and the Feldspar project [17] which targets GPGPUs for high-performance signal processing using a DSL approach.

DSLs in Finance. Financial applications have been identified as a promising DSL area relatively early. Researchers have successfully modeled and analysed financial instruments [35], commercial contracts [2], and risk management [6] using DSL technology. The French company LexiFi, one of the industrial partners in HIPERFIT, has matured the research on financial DSLs [35] into the language MLFi [27], which is embedded into OCaML as a combinator library for describing contracts and valuation (called a "domain-specific embedded language", DSEL).

The hallmark feature of such contract languages is that they allow more complex instruments/contracts/risk models to be built up by composing simpler, often reusable, components that can be shared amongst different instruments. Also, the same domain-specific descriptions enable different interpretations. For instance, a description of a financial instrument in MLFi can be used both for pricing the instrument and for backoffice automation; that is, managing when options and obligations described in the instrument are to be exercised and when payments are to be made or received.

Project Goal: DSL Framework for Finance. The general goal of DSLs is to support fast implementation, extensibility, reuse across financial institutions, maintainability and low total cost of ownership (TCO) for the domain expert as a user. We want to create a framework for financial information applications which covers various applications: reporting to auditors and public authorities, data communication with clearing houses, internal reporting and statistics, computations for the purpose of internal risk management, and flexible integration for standard routines such as accounting and confirmation processing.

DSLs for financial instruments are commonly used in many companies today, but often mix contract and valuation aspects. A crucial goal of HIPERFIT is to design similarly expressive languages to describe the stochastic models and computational valuation methods, and to achieve clear separation and interfaces towards a universal valuation engine. We will investigate existing DSL approaches in the different areas and experiment with combining them to identify the lines of separation and useful language features.

4.2 Parallel Functional Programming in HIPERFIT

Why Parallel Functional Programming Matters[1]

Functional programs are easy to read and understand, program construction and code reuse are simplified (glue), and programs are transformed, optimised and formally reasoned about with relative ease. More specific to parallel computations, the absence of side effects makes data dependencies and inherent parallelism manifest, (purely) functional parallel programs have deterministic semantics irrespective of the evaluation order, and reduction semantics is inherently parallel. Last but not least, higher-order functions can nicely describe common parallelisation patterns as skeletons [15,38], without the reader getting lost in technical details or particularities of the concrete algorithm. In all, irrespective of the concrete programming model, the high level of abstraction provided by functional languages makes them suitable languages to conceptually describe parallelism, in an executable specification.

Models, Paradigms and Classification. A number of programming models for parallel functional programming have been developed. They can be categorised along different aspects of programming and implementation. A good criterion for classifying parallel programming models is the *degree of explicitness*: how much parallelism needs to be controlled and specified by the programmer. Skillicorn and Talia [41] subdivide explicitness along several aspects: decomposition, mapping, communication, and synchronisation, as increasing degrees of explicitness for parallel subcomputations.

The main credo in functional languages being high abstraction, it is not surprising that most approaches to parallelism try to limit the programmer's control of parallelism. Parallelism should ideally be non-invasive, i.e. not require large changes to a program's source code. In the extreme, inherent parallelism exploited stems from the reduction semantics, for example in *parallel Haskell* (pH [1]): lazy graph reduction is changed to eager evaluation for performance. However, experience has shown that such completely implicit approaches are of limited use. The predominant category is a mid-level of "controlled parallelism" [23], where programmers specify parallelism, while details are left to the language implementation. In Figure 2, we provide a categorisation of parallel functional languages that expands this semi-explicit mid-level further into subcategories. As another aspect, the vertical axis in the figure shows to what extent units of computation in parallel programs are *explicitly interacting*.

One classical approach is to parallelise operations over special bulk data types – data parallel languages. Examples are NESL [12], Data-parallel Haskell [14], and its newer variant RePA [25]. Language extensions targeting GPGPUs [29,13] also fall in this category of type-driven parallelism.

Slightly more powerful, and more involved, is to *indicate inherent parallelism* in a functional program by annotations or special evaluation combinators, to inform compiler and runtime system about whether an independent computation *should* be done in parallel. This is the model of Glasgow parallel Haskell

---

[1] In reverence to Backus [7], Hughes [24] and Hammond/Michaelson [23, Introduction].

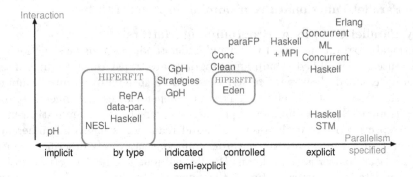

Fig. 2. Parallel Haskells and other functional languages classified

(GpH) [44]. Evaluation strategies built on GpH [43] (recently overhauled [31]) provide slightly more control, enabling the programmer to force evaluation of subexpressions to a certain degree (in parallel or sequentially). This facilitates opportunistic parallel evaluation. It does not guarantee parallelism, however. In contrast, parallelism annotations used in Concurrent Clean [37] have mandatory operational semantics, providing *controlled* parallelism. The programmer explicitly specifies parallel scheduling; programs using controlled parallelism are indeed parallel and expose their parallel behaviour. Skeleton-based parallelisation [15] could be included in this category since, commonly, the programmer has to explicitly choose the algorithmic pattern implemented by a certain skeleton, and to follow it. However, we prefer to categorise them as implicit (likewise Skillikorn and Talia [41]), since a skeleton's parallel implementation is entirely hidden in libraries. Other examples of controlled functional parallelism are Hudak's para-functional programming approach and successors [33], and the language Eden [28]. Often we find the concept of *processes* and *channels* between them to define process networks. The language Eden [28] is the major representative of this approach in the Haskell world. Eden retains a mostly [10] functional interface, with a notion of processes specified by their input-output mapping, and implicitly connected via channels which may transfer data as *streams*. It has been demonstrated [9,8,5] that Eden provides good support for skeleton-based programming, both for the skeleton user and as an implementation language.

Languages like Concurrent Clean and Eden are still (mostly) implicit about the communication details and synchronisation. Going even further, we find functional languages with *explicit message-passing and concurrency*. Examples using message passing are Concurrent ML [39], Haskell-MPI, and notably Erlang [3]. Concurrent Haskell [36] and Haskell transactional memory (STM) use shared memory, where threads communicate via shared mutable variables. A side remark on our categorisation: While interaction and explicitness of parallelism are mostly correlated, Haskell STM is the notable "outlier". There are no STM constructs for interaction between concurrent threads.

In general, *concurrency* is a programming model which allows to separate independent (usually effectful) computations into multiple (sometimes interacting) execution threads. Historically, this aims at supporting responsive distributed and interactive systems, which is also useful in the absence of actual parallel execution. Concurrency constructs are often also used to achieve genuine *parallelism*, speeding up a computation by executing its computational steps simultaneously ("in parallel") on computers with multiple processing units – and guaranteeing to do so. In contrast to this, concurrency can be understood as *sequential* computation, but with internal nondeterministic choices for selecting the next step. This is done by splitting the computation in a set of (sequential) *threads* or (sequential) *processes* (threads with shared memory). Assuming the implementation executes threads in parallel, concurrency can be a good implementation tool for parallel algorithms. Experience has shown that the large degree of control offered by concurrency abstractions and explicit message passing can prove useful for advanced parallel functional programming [10]. Functional languages also allow for more deterministic models to implement parallelism.

Project Goal: Tailored Parallel Functional Language. Within HIPERFIT, we aim to develop a functional language that can be productively used to express computations in mathematical finance, and which exposes inherent parallelism in these computations. Driven by the application domain of financial modelling, we will identify common computation patterns and their potential for parallelisation. Potentially parallel computations should be easy to extract and transform into explicitly parallel operations on a variety of modern parallel platforms.

In Figure 2, we have sketched the functional programming languages we expect to be most relevant for HIPERFIT. Apart from functional languages we also expect to draw on the heritage of classical bulk-data programming languages such as APL, SETL and SQL. Principally, data parallelism [12] appears to be a good match for the HIPERFIT application domain: it enables concise and long-term maintainable specifications of a wide variety of inherently parallelisable computations, without committing to any particular implementation strategy or execution environment. It facilitates correctness proofs and performance estimates, and, under eager evaluation, it has a useful compositional parallel cost model. Pure data parallelism, on the other hand, is less suitable for loosely-coupled systems. We therefore expect to also use more explicit and coarse-grained programming models (like e.g. Eden), however avoiding the burden of explicit message-passing and using implementation skeletons where possible.

At a later stage, we expect the DSL development for financial models to yield additional or modified requirements. Useful abstractions and patterns of parallelism will be identified from working on concrete projects. Ultimately, our language should support specific typical operations tailored to the application domain, risk analysis and valuation in a financial context, but without hard-wiring the application domain into it.

4.3 Support for Multicore and Novel Parallel Hardware

In the previous section, we have motivated our functional approach by a number of historic achievements of relevance, based on more than 20 years of research in parallel functional programming. Yet, it is interesting to see how much the availability of advanced GPGPU hardware in practice changes the scientific landscape. GPGPUs are made for SIMD-style parallel computations with minor memory requirements. Parallel software has often been built as a match to existing well-performing and well-understood hardware. Functional approaches claim to capture parallelism at a more abstract level, but recent publications about GPGPU programming in functional languages focus exactly on these simple embarrasingly parallel problems, where quick success can be expected.

Especially for accelerating financial simulations, the approach of modern GPGPUs appears promising; we already know that Monte Carlo methods can get massive speedups, due to their simple structure. This holds not only for finance, but also for various scientific applications using Monte Carlo simulations, for instance particle physics and computational geo-science. Today, we find several language bindings to GPGPU accelerators in the Haskell research community. They realise easy data parallelism on specially designated parallel vectors (Nikola [29]) or arrays (Accelerate [13]). These research prototypes deliver important insight for future GPGPU language design and pragmatics, but we still have a way to go towards making this research software work in practice for the average programmer or domain expert. And as mentioned, we observe an antithetic trend in scientific computation: scientists of various disciplines choose to operate at the lowest abstraction level API, Cuda C code.

Before GPGPUs became the prodigy of parallelism, a first wave of interest for parallelism was induced by *multicore CPUs*. Having several cores is a mere normality today, yet major functional languages have only recently optimised their multicore support. The high level of the languages, and implementation traditions, makes it sometimes very hard to optimise locality, but promising results have been obtained [5,11,30], and even entire new projects for multicore were set up, for instance Manticore [20]. With the movement towards OpenCL [34], both multicore processors, GPUs, and future heterogenous manycore architectures can be captured in a single computational idiom. OpenCL is supported by major manufacturers of novel hardware, and HIPERFIT will likely contribute to advancing its development and use as an intermediate target language.

Another recent effort is the initiative to make parallel Haskell apt for widespread commercial use, initiated by the Well-Typed consultancy and sponsors [4]. One of the first activities was to revive Haskell-MPI (from 2001) – which seems to be a major industrial demand, while some researchers consider message passing "harmful" [22]. Aiming at a higher hardware abstraction level, the latest efforts of that project are into performance analysis tool support [16].

Various activities on parallel Haskell are going on and in diverse directions. We believe that there is still important work to do, however. Our intention with HIPERFIT in this direction is to advertise and test various existing approaches through prototype implementations. We will closely follow and adopt the latest research in parallel functional programming, and at the same time continue work on our own high-performance backend, providing as general a platform for processing bulk data as we can realise.

5   Project Start and First Activities

Integrating Valuation and Contract Specification. The major use case of existing contract specification languages is *valuation (pricing)*: determining the value of a financial contract at any point in time, based on a stochastic model of the future. Existing contract languages have usually been developed together with a valuation semantics from the start. Based on a probabilistic model of unknown variables (for instance, modelling changes in interest rate for zero-coupon bonds), a range of possible outcomes and their probabilities is computed. A simple stochastic method for valuation is Monte Carlo simulation, which is inherently parallel by nature. More advanced methods might lead to a large number of possible outcomes and are thus computationally intensive; again massive parallelisation can hopefully lead to faster results.

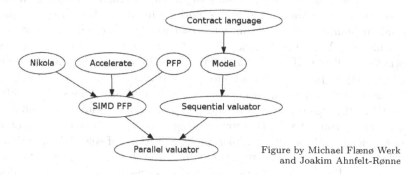

Figure by Michael Flænø Werk and Joakim Ahnfelt-Rønne

Fig. 3. Integration Overview for Contracts, PFP, and Data Parallelism

As one strand of HIPERFIT activities, we are evaluating existing GPGPU support in Haskell, namely the Nikola [29] DSEL and the accelerated Haskell array library [13], to offload vector computations to a GPGPU. Figure 3 gives an overview of the evaluated technologies. A recently concluded Master's thesis in HIPERFIT prototypes a Haskell system that combines existing technologies and applies them to accelerated stochastic contract valuation. Another strand is a domain-specific approach to Probabilistic Functional Programming (PFP) [18]. This DSEL separates the method of evaluation from the stochastic model and is thus helpful in structuring the implementation of our intended parallel valuation engine. Ultimately, we aim at producing a fully modular valuation engine, where instruments (contracts) and models (stochastic processes) are specified independently.

Port of Data.Array.Accelerate to OpenCL. In view of our general goal to use and produce open standards and open source software in HIPERFIT, we would like to pave the way towards using the standardized OpenCL [34] rather than the proprietary Cuda for GPGPU computations. We are therefore porting Data.Array.Accelerate [13] to OpenCL. The technology for this accelerated array library is well understood; we expect to mainly solve technical and engineering hurdles here. As a by-product, a new library of OpenCL bindings will be created. At a later time, we might also be able to maturate the Nikola [29] research to better usability by non-experts, and port it to OpenCL as well.

As discussed earlier (see Section 4.3), the GPU platform and programming model appears to be tailored, if not rigidly limited, to data parallelism. Control structures are very limited, memory accesses are entirely explicit, recursion is not possible, branching constructs execute both alternatives. On the other hand, precisely these properties could provide the magic wand for cost analysis and thereby performance prediction of parallelised valuation code. In view of this long-term goal, it is a strategic decision to generate know-how about GPU bindings, involving embedded compilation, in the context of HIPERFIT.

Other Activities. Work has also started in other research areas of HIPERFIT. To give a general idea of what our case-based working methodology looks like in practice, we mention a few other activities. One interesting area is to parallelise random number generation in a reproducible manner, for use in Monte Carlo simulations. A HIPERFIT project is investigating existing research to extract best practice on using GPGPUs for this problem. In a second strand of activities, we aim to extract patterns and common usage from existing in-house bank software, by inspecting and parallelising kernel routines of an in-house C++ library. In another project, we want to take the perspective of an informed economist on the topic of instrument valuation, by creating a survey and classification of financial instruments and models. Parallel implementations of selected valuation models will follow, which can be structured to reflect the generalities that have been identified. The implementation work also serves to evaluate other declarative parallel languages (to be determined) and to identify recurring patterns and potentially useful features for later DSL development.

6   Conclusions

We have presented motivation, goals and methods of the HIPERFIT research center, a joint activity of researchers in mathematical finance, programming languages, parallel computing, and computer systems in collaboration with Finance IT professionals. In order to meet new and increasing computational needs of a complex global industry of major impact, HIPERFIT aims at integrated solutions that transcend a single researcher's field of expertise, and explicitly fosters interdisciplinarity and practical relevance through its paradigm of case-driven research themes.

We want to develop advanced new methods in mathematical finance and work towards a framework of domain-specific languages to express financial instruments, models and valuation methods. Parallelisation techniques using a functional approach should both lead to efficient parallel execution on novel hardware, and leave the code accessible for proofs of semantic properties and, to some extent, performance predictions.

The goals of HIPERFIT which relate to programming languages appear to carry the highest risk of achieving practical impact, but arguably also promise the best long-term investment. Past research on parallelism concepts has often come to success and innovation by focusing on particular application domains. Immediate practical use and challenging problems derived from practice are a good touch-stone for research. Especially because of the unique combination of advanced programming language technology and parallelism envisioned in HIPERFIT, we consider it an exciting opportunity to perform and promote research in DSLs and parallel functional programming, and hope to make it one of its major showcases.

The HIPERFIT Website: http://www.hiperfit.dk.

References

1. Aditya, S., Arvind, A.L., Maessen, J.W., Nikhil, R.S.: Semantics of pH: A parallel dialect of Haskell. In: Hudak, P. (ed.) Proceedings of the Haskell Workshop, La Jolla, USA, pp. 35–49 (1995)
2. Andersen, J., Elsborg, E., Henglein, F., Simonsen, J.G., Stefansen, C.: Compositional specification of commercial contracts. International Journal on Software Tools for Technology Transfer (STTT) 8(6), 485–516 (2006)
3. Armstrong, J., Virding, R., Wikström, C., Williams, M.: Concurrent Programming in ERLANG., 2nd edn. Prentice Hall, Hertfordshire (1996)
4. Astapov, D.: Parallel Haskell project underway. Blog post (October 2010), http://www.well-typed.com/blog/48
5. Aswad, M., Trinder, P., Al Zain, A.D., Michaelson, G., Berthold, J.: Low Pain vs. No Pain Multicore Haskells. In: Horváth, Z., Zsók, V., Achten, P., Koopman, P. (eds.) Trends in Functional Programming (TFP 2009), pp. 49–64. Intellect, Exeter (2010)
6. Augustsson, L., Mansell, H., Sittampalam, G.: Paradise: A two-stage DSL embedded in Haskell. In: ICFP 2008, Proceedings of the 13th ACM SIGPLAN International Conference on Functional Programming, pp. 225–228. ACM, New York (2008)
7. Backus, J.: Can programming be liberated from the von neumann style. Communications of the ACM 21(8), 613–641 (1978)
8. Berthold, J., Dieterle, M., Loogen, R.: Implementing Parallel Google Map-Reduce in Eden. In: Sips, H., Epema, D., Lin, H.-X. (eds.) Euro-Par 2009. LNCS, vol. 5704, pp. 990–1002. Springer, Heidelberg (2009)
9. Berthold, J., Dieterle, M., Loogen, R., Priebe, S.: Hierarchical Master-Worker Skeletons. In: Hudak, P., Warren, D.S. (eds.) PADL 2008. LNCS, vol. 4902, pp. 248–264. Springer, Heidelberg (2008)

10. Berthold, J., Loogen, R.: Parallel Coordination Made Explicit in a Functional Setting. In: Horváth, Z., Zsók, V., Butterfield, A. (eds.) IFL 2006. LNCS, vol. 4449, pp. 73–90. Springer, Heidelberg (2007)

11. Berthold, J., Marlow, S., Hammond, K., Al Zain, A.: Comparing and Optimising Parallel Haskell Implementations for Multicore Machines. In: Enokido, T., et al. (eds.) 3rd Int. Workshop on Advanced Distributed and Parallel Network Applications (ADPNA 2009). IEEE (2009); (previously presented at IFL 2008)

12. Blelloch, G.: Programming parallel algorithms. CACM 39(3), 85–97 (1996)

13. Chakravarty, M.M., Keller, G., Lee, S., McDonell, T.L., Grover, V.: Accelerating Haskell array codes with multicore GPUs. In: DAMP 2011: Proceedings of the Sixth Workshop on Declarative Aspects of Multicore Programming, pp. 3–14. ACM, New York (2011)

14. Chakravarty, M., Leshchinskiy, R., Jones, S.P., Keller, G., Marlow, S.: Data parallel Haskell: A status report. In: DAMP 2007: Workshop on Declarative Aspects of Multicore Programming, pp. 10–18. ACM, New York (2007)

15. Cole, M.I.: Algorithmic Skeletons: Structured Management of Parallel Computation. Research Monographs in Parallel and Distributed Computing. MIT Press, Cambridge (1989)

16. Coutts, D.: Spark visualisation in threadscope. In: Contribution to the Haskell Implementors' Workshop 2011, Tokyo (September 2011)

17. Dévai, G., Tejfel, M., Gera, Z., Páli, G., Nagy, G., Horváth, Z., Axelssony, E., Sheeran, M., Vajda, A., Lyckegård, B., Persson, A.: Efficient code generation from the high-level domain-specific language Feldspar for DSPs. In: ODES-8, 8th Workshop on Optimizations for DSP and Embedded Systems, Toronto (April 2010)

18. Erwig, M., Kollmansberger, S.: Probabilistic functional programming in Haskell. J. of Functional Programming 16(1), 21–34 (2006)

19. FCIC: The financial crisis inquiry report. Tech. rep., Financial Crisis Inquiry Report Commission (January 2011), http://www.fcic.gov/report

20. Fluet, M., Rainey, M., Reppy, J., Shaw, A., Xiao, Y.: Manticore: A Heterogeneous Parallel Language. In: Glew, N., Blelloch, G.E. (eds.) DAMP 2007: Workshop on Declarative Aspects of Multicore Programming, Nice, France, pp. 37–44 (2007)

21. Glasserman, P.: Monte Carlo methods in financial engineering. Applications of Mathematics, vol. 53. Springer, New York (2004)

22. Gorlatch, S.: Send-receive considered harmful: Myths and realities of message passing. ACM TOPLAS 26(1), 47–56 (2004)

23. Hammond, K., Michaelson, G. (eds.): Research Directions in Parallel Functional Programming. Springer, London (2000)

24. Hughes, J.: Why functional programming matters. The Computer Journal 32(2), 98–107 (1989)

25. Keller, G., Chakravarty, M.M., Leshchinskiy, R., Peyton Jones, S., Lippmeier, B.: Regular, shape-polymorphic, parallel arrays in Haskell. In: ICFP 2010: Proceedings of the 15th ACM SIGPLAN International Conference on Functional Programming, pp. 261–272. ACM, New York (2010)

26. Lewis, J.: Cryptol: specification, implementation and verification of high-grade cryptographic applications. In: FMSE 2007: Proceedings of the ACM Workshop on Formal Methods in Security Engineering, p. 41. ACM, New York (2007)

27. LexiFi: Contract description language (MLFi). Web page and white paper, http://www.lexifi.com/technology/contract-description-language

28. Loogen, R., Ortega-Mallén, Y., Peña-Marí, R.: Parallel Functional Programming in Eden. Journal of Functional Programming 15(3), 431–475 (2005)

29. Mainland, G., Morrisett, G.: Nikola: embedding compiled GPU functions in Haskell. In: Haskell 2010: Proceedings of the Third ACM SIGPLAN Symposium on Haskell, pp. 67–78. ACM, New York (2010)
30. Marlow, S., Jones, S.P., Singh, S.: Runtime Support for Multicore Haskell. In: ICFP 2009: Proceedings of the 14th ACM SIGPLAN International Conference on Functional Programming, New York, pp. 65–78 (2009)
31. Marlow, S., Maier, P., Loidl, H.W., Aswad, M.K., Trinder, P.: Seq no more: Better strategies for parallel Haskell. In: Haskell 2010: Proceedings of the Third ACM SIGPLAN Symposium on Haskell, pp. 91–102. ACM, New York (2010)
32. Mernik, M., Heering, J., Sloane, A.M.: When and how to develop domain-specific languages. ACM Computing Surveys 37(4), 316–344 (2005)
33. Mirani, R., Hudak, P.: First-class monadic schedules. ACM TOPLAS 26(4), 609–651 (2004)
34. Munshi, A.: The OpenCL Specification. Khronos OpenCL Working Group (2010), http://www.khronos.org/opencl/
35. Peyton Jones, S., Eber, J.M., Seward, J.: Composing contracts: an adventure in financial engineering (functional pearl). In: ICFP 2000: Proceedings of the Fifth ACM SIGPLAN International Conference on Functional Programming, pp. 280–292. ACM, New York (2000); (Later extended to a book chapter)
36. Peyton Jones, S., Gordon, A., Finne, S.: Concurrent Haskell. In: Proceedings of POPL 1996, pp. 295–308. ACM, New York (1996)
37. Plasmeijer, M., van Eekelen, M.: Functional Programming and Parallel Graph Rewriting. Addison-Wesley, Reading (1993)
38. Rabhi, F.A., Gorlatch, S. (eds.): Patterns and Skeletons for Parallel and Distributed Computing. Springer, London (2003)
39. Reppy, J.H.: Concurrent Programming in ML. Cambridge Univ. Press (1999)
40. Securities and Exchange Commission: Proposed rule: Asset backed securities (2010), http://www.sec.gov/rules/proposed/2010/33-9117.pdf
41. Skillicorn, D.B., Talia, D.: Models and languages for parallel computation. ACM Computing Surveys 30(2), 123–169 (1998)
42. Sobral, J.L., Monteiro, M.P.: A domain-specific language for parallel and Grid computing. In: DSAL 2008: Proceedings of the 2008 AOSD Workshop on Domain-Specific Aspect Languages, pp. 2:1–2:4. ACM, New York (2008)
43. Trinder, P., Hammond, K., Loidl, H.W., Peyton Jones, S.: Algorithm + Strategy = Parallelism. J. of Functional Programming 8(1), 23–60 (1998)
44. Trinder, P., Hammond, K., Mattson Jr., J., Partridge, A., Peyton Jones, S.: GUM: a Portable Parallel Implementation of Haskell. In: PLDI 1996, pp. 78–88. ACM, New York (1996)
45. Diderot project. Website (2010), http://diderot-language.cs.uchicago.edu/

Thread-Safe Priority Queues
in Haskell Based on Skiplists

Michael Lesniak

University of Kassel
Research Group Programming Languages / Methodologies
Wilhelmshöher Allee 73
Kassel, Germany
mlesniak@uni-kassel.de

Abstract. Although thread-safe priority queues are fundamental building blocks for many parallel algorithms, there are currently no scalable
implementations available in Haskell. An efficient structure to implement priority queues is the skiplist, which is a multi-level linked list
with shortcuts. We developed three thread-safe skiplist variants, based
on locks, software transactional memory, and atomic compare-and-swap,
respectively. In our benchmarks, the lock-based and compare-and-swap
variants scaled about equally well, while the transactional variant was
by several orders of magnitude slower.

1 Introduction

Priority queues are well-known data structures to store and retrieve elements
from some ordered set [1]. They support at least two operations: *insert* adds an
element to the queue, and *deleteMin* removes and returns the minimal element.
Priority queues are used in many parallel algorithms, where they need to be
thread-safe.

Unfortunately there are currently no scalable thread-safe priority queue
implementations available in Haskell. The main contribution of this paper is providing implementations based on skiplists [2], which are multi-leveled linked list
data structures with shortcuts to randomly chosen elements. According to Pugh
and others [3–6], both lock-based and lock-free variants of skiplists are superior
in performance to classic approaches such as the thread-safe binary heap [7]. We
implemented three variants of skiplists. One ensures thread-safety with explicit
locking, while the others are lock-free and based on software transactional memory and atomic compare-and-swap operations, respectively. As common in related
literature, we benchmarked the different variants using random (but reproducible)
insert and deleteMin operations with and without computational load in-between.
Additionally, we compared them with a naive coarse-locked heap. Unlike many
other implementations of thread-safe priority queues our queues fully support duplicates, i.e., multiple elements may have the same key, as they are frequently
needed in practice. We tested the correctness of our implementations with Johnson's algorithm [8] for the single-source shortest path problem in sparse graphs.

R. Peña and R. Page (Eds.): TFP 2011, LNCS 7193, pp. 114–129, 2012.
© Springer-Verlag Berlin Heidelberg 2012

To briefly state our results, the lock-based and atomic compare-and-swap (CAS) variants scale comparably well, although the CAS variant is slower in absolute terms. The transactional variant is always slower by several orders of magnitude, except when the computational load is so high that the synchronization time is negligible. Surprisingly, the heap-based variant scales comparably well due to its better cache locality.

The full source code of our implementations, as well as the shell scripts for benchmarking and the raw benchmark results can be found at the author's software repository [9].

The rest of the paper is structured as follows. Section 2 describes the sequential skiplist that we based our work on. Section 3 describes the different concurrent skiplist variants in detail. Section 4 explains our benchmarks and discusses the experimental results. Section 5 reviews related work and Section 6 concludes and gives an outlook to future work.

2   Skiplists

In this section we briefly explain the non-optimized variant of the sequential skiplist data structure first described and analyzed by Pugh [2]. For simplification, we postpone details of handling duplicates to the next section.

A skiplist is basically an ordered linked list with additional randomly chosen shortcuts (see Figure 1). The shortcuts speed up searches, and thus also inserts

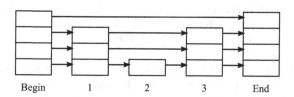

Begin   1   2   3   End

Fig. 1. A skiplist of height 4 storing keys 1, 2 and 3. The elements with keys 1 and 3 have height 3, element with key 2 has height 1. There is no element with height 4.

and deletes by allowing to skip over a number of elements in one step (see Figure 2). The search operation starts at the initial node of the list at its highest level. It walks through nodes on the particular level until the following node has a larger or equal key. In this case, the search continues on the preceding level. The insert and delete operations use the (stored) predecessors at each level to perform the well-known operations for linked-lists. The deleteMin simply deletes and returns the first element on level 1. On insertion, the height of each node is randomized such that 50% have height 1, 25% have height 2 and so on. That way, skiplists have a probabilistic time complexity of $O(\log n)$ for search, insert and delete and a worst-case time complexity of $O(n)$, where n is the number of stored elements.

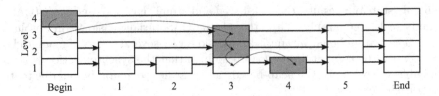

Fig. 2. Search for the element with key 4. By using the shortcut on level 3, keys 1 and 2 are skipped. The dashed arrows show the search order. Note that the search looks ahead to the next node. The gray-shaded boxes mark the predecessors of the found node on each level.

3   Concurrent Skiplist Variants

In this section we first explain the `PriorityQueue` typeclass common to all implementations, and then describe our three variants of concurrent skiplists. The following presentation is occasionally simplified; further details can be found in the source code or the referenced papers, respectively.

3.1   The PriorityQueue Typeclass

To ease experimentation and later usage, we defined a common typeclass with functional dependencies [10] which is implemented by all skiplist variants:

```
class Ord p => PriorityQueue pq p v | pq -> p, pq -> v where
    deleteMin :: pq -> IO (Maybe (p,v))
    insert    :: p  -> v -> pq -> IO ()
```

The `deleteMin` function returns the key and value of the minimal element or `Nothing` if the queue is currently empty. The `insert` function adds a key and its value to the queue. In contrast to many other concurrent variants of skiplists, we decided to support duplicates, although it increases the difficulty of a correct implementation. The motivation was that many real-world problems, e.g. Johnson's algorithm, need duplicates to function correctly. All implementations can be modified to simply overwrite the value when a given key already exists. All implementations evaluate keys and values lazy. Since the insertion of an element needs to evaluate its key to find the correct position, this does not influence correctness.

3.2   Lock-Based Skiplists

Our lock-based implementation is based on the original lock-based concurrent variant of Pugh [6]. It has the advantage that a thread only needs to lock a small portion of the skiplist and only for a short time to insert or delete a node, and that traversal does not need locking at all. Base types are shown in Figure 3. Each skiplist is initially empty and all pointers of the beginning node `skipBegin`

```haskell
data (Ord p) => Skiplist p v = Skiplist {
    skipBegin  :: Node p v,
    skipEnd    :: Node p v
}

data (Ord p) => Node p v = Node {
    nodeValue   :: NodeValue p v,
    nodeId      :: Unique,
    nodeGarbage :: IORef Bool,
    nodePointer :: Pointers p v,
    nodeLevel   :: Lock Level,
}

data NodeValue p v = Value (p,v) | Begin | End deriving Eq
type Level          = Int
type Pointers p v  = IOArray Level (Lock (Node p v))

data Lock a = Lock {
    lockValue :: IORef (Maybe a),
    lockLock  :: MVar ()
}
```

Fig. 3. Base types for the lock-based skiplist implementation

point to the end node `skipEnd`. Each `Node` holds its key-value pair (if it is not the beginning or end node), a unique id to handle duplicates, a deletion marker to signal deletion to other threads, its height, and references to its successors at each level.

Pugh's algorithm requires both the support of concurrent read access to shared values and their exclusive locking such that other threads trying to lock are blocked (but are still allowed to read the value). We defined a type `Lock` which encapsulates a (possibly empty) modifiable value in an `IORef`, and use an `MVar` to achieve the blocked locking [11]. Since the (sequential) insert and delete operations work on a level by level basis, locking is mainly used to control the shared access to the successor pointers of each node as follows. Both operations first create a vector of predecessor nodes (as marked in Figure 2).

The **insert** operation inserts the created node level by level, beginning with level 1: after locking the successor pointer of the predecessor on the current level, it sets the pointer to the newly created node and the successor of the new node to the former successor (see Figure 4).

To implement deleteMin we use a more general helper function called `delete` that allows deletion of arbitrary keys. It starts by checking the current status of a node's possible deletion: if `nodeGarbage` is false, no other thread deletes the node and it is set. Otherwise deletion is stopped and may be repeated by searching for another node with the same key. The found node is then removed level by level, starting with the highest one. Note that pointers on levels larger

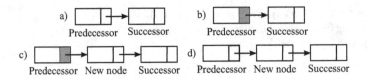

Fig. 4. Locking to insert a node into the list on a particular level. a) initial state b) Lock of successor pointer of the predecessor c) insertion of new node d) unlocking of the locked pointer.

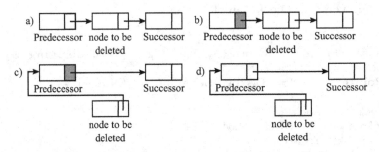

Fig. 5. Deleting and locking of a node on a particular level. a) initial state b) Lock of successor pointer of the predecessor c) setting new successor pointer of the predecessor and creating the backreference d) unlocking of the locked pointer.

than 1 are solely shortcuts and removing them does not lead to a (partially) corrupted skiplist. A node is thus deleted when it is removed from level 1. Since other threads could possibly be traversing through the node currently being deleted, a backreference is used to allow continuous traversal (see Figure 5). The approach of marking nodes to be deleted is an optimization to marking, threads would concurrently try to delete the node on its different levels, leading to successfully.

The `deleteMin` operation simply reads the key of the successor of the beginning node and tries to delete it. If it is successful, this element can be returned. If not, another thread deleted the element simultaneously and the operation is restarted.

Since insert proceeds level-wise and threads are allowed to insert duplicates, there is no guarantee of the order of elements on each level (see Figure 6). When a particular key is deleted it is crucial that the correct predecessor pointers on each level are modified. To solve this problem we added an unique identifier to each node, such that a search can find all correct predecessors on each level (see Figure 7): In the given example assume we need to find the correct predecessors of the node with key 2. On the top level the list traversal finds it in front of the node with the unique key (1), such that further traversals will now search predecessors which point to nodes with the same unique key.

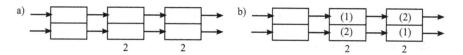

Fig. 6. a) External representation of a skiplist with two keys 2 b) Internal representation. Values in brackets show the unique identifiers.

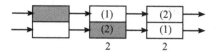

Fig. 7. By using unique identifiers, the predecessors for key 2 with identifier (1) can be found. They are marked in gray.

3.3   Software Transactional Memory Based Skiplists

Since lock-based programming has well-known drawbacks like deadlocks and difficult debugging, interest in alternative approaches has risen in the last years. Software Transactional Memory (STM), coming historically from database research, uses the idea of *transactions* to allow concurrent access to shared data structures [12]; instead of locking, functions access shared data structures in transactions and the runtime systems takes care of consistency issues, e.g. by restarting transactions in case of conflicts. To restrict the number of variables that the parallel runtime system needs to take care of, (transactional) shared values in Haskell are wrapped in a TVar and their use (i.e. reading and writing) is only allowed inside an STM monad [13]. We developed two variants of the STM skiplist: a naive one where the whole functionality for each operation is enclosed in one atomic block, and a more sophisticated one where we divided the different actions of each operation into independent blocks.

The data structures for the STM variants are similar to the lock-based ones shown in Figure 3. Instead of IORefs and MVars to control mutable variables and locks, TVars are used (see Figure 8).

In the naive variant there is no need for a shared variable containing the deletion state since this is handled implicitly by the underlying transaction model. It therefore allows to easily model the sequential variant, since the algorithms and approaches can be transcribed directly by simply changing mutable variables to TVars and enclosing the operations in an atomic block. As we discuss and explain in Section 4, the performance of this variant is rather bad due to the possibly long duration of each transaction and resulting high probability of conflicts and restarts.

A more reasonable approach is to divide the transactions into independent sub-transactions and thus to partially remodel the lock-based variant. Both the insert and delete operations have now two phases, transactionally independent from an STM point of view: in the first phase the predecessors for the correct position are found and, in the case of deletion, the corresponding node is marked

```
data (Ord p) ⇒ Skiplist p v = Skiplist {
    skipBegin  :: Node p v,
    skipEnd    :: Node p v
}

data (Ord p) ⇒ Node p v = Node {
    nodeValue    :: NodeValue p v,
    nodeId       :: Unique,
    nodePointer  :: Pointers p v,
    nodeLevel    :: TVar Level,
}

type Pointers p v  = TArray Level (Node p v)
```

Fig. 8. Base types for the STM-based skiplist implementation

as to be deleted. In the second phase, the new node is inserted at the correct position or removed, respectively; for each level a new transaction (for the second phase) is started.

Although it would be possible to further dissect the level-based transactions, i.e. approaching the lock-based solution further, this would (in our opinion) conflict with the overall idea of transaction-based synchronization and its promise to simplify parallel programming.

3.4 Skiplists Based on Atomic Compare and Swap Operations

While lock-based implementations of thread-safe data structures are conceptually easy to comprehend, they imply the problems mentioned in the beginning of the last section.

As a second alternative, lock-free synchronization with atomic compare-and-swap operations promises to deliver better performance as compared to transaction-based synchronization due to greater control of the operations. We used ideas for a lock-free implementation of linked lists from Harris and Fomitchev [3, 14]. To guarantee consistency of shared variables, atomic compare-and-swap (CAS) and test-and-set (TAS) operations are used. A CAS checks if the shared variable contains a particular value (usually the value of the variable read previously) and if and only if it does, swaps it with a new one. A TAS applies a function to the current value and swaps with the new value if the return value of the function is true. In both cases a returned flag indicates success. Haskell code for both CAS (from [15]) and TAS for modifying shared IORefs is shown in Figure 9.

Types are slightly modified as compared to Figure 3. Since we are not able to lock nodes currently being changed but still need a mechanism to at least

```
atomCAS  ::  Eq a ⟹ IORef a −> a −> a −> IO Bool
atomCAS ptr old new = atomTAS ptr (==old) new

atomTAS  ::  Eq a ⟹ IORef a −> (a −> Bool) −> a −> IO Bool
atomTAS ptr test new = do
    atomicModifyIORef ptr $ \cur −>
        if test cur then (new, True) else (cur, False)
```

Fig. 9. Atomic compare-and-swap and test-and-set functions

```
data Mark         = Marked | Unmarked deriving Eq
type Pointer p v  = (Mark, Node p v)
type Pointers p v = IOArray Level (IORef (Pointer p v))
```

Fig. 10. Modification of pointers to allows annotation with a 'currently modified'-flag

check their modification, we extend a reference (pointer) with a flag. By using a single CAS to set the flag from Unmarked to Marked, a node is marked to signal its removal state. Many low-level implementations modify the least significant bits of a memory address instead [3, 16, 14], but this architecture- and compiler-dependent approach is obviously not directly possible in Haskell (with IORefs). Instead, a pointer now contains a tuple as shown in Figure 10 and is changed as described below.

The insert and delete operations use methods described by Harris for handling lock-free linked lists [14]. We extend them to work on multiple levels (i.e. deletion works level-wise downwards and insertion upwards), as explained in Section 3.2.

Both operations start by creating the vector of predecessors and then working level-wise in the specified direction. While insertion is similar to Figure 4, deletion using CAS is more complicated, since interfering insertions can lead to corrupt data structures (see Figure 11). The solution is to split the deletion in two phases: one marks the node to be deleted logically, such that concurrent insertions skip these nodes, and the following phase removes the node physically. The delete operation works therefore as follows: first, the node to be deleted is searched and logically deleted by marking the successor pointer of its predecessor using CAS; it repeats if the CAS fails. It is then physically deleted (also using CAS) by setting the pointer of the predecessor node to the successor of the deleted node, if possible. If a concurrent operation changed the pointers and the CAS failed, delete removes the node by searching for the key as indicated below.

The key function used by both operations is the search for the predecessor and successor of a node: while searching for these nodes the search also deletes nodes that it traverses and which have been marked for removal by other threads (see Figure 12).

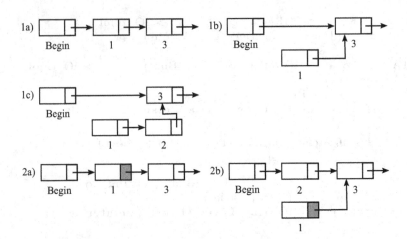

Fig. 11. Consistency problems with concurrent deletion of node 1 and insertion of node 2: 1a) initial state 1b) Using a single CAS (modifying the successor of the Begin-node) 1c) Concurrent insertion can lead to unreachable newly inserted nodes. Solution using a two-phase deletion: 2a) Deletion phase 1: logically mark the node as to be deleted 2b) After physical deletion and concurrent insertion.

3.5   Testing the Implementations

Developing concurrent algorithms is tremendously difficult. Hard to find errors, e.g. those corrupting the data structure instead of leading to a clearly visible error (like a deadlock) can be easily overlooked. While proving the correctness of an actual implementation is desirable, it is still a topic of ongoing research [17]. To challenge the different skiplist variants and at least test their desired functionality, we implemented Johnson's algorithm [8], which calculates the single-source shortest path (SSSP) in sparse graphs in parallel using a thread-safe priority queue as its basic data structure. This algorithm uses both insert and deleteMin operations in a realistic scenario, stresses the duplicate key support (since many duplicate keys occur) and allows easy comparison with a desired outcome: For reference, we developed a simple sequential implementation. We ran each test a few hundred times with different seeds and graph sizes for all four skiplist implementations. We did not use the algorithm for performance measurement: Since the amount of work per extracted element is exceptionally low, Johnson's algorithm can be improved in this respect (and it is very reasonable to do so in a real-world application). These improvements are a research topic on its own right [18, 19] and out of scope of this paper.

A common tool for testing in Haskell is Quickcheck [20], however it is primarily aimed at pure code and not appropriate for concurrent code using the IO-monad. In particular, its strength of automatic test case generation (e.g. finding minimal examples) does not necessarily apply to non-deterministic bugs that are commonly found in concurrent programs.

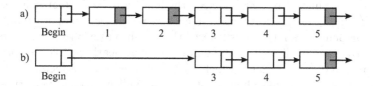

Fig. 12. Representation of deleting traversed nodes in a search for a node with key 3. a) initial state. The marked nodes were marked by other threads b) state after traversal. The search function returns the beginning node as the predecessor and node 4 as the successor. Non-traversed nodes (e.g. node 5) are not influenced.

4   Benchmarks

We ran experiments on a 2.3 GHz 16-core AMD Opteron 6134 with 32 GB RAM running a Linux-kernel 2.6.38-8 with GHC 7.0.3. Interpretation of the experimental outcomes was limited, since there is no parallel profiler for Haskell's parallel runtime system, and Threadscope [21] primarily provides information regarding the garbage collector and overall processor utilization. Garbage collection times were negligible and ranged from 1% up to 10% for all benchmarks.

We examined two scenarios: First we tested the scalability of the implementations with a benchmark adapted from the literature. Second we examined the speedup using a synthetic benchmark mirroring divide-and-conquer algorithms. As stated in Section 3.5 we deliberately did not implement a real algorithm, since the design space even for quite simple algorithms is huge and currently unexplored in Haskell. In addition to the variants described in Section 3 we implemented a sequential heap with arrays [1] and protected by a single MVar (thus implementing a coarse lock). The implementation allocates an array that is large enough to store all values, eliminating the need to dynamically resize.

In our scalability benchmarks each concurrent thread performs 1000 initial insertions, followed by 10000 operations, chosen with a 50% probability to be deleteMin or insert. Keys were randomly chosen from the interval $(0, 10^6)$. These values and probabilities were taken from other papers, e.g. [3]. We re-run each benchmark three times and report the average execution times. Since the thread-specific random number generators are (re-)initialized with the same initial (but thread-specific) seed, the same sequential operations are performed in all runs and implementations, guaranteeing reproducibility. Since *each* threads performs 11000 operations, the total number of operations increases with the number of threads and *scalability* is examined. We performed three experiments with varying workload after each deleteMin operation:

In the most realistic scenario the thread that executed deleteMin receives the key-value k and computes π on $\frac{k}{35000}$ digits. For $k = 10^6$ this calculation takes 0.002s, which is a reasonable amount of computational work. Results are shown in Figure 13; keep in mind that the time-axes in all figures are logarithmic and we do not show times over 1000s to keep the lower graphs distinguishable. Both transactional variants perform bad, since the amount of computational work can not compensate for the overhead of the synchronization model, nevertheless the advantage of dissecting the transactions is clearly visible. Surprisingly the compare-and-swap variant, which was motivated by the fact that it does not explicitly lock and thus should outperform explicit locking, performs magnitudes of orders better than the transactional variants but about three times slower than the lock-based and heap variants. This can be explained by the very high abstraction level of the atomic compare-and-swap operations using IORefs (see Section 6). While the good scalability of the lock-based variant was expected (since the implementation does not hold any global lock and MVars are widely used and optimized) we were surprised by the good scalability of the heap-based variant. While its coarse locking hurts performance, this drawback is more than compensated by a simpler memory layout: all operations are done on a continuously allocated memory block (array) that provides for much better spatial locality and cache usage than the small data chunks of skiplists.

To see the influence of high contention, we omitted the workload in a second experiment. The results are shown in Figure 14. Not surprisingly, the transactional variants perform quite bad since transactions are restarted (overall or on a per level basis) very often. The compare-and-swap variant still scales well. Although both the heap and the lock-based variant scale better than the others, concurrent accesses to the heap occur so often that the cache advantage (mentioned above) disappears.

Since the amount of computational load plays a major role, it is interesting to look at the scalability when its is even higher. We experimented with computing π on $\frac{k}{2000}$ digits (about 0.035s for $n = 10^6$) and additionally reduced the number of initial insertions and operations. Results are shown in Figure 15. While the different variants converge, the overall ranking stays the same.

Our second scenario, the synthetic speedup benchmark, initially fills a priority queue with 10000 random elements. Computation takes up to 0.002s per element using the π calculation mentioned above. If an element is extracted from the queue for the first time, it is additionally reinserted two times with half its value (halving its next computation time), thus mirroring a divide-and-conquer algorithm. The results are shown in Figure 16; since the transactional variants performed bad, they are not fully shown in this graph. In accordance to the scalability results we see that the lock-based variant and the heap have the best speedup although the compare-and-swap variant is quite close. Both transactional variants show a small speedup but are three orders of magnitudes slower.

Summarizing, both the lock-based variant and the heap-based variant perform best. Since the lock-based variant scales better, it should be favored especially on future large multicore and manycore systems. The compare-and-swap variant also shows good scalability but the constant factors need to be improved to be

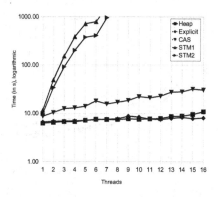

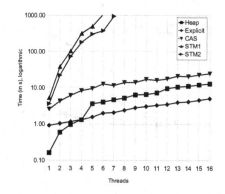

Fig. 13. Scalability of priority queue implementations with computational load

Fig. 14. Scalability of priority queue implementations without computational load

competitive. The transactional variants are not feasible under high contention, but they still provide for an easy-to-develop alternative in scenarios with lower contention.

4.1   Additional Comparisons: Difficulty and Code Size

Finally we look at our experiences regarding two non-performance oriented metrics: programming expense and code size.

The naive transactional variant was by far the easiest to develop. As stated in Section 3.3 a thread-safe variant could be developed by swapping mutable variables with TVars. The dissected transactional variant follows closely. Although we had to implement dissected level-based traversal, we still did not need to pay attention to synchronization problems such as deadlocks. The lock-based variant was more difficult to develop, despite the fact that it was the most researched one and the author was experienced in this approach. It had the well-known problems of rarely occurring deadlocks and thus difficult debugging. An advantage of the lock-based approach is clear semantics: if a potential source for a bug has been found, it is rather easy to reason about the behavior of the program and the source of the error. The compare-and-swap variant was the most difficult to develop: programming errors did not lead to observable deadlocks but more often to a slightly corrupted data structure which could lead to errors much later in the execution, making debugging and reasoning about potential errors very difficult.

While the code size heavily depends on the developer's programming style, a comparison gives another view on the complexity of the implementations. We counted all lines in each variant without comments or empty lines. The transactional variants STM1 and STM2 were comparable with 237 and 250 lines of code, respectively. Both other variants were significantly larger with 401 lines each.

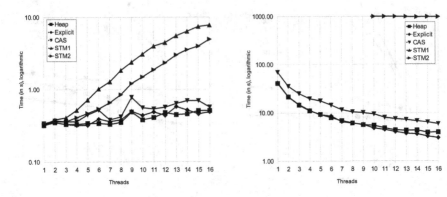

Fig. 15. Scalability of priority queue implementations with larger computational load

Fig. 16. Speedup of different priority queue implementations

5 Related Work

An extensive amount of research has been done for performant and thread-safe implementations of priority queues. Traditionally they are implemented using binary heaps [1]. A well-known parallel variant which uses locks is described by Hunt [7]. A general survey of thread-safe priority-queue implementations and a discussion of their properties has been done by Bauer et al. [22].

A sequential and lock-based skiplist were initially developed by Pugh [2, 6]. Both implementations showed a superior performance as compared to binary heaps. An extensive discussion of the performance characteristics of lock-based priority queues using skiplists has been done by Lotan et al. [4]. An algorithmic performance analysis for lock-free linked lists (and an outlook on skiplists) is described by Fomitchev [3]. Experimental results and a comparison of the performance of lock-free implementations with lock-based variants (Hunt, Lotan-Shavit) are discussed by Sundell [5]. Both works build on the implementation of lock-free linked lists as described by Harris [14], which itself was an algorithmic improvement for the original work on this subject from Valois [16].

Sulzmann et al. analyzed the performance of concurrent linked list implementations in Haskell [15]. Like our work, they discuss synchronization using MVars, IORefs and STM, but their benchmark depends more on GHC's internal thread scheduling. In contrast to the results discussed and explained in Section 4, the lock-free CAS implementation outperformed the other variants.

Although priority queues are fundamental for many parallel algorithms, there is as far as we know no prior literature about thread-safe priority queue implementations in Haskell. The common way to implement them is to protect a pure data structure [23] with a coarse thread-safe container (e.g. an MVar or IORef), which for example has been done in the new GHC 7 IO manager [24]. One possible reason for the lack of research is that they still work on a fairly low abstraction level. Haskell provides alternatives which allow for a more abstract formulation of parallel algorithms for the price of not being able to transcribe well-known solutions found for traditional parallel systems. Intel's Concurrent Collections provide a graph-based framework for formulating parallel algorithms [25], data parallel Haskell allows to implicitly evaluate parallel array algorithms [26] and the `par`-functions allows semi-implicit parallelization of functions, such that the compiler takes care of the (manual) synchronization done in this work [27].

6   Conclusion and Future Work

We have implemented thread-safe skiplists in Haskell, based on lock-based and lock-free synchronization techniques. Our lock-based variant uses `MVars`, whereas the lock-free variants use software transactional memory (STM) and atomic compare-and-swap operations, respectively. For STM, we developed two variants: a naive transformation of the sequential implementation and another that dissects the transactions into independent parts. We checked the correctness of all variants with Johnson's algorithm for the single source shortest path problem on sparse graphs, comparing the results with a reference implementation. Each implementation was benchmarked using synthetic randomized operations that allowed reproducible results.

The lock-based variant was the fastest and since it does not use any global lock we think that it will continue to scale well with more cores. Surprisingly, for many scenarios with low contention an implementation using a coarse-locked heap performs comparably well (although we expect that to change with more concurrent threads) and is easy to develop. The compare-and-swap variant scaled well but its absolute performance suffered from a currently slow atomic compare-and-swap operation. Until a more performant compare-and-swap operation for mutable variables is developed (see below) we can only warn against implementing lock-free models using this synchronization model, since its absolute performance is (not yet) on par with a well-tuned lock-based variant. Although being the easiest to develop, the transaction-based implementations do not seem to be a good choice for synchronization of thread-safe data structures since their initial overhead in combination with high synchronization costs under high contention is too high.

Future work may address different related topics: first, despite their sole use as priority queues in this work, skiplists are general dictionary structures. A comparison of their concurrent performance for arbitrary insertions and deletions seems interesting. Second, GHC does not support real (fast) atomic compare-and-swap operations using high-level abstractions. Implementing an extension on top of `IORefs` using the foreign function interface (FFI) to use GCC's atomic operations [28] would greatly improve the performance of the CAS skiplist implementation. Additionally it would allow to implement highly scalable lock-free algorithms as building blocks for concurrent algorithms. Third, implementing and analyzing other thread-safe data structures (e.g. variants of finger trees) looks interesting and is largely unresearched. Fourth, the current rise of (experimental) manycore architectures poses the question of the scalability of our implementations to many more cores. This could be examined using Intel's ManyCore Lab [29] and its experimental Haskell support.

Acknowledgments. We would like to thank the reviewers of the TFP 2011 student feedback committee and the final reviewers for their helpful and detailed comments and Claudia Fohry for comments on a preliminary version of this paper.

References

1. Cormen, T.H., Leiserson, C.E., Rivest, R.L., Stein, C.: Introduction to Algorithms. MIT Press (2001)
2. Pugh, W.: Skip lists: a probabilistic alternative to balanced trees. Commun. ACM 33, 668–676 (1990)
3. Fomitchev, M., Ruppert, E.: Lock-free linked lists and skip lists. In: Proceedings of the Twenty-Third Annual ACM Symposium on Principles of Distributed Computing, PODC 2004, pp. 50–59. ACM, New York (2004)
4. Lotan, I., Shavit., N.: Skiplist-based concurrent priority queues. In: Proc. of the 14th International Parallel and Distributed Processing Symposium (IPDPS), pp. 263–268 (2000)
5. Sundell, H., Tsigas, P.: Fast and lock-free concurrent priority queues for multi-thread systems. J. Parallel Distrib. Comput. 65, 609–627 (2005)
6. Pugh, W.: Concurrent maintenance of skip lists. Technical report, College Park, MD, USA (1990)
7. Hunt, G.C., Michael, M.M., Parthasarathy, S., Scott, M.L.: An efficient algorithm for concurrent priority queue heaps. Inf. Process. Lett. 60, 151–157 (1996)
8. Kumar, V., Grama, A., Gupta, A., Karypis, G.: Introduction to parallel computing: design and analysis of algorithms. Benjamin-Cummings Publishing Co., Inc., Redwood City (1994)
9. GitHub: repository with source code (available May 2011), http://github.com/mlesniak/haskell-priorityqueue
10. Jones, M.P.: Type Classes with Functional Dependencies. In: Smolka, G. (ed.) ESOP 2000. LNCS, vol. 1782, pp. 230–244. Springer, Heidelberg (2000)
11. Jones, S.P., Gordon, A., Finne, S.: Concurrent haskell, pp. 295–308. ACM Press (1996)
12. Shavit, N., Touitou, D.: Software transactional memory. In: Proceedings of the Fourteenth Annual ACM Symposium on Principles of Distributed Computing, PODC 1995, pp. 204–213. ACM, New York (1995)
13. Harris, T., Marlow, S., Peyton-Jones, S., Herlihy, M.: Composable memory transactions. In: PPoPP 2005: Proceedings of the Tenth ACM SIGPLAN Symposium on Principles and Practice of Parallel Programming, pp. 48–60. ACM, New York (2005)
14. Harris, T.L.: A Pragmatic Implementation of Non-blocking Linked-Lists. In: Welch, J.L. (ed.) DISC 2001. LNCS, vol. 2180, pp. 300–314. Springer, Heidelberg (2001)
15. Sulzmann, M., Lam, E.S., Marlow, S.: Comparing the performance of concurrent linked-list implementations in haskell (abstract only). SIGPLAN Not. 44, 9 (2009)

16. Valois, J.D.: Lock-free linked lists using compare-and-swap. In: Proceedings of the Fourteenth Annual ACM Symposium on Principles of Distributed Computing, PODC 1995, pp. 214–222. ACM, New York (1995)

17. Stolz, V., Huch, F.: Runtime verification of concurrent haskell programs. In: Proceedings of the Fourth Workshop on Runtime Verification, pp. 201–216. Elsevier Science Publishers (2004)

18. Papaefthymiou, M., Rodrigue, J.: Implementing parallel shortest-paths algorithms. In: Bhatt, S.N. (ed.) Parallel Algorithms. DIMACS Series in Discrete Mathematics and Theoretical Computer Science, vol. 30, pp. 59–68. American Mathematical Society (1997)

19. Subramanian, S.: Parallel and dynamic shortest-path algorithms for sparse graphs. Technical report, Providence, RI, USA (1995)

20. Claessen, K., Hughes, J.: Quickcheck: A lightweight tool for random testing of haskell programs. In: ICFP, pp. 268–279. ACM Press, New York (2000)

21. Jones, D., Marlow, S., Singh, S.: Parallel performance tuning for haskell. In: Haskell 2009: Proceedings of the Second ACM SIGPLAN Symposium on Haskell. ACM (2009)

22. Dragicevic, K., Bauer, D.: A survey of concurrent priority queue algorithms. In: IPDPS, pp. 1–6. IEEE (2008)

23. Okasaki, C.: Purely functional data structures. Cambridge University Press, Cambridge (1998)

24. O'Sullivan, B., Tibell, J.: Scalable i/o event handling for ghc. In: Proceedings of the Third ACM Haskell Symposium on Haskell 2010, pp. 103–108. ACM, New York (2010)

25. Newton, R., Chen, C.P., Marlow, S.: Intel concurrent collections for haskell. Submitted to the Haskell Symposium 2010 (2010)

26. Chakravarty, M.M.T., Leshchinskiy, R., Jones, S.P., Keller, G., Marlow, S.: Data parallel haskell: a status report. In: Proceedings of the 2007 Workshop on Declarative Aspects of Multicore Programming, DAMP 2007, pp. 10–18. ACM, New York (2007)

27. Marlow, S., Peyton Jones, S., Singh, S.: Runtime support for multicore haskell. SIGPLAN Not. 44(9), 65–78 (2009)

28. Wicke, G.: The bits-atomic package on hackage,
    http://hackage.haskell.org/package/bits-atomic

29. Intel Manycore Testing Lab,
    http://software.intel.com/en-us/articles/intel-many-core-testing-lab/

Adams' Trees Revisited
Correctness Proof and Efficient Implementation

Milan Straka

Department of Applied Mathematics, Charles University in Prague, Czech Republic
`fox@ucw.cz`

Abstract. We present a correctness proof of Adams' trees of bounded balance, which are used in Haskell to implement `Data.Map` and `Data.Set`. Our analysis includes the previously ignored `join` operation, and also guarantees trees with smaller depth than the original one. Because the Adams' trees can be parametrized, we use benchmarking to find the best choice of parameters. Finally, a saving memory technique based on introducing additional data constructor is evaluated.

Keywords: Data structures, balanced binary search trees, Haskell.

1 Introduction

Adams' trees, or *trees of bounded balance* ω, shortly *BB-ω* trees, are binary search trees introduced in [1] and [2]. These trees are a popular choice for implementing purely functional search structures: They are used in Haskell to implement the `Data.Map` and `Data.Set` modules, which are part of the standard data structure library `containers` [10]. BB-ω trees are also used in data structure libraries in Scheme and SML. According to the measurements in [9], their performance is comparable to other alternatives such as AVL trees [3] or red-black trees [4].

Every node of BB-ω tree has subtrees of relative size bounded by ω. This balance condition guarantees logarithmic depth, which is asymptotically optimal.

The only corectness proof (published in [1]) has several serious flaws – it wrongly handles `delete` and it does not consider `join`. Recently a proof of a tree similar to BB-ω tree appeared in [5], presented using Coq Proof Assistant.

Our contributions are as follows:

- We present a correctness proof of BB-ω trees. In particular, we investigate the space of parameters and prove correctness for several chosen parameters: for all integral parameters and also for parameters that guarantee trees with smallest depth. Our analysis guarantees trees with lower depths than the original one and also considers previously ignored `join` operation.
- We show that the depth of BB-ω trees is better than the known upper bound.
- Because the BB-ω trees are parametrized, we perform several benchmarks to find the best choice of parameters.
- In order to save memory, we evaluate the technique of introducing additional data constructor representing a tree of size one. This allows us to save 20-30% of memory and even decreases the time complexity.

R. Peña and R. Page (Eds.): TFP 2011, LNCS 7193, pp. 130–145, 2012.

2   BB-ω Trees

We expect the reader to be familiar with binary search trees, see [6] for a comprehensive introduction.

Definition 1. *A binary search tree is a tree of bounded balance ω, denoted as BB-ω tree, if in each node the following balance condition holds:*

$$\text{size of the left subtree} \leq \omega \cdot \text{size of the right subtree},$$
$$\text{size of the right subtree} \leq \omega \cdot \text{size of the left subtree}, \tag{1}$$
$$\text{if one subtree is empty, the size of the other one is at most 1}.$$

Consider a BB-ω tree of size n. The size of its left subtree is ω times the size of its right subtree, so the size of the left subtree is at most $\frac{\omega}{\omega+1}n$. Therefore the size of a BB-ω tree decreases by at least a factor of $\frac{\omega}{\omega+1}$ at each level, which implies that the maximum depth of a BB-ω tree with n nodes is bounded by $\log_{(\omega+1)/\omega} n = \frac{1}{\log_2(1+1/\omega)} \log_2 n$. Detailed analysis is carried out in Section 6.

The exception for empty subtrees in the definition of balance condition is not elegant, but from the implementation point of view it is of no concern – empty subtrees are usually represented by a special data constructor and are treated differently anyway. Nevertheless, some modifications to the balance condition have been proposed to get rid of the special case – most notably to use the size of a subtree increased by one, which was proposed in [8]. We therefore define a generalized version of the balance condition, which comprises both cases:

$$\text{size of the left subtree} \leq \max(1, \omega \cdot \text{size of the right subtree} + \delta),$$
$$\text{size of the right subtree} \leq \max(1, \omega \cdot \text{size of the left subtree} + \delta). \tag{2}$$

The parameter δ is a nonnegative integer and if it is positive, the special case for empty subtrees is no longer necessary. Notice that the definition with sizes increased by one is equivalent to the generalized balance condition with $\delta = \omega - 1$.

An implementation of a BB-ω tree needs to store the size of a subtree of every node, which results in the following data-type:

```
data BBTree a = Nil            -- empty tree
              | Node           -- tree node
                (BBTree a)     -- left subtree
                Int            -- size of this tree
                a              -- element stored in the node
                (BBTree a)     -- right subtree
```

We also provide a function **size** and a smart constructor **node**, which constructs a tree using a left subtree, a key, and a right subtree. The balance condition is not checked, so it is upon the caller to ensure its validity.

```
size :: BBTree a -> Int
size Nil = 0
size (Node _ s _ _) = s

node :: BBTree a -> a -> BBTree a -> BBTree a
node left key right = Node left (size left + 1 + size right) key right
```

3 BB-ω Tree Operations

Locating an element in a BB-ω tree works as in any binary search tree:

```
lookup :: Ord a => a -> BBTree a -> Maybe a
lookup k Nil = Nothing
lookup k (Node left _ key right) = case k 'compare' key of
                                     LT -> lookup k left
                                     EQ -> Just key
                                     GT -> lookup k right
```

When adding and removing elements to the tree, we need to ensure the validity of the balance condition. We therefore introduce another smart constructor balance with the same functionality as node, which in addition ensures the balance condition. To achieve efficiency, certain conditions apply when using balance. We postpone further details until Section 4.

With such a smart constructor, the implementation of insert and delete is straightforward. Assuming the balance smart constructor works in constant time, insert and delete run in logarithmic time.

```
insert :: Ord a => a -> BBTree a -> BBTree a
insert k Nil = node Nil k Nil
insert k (Node left _ key right) = case k 'compare' key of
                                     LT -> balance (insert k left) key right
                                     EQ -> node left k right
                                     GT -> balance left key (insert k right)

delete :: Ord a => a -> BBTree a -> BBTree a
delete _ Nil = Nil
delete k (Node left _ key right) = case k 'compare' key of
                                     LT -> balance (delete k left) key right
                                     EQ -> glue left right
                                     GT -> balance left key (delete k right)
  where glue Nil right = right
        glue left Nil = left
        glue left right
          | size left > size right = let (key', left') = extractMax left
                                     in node left' key' right
          | otherwise              = let (key', right') = extractMin right
                                     in node left key' right'

        extractMin (Node Nil _ key right) = (key, right)
        extractMin (Node left _ key right) = case extractMin left of
          (min, left') -> (min, balance left' key right)

        extractMax (Node left _ key Nil) = (key, left)
        extractMax (Node left _ key right) = case extractMax right of
          (max, right') -> (max, balance left key right')
```

When representing a set with a binary search tree, additional operations besides inserting and deleting individual elements are needed. Such an operation is join. The join operation is also a smart constructor – it constructs a tree using a key and left and right subtrees. However, it poses no assumptions on the sizes of given balanced subtrees and produces a balanced BB-ω tree. The `join` operation is useful when implementing **union**, **difference** and other set methods.

By utilizing the **balance** smart constructor once more, it is straightforward to implement the `join` operation. Again, assuming **balance** works in constant time, `join` runs in logarithmic time.

```
join :: BBTree a -> a -> BBTree a -> BBTree a
join Nil key right = insertMin key right
  where insertMin key Nil          = Node Nil 1 key Nil
        insertMin key (Node l _ k r) = balance (insertMin key l) k r

join left key Nil = insertMax key left
  where insertMax key Nil          = Node Nil 1 key Nil
        insertMax key (Node l _ k r) = balance l k (insertMax key r)

join left@(Node ll ls lk lr) key right@(Node rl rs rk rr)
  | ls > omega * rs + delta = balance ll lk (join lr key right)
  | rs > omega * ls + delta = balance (join left key rl) rk rr
  | otherwise               = node left key right
```

4 Rebalancing BB-ω Trees

We restore balance using standard single and double rotations. These are depicted in Fig. 1. The code for these rotations is straightforward, the L or R suffix indicates the direction of the rotation (both rotations in the Fig. 1 are to the left).

Because we want the **balance** function to run in constant time, we introduce following assumption – the **balance** can be used on subtrees that previously fulfilled the balance condition and since then one **insert**, **delete** or `join` operation was performed. So far all implementations fulfilled this condition.

Using this assumption, the **balance** function restores balance using either a single or a double rotation – but a question is which one to choose. If we perform a left rotation as in Fig. 1, a double rotation split the left son of the right subtree into two subtrees, but a single rotation keeps it unaffected. Therefore we choose the type of a rotation according to the size of the left son of the right subtree.

Formally, we use a parameter α[1], which we use as follows: When we want to perform a left rotation, we examine the right subtree. If its left son is strictly smaller than α-times the size of its right son, we perform a single rotation, and otherwise a double rotation. The implementation follows:

```
balance :: BBTree a -> a -> BBTree a -> BBTree a
balance left key right
  | size left + size right <= 1 = node left key right
  | size right > omega * size left + delta = case right of
      (Node rl _ _ rr) | size rl<alpha*size rr -> singleL left key right
                       | otherwise             -> doubleL left key right
```

---

[1] Our α is the inverse of α from [1].

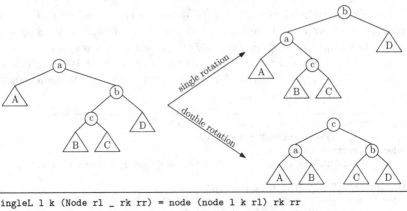

```
singleL l k (Node rl _ rk rr) = node (node l k rl) rk rr
singleR (Node ll _ lk lr) k r = node ll lk (node lr k r)
doubleL l k (Node (Node rll _ rlk rlr) _ rk rr) =
  node (node l k rll) rlk (node rlr rk rr)
doubleR (Node ll _ lk (Node lrl _ lrk lrr)) k r =
  node (node ll lk lrl) lrk (node lrr k r)
```

Fig. 1. Single and double rotations

```
| size left > omega * size right + delta = case left of
    (Node ll _ _ lr) | size lr<alpha*size ll -> singleR left key right
                     | otherwise            -> doubleR left key right
| otherwise = node left key right
```

5   Choosing the Parameters ω, α and δ

We call the parameters (ω, α, δ) *valid*, if `balance` can always restore the balance condition after one `insert`, `delete` or `join` operation.

Ideally we would classify all parameters (ω, α, δ) as either valid or not valid, but it is difficult to come up with complete characterization. The reason is that when dealing with small trees, rebalancing relies on the fact that all subtrees have integral sizes – i.e., it is fine that node with subtrees of sizes 1.5 and 2.5 cannot be rebalanced, because it does not exist.

Instead of complete characterization, we therefore rule out parameters which are definitely not valid and then prove the validity only for several chosen parameters. It is easy to see that $\omega \geq 5$ and $\omega = 2$ are not valid for any α in the sense of the original balance condition, i.e., with $\delta = 0$: In the situation in Fig. 2 neither single nor double rotation can restore balance.

To get a more accurate idea, we evaluated validity of parameters on all trees up to size of 1 million – the results are displayed in Fig. 3. The code used to generate this figure is listed in Appendix A. When choosing the parameters, the value of ω is the most important, because it defines the height of the tree. On

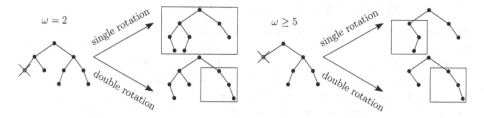

Fig. 2. Parameters $\omega = 2$ and $\omega \geq 5$ are not valid for any α and $\delta = 0$

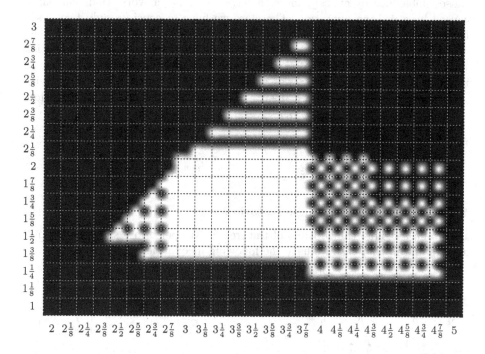

Fig. 3. The space of parameter (ω, α, δ). The values of ω and α are displayed on the x and y axis, respectively. Every dashed square consists of four smaller squares, which correspond to the δ values $\begin{smallmatrix} 0 & 1 \\ 2 & 3 \end{smallmatrix}$. Black denotes non-valid parameters, white denotes parameters which are valid for trees of size up to 1 million. For example, when $\omega = 4$ and $\alpha = 2$, $\delta \in \{0, 3\}$ is valid and $\delta \in \{1, 2\}$ is not valid.

the other hand, the value of α is quite unimportant – it affects only the internal implementation of `balance`. The value of δ is kept as low as possible, since higher values of δ increases imbalance of BB-ω trees.

After inspection of Fig. 3 we have chosen integer parameters $(\omega = 3, \alpha = 2, \delta = 0)$ and $(\omega = 4, \alpha = 2, \delta = 0)$ and also parameters $(\omega = 2.5, \alpha = 1.5, \delta = 1)$, where the value of ω is the smallest possible. The last parameters are not integral, but we can perform multiplication by ω or α using right bit shift.

5.1　Validity of $w = 2.5$, $w = 3$ and $w = 4$

We now prove the validity of chosen parameters ($\omega = 2.5, \alpha = 1.5, \delta = 1$), ($\omega = 3, \alpha = 2, \delta = 0$) and ($\omega = 4, \alpha = 2, \delta = 0$). Because the values of α and δ are determined by ω, we identify these sets of parameters only by the value of ω.

Consider performing `balance` after the balance is lost. Without loss of generality assume the right subtree is the bigger one and denote n and m the sizes of the left and right subtrees, respectively. We will use the notation of the tree size and the tree itself interchangeably.

Because the balance is lost, we have now $\omega n + \delta < m$. The `insert` operation causes imbalance by exactly one element, so it is never worse than imbalance caused by a `delete` operation. Therefore we have to consider only two possibilities how the imbalance was caused – `delete` or `join` operation. If the last operation was `delete`, we know that $\omega n + \delta \geq m - \omega$. If the last operation was `join` with the subtree of size z, we know that $\omega n + \delta \geq m - z$. During the `join` operation the tree z was small enough to be recursively joined with subtree m, so we have $\omega z + \delta < n + 1 + (m - z)$, so $z < \frac{n+1+m-\delta}{\omega+1}$ and therefore

$$m - \frac{n+m+1-\delta}{\omega+1} < \omega n + \delta, m < \frac{\omega+1}{\omega}\left(\omega n + \delta + \frac{n+1-\delta}{\omega+1}\right), m < \frac{\omega+1}{\omega}\left(\omega n + \frac{n+\omega\delta+1}{\omega+1}\right),$$
$$m < \left(\omega + 1 + \frac{1}{\omega}\right)n + \delta + \frac{1}{\omega}. \text{ To summarize:}$$

$$\overset{(A)}{m > \omega n + \delta}, \quad \overset{(B_{del})}{m - \omega \leq \omega n + \delta}, \quad \overset{(B_{join})}{m < \left(\omega + 1 + \frac{1}{\omega}\right)n + \delta + \frac{1}{\omega}}.$$

5.2　Correctness of a Single Rotation

Let x and y denote the subtrees of the tree m. We perform a single rotation iff $x < \alpha y$ and in that case we have the following inequalities:

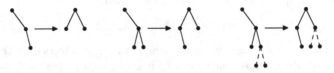

$$\overset{(C)}{\omega x + \delta \geq y \Rightarrow (\omega + 1)x + \delta \geq m - 1},$$
$$\overset{(D)}{x < \alpha y \Rightarrow x < \frac{\alpha}{\alpha+1}(m-1)}, \quad \overset{(E)}{y > \frac{1}{\alpha+1}(m-1)}.$$

At first we need to solve the cases where n, x or y are zero, as the balance condition is different in that case. All such cases are shown in Fig. 4.

Fig. 4. Cases when n, x or y are zero and a single rotation is performed

In the case when all subtrees are nonempty, we need to validate the balance condition in each of the two new trees:

- $wn + \delta \geq x$ after **delete**: $x \overset{(D)}{<} \frac{\alpha}{\alpha+1}(m-1) \overset{(B_{del})}{\leq} \frac{\alpha}{\alpha+1}(wn+\delta+w-1)$

- $wn + \delta \geq x$ after **join**: $x \overset{(D)}{<} \frac{\alpha}{\alpha+1}(m-1) \overset{(B_{join})}{<} \frac{\alpha}{\alpha+1}\left((w+1+\frac{1}{w})n+\delta+\frac{1}{w}-1\right)$

- $wx + \delta \geq n$: $n \overset{(A)}{<} \frac{m-\delta}{w} \overset{(C)}{\leq} \frac{w+1}{w}x + \frac{1}{w}$

- $w(n+1+x)+\delta \geq y$: $y \leq wx + \delta$

- $wy + \delta \geq n+1+x$: $n+1+x = n+m-y \overset{(A)}{\leq} \frac{m-1}{w} + m - y = m\frac{w+1}{w} - y - \frac{1}{w} \overset{(E)}{<}$ $((\alpha+1)y+1)\frac{w+1}{w} - y - \frac{1}{w} = \frac{(\alpha+1)(w+1)-w}{w}y+1$. Here we used the fact that when w is an integer, $m \overset{(A)}{\geq} wn+\delta+1$, so we have $m \overset{(A)}{\geq} wn+1$.

The third and the fourth inequalities obviously hold. To see that also the first, second and fifth inequalities hold, we evaluate the resulting inequalities and use the fact that the tree sizes are positive integers:

	$wn + \delta \geq x$ after **delete**	$wn + \delta \geq x$ after **join**	$wy + \delta \geq n+1+x$
$w = 2.5$	$x < \frac{3}{2}n + \frac{3}{2}$	$x < \frac{117}{50}n + \frac{6}{25}$	$n+1+x < \frac{5}{2}y + 1$
$w = 3$	$x < 2n + \frac{4}{3}$	$x < \frac{26}{9}n - \frac{4}{9}$	$n+1+x < 3y + 1$
$w = 4$	$x < \frac{8}{3}n + 2$	$x < \frac{7}{2}n - \frac{1}{2}$	$n+1+x < \frac{11}{4}y + 1$

The linear coefficients are always less or equal the required ones and it is simple to verify that all inequalities hold also for small integer sizes.

5.3   Correctness of a Double Rotation

When performing a double rotation, we have the following inequalities:

$$\text{any child } a \text{ of } b \Rightarrow (w+1)a + \delta \overset{(C)}{\geq} b - 1,$$
$$\text{any child } a \text{ of } b \Rightarrow (w+1)a \overset{(D)}{\leq} w(b-1) + \delta,$$
$$x \geq \alpha y \overset{(E)}{\Rightarrow} x \geq \frac{\alpha}{\alpha+1}(m-1), \quad y \overset{(F)}{\leq} \frac{1}{\alpha+1}(m-1).$$

Once again we need to solve the cases when n, y, s or t are zero – we enumerate these cases in Fig. 5.

Fig. 5. Cases when n, y, s or t are zero and a double rotation is performed

When all subtrees are nonempty we create three new trees, so we have to check six inequalities:

$- wn + \delta \geq s$ after delete: $s \overset{(D)}{\leq} \frac{\omega}{\omega+1}(x - 1 + \frac{\delta}{\omega}) \overset{(D)}{\leq} \frac{\omega}{\omega+1}(\frac{\omega}{\omega+1}(m - 1 + \frac{\delta}{\omega}) - 1 +$

$\frac{\delta}{\omega}) \overset{(B_{del})}{\leq} \frac{\omega}{\omega+1}(\frac{\omega}{\omega+1}(wn + \delta + \omega - 1 + \frac{\delta}{\omega}) - 1 + \frac{\delta}{\omega}) = \frac{\omega^3}{(\omega+1)^2}n + \frac{\omega^3 + \delta\omega^2 - \omega^2 + \delta\omega}{(\omega+1)^2} + \frac{\delta - \omega}{\omega+1}$

$- wn + \delta \geq s$ after join: $s \overset{(D)}{\leq} \frac{\omega}{\omega+1}(x - 1 + \frac{\delta}{\omega}) \overset{(D)}{\leq} \frac{\omega}{\omega+1}(\frac{\omega}{\omega+1}(m - 1 + \frac{\delta}{\omega}) - 1 +$

$\frac{\delta}{\omega}) \overset{(B_{join})}{<} \frac{\omega}{\omega+1}(\frac{\omega}{\omega+1}((\omega + 1 + \frac{1}{\omega})n + \delta + \frac{1}{\omega} - 1 + \frac{\delta}{\omega}) - 1 + \frac{\delta}{\omega}) = \frac{\omega^3 + \omega^2 + \omega}{(\omega+1)^2}n +$

$\frac{\delta\omega^2 - \omega^2 + \delta\omega + \omega}{(\omega+1)^2} + \frac{\delta - \omega}{\omega+1}$

$- ws + \delta \geq n$: $n \overset{(A)}{<} \frac{1}{\omega}(m - \delta) \overset{(E)}{\leq} \frac{1}{\omega}(\frac{\alpha+1}{\alpha}x + 1 - \delta) \overset{(C)}{\leq} \frac{1}{\omega}(\frac{\alpha+1}{\alpha}((\omega + 1)s + \delta +$

$1) + 1 - \delta) = \frac{\omega+1}{\omega}\frac{\alpha+1}{\alpha}s + \frac{\delta+1}{\omega}\frac{\alpha+1}{\alpha} + \frac{1-\delta}{\omega}$

$- wt + \delta \geq y$: $y \leq \frac{x}{\alpha} \overset{(C)}{\leq} \frac{\omega+1}{\alpha}t + \frac{\delta+1}{\alpha}$

$- wy + \delta \geq t$: $t \overset{(D)}{\leq} \frac{\omega(x-1)+\delta}{\omega+1} \leq \frac{\omega(\omega y + \delta - 1) + \delta}{\omega+1} = \frac{\omega^2}{\omega+1}y + \delta - \frac{\omega}{\omega+1}$

$- \omega(n + 1 + s) + \delta \geq t + 1 + y$ after delete: $\omega(n + 1 + s) + \delta \geq \omega(n+1) + t \overset{(B_{del})}{\geq}$
$m - \delta + t \geq x - \delta + 1 + y + t$

$- \omega(n + 1 + s) + \delta \geq t + 1 + y$ after join: $t + 1 + y \leq ws + \delta + 1 + y \overset{(F)}{\leq} ws + \delta + 1 +$

$\frac{m-1}{\alpha+1} \overset{(B_{join})}{<} ws + \delta + 1 + \frac{(\omega+1+\frac{1}{\omega})n + \delta + \frac{1}{\omega} - 1}{\alpha+1} = \frac{\omega^2 + \omega + 1}{\omega(\alpha+1)}n + 1 + \frac{\omega(\delta-1)+1}{\omega(\alpha+1)} + ws + \delta$

$- \omega(t + 1 + y) + \delta \geq n + 1 + s$: $n + 1 + s \overset{(A)}{<} \frac{m}{\omega} + 1 + s \leq \frac{m}{\omega} + 1 + wt + \delta \overset{(C)}{\leq}$
$wt + \delta + 1 + \frac{(\omega+1)y + \delta + 1}{\omega} = wt + \frac{\omega+\delta+1}{\omega} + \frac{\omega+1}{\omega}y + \delta$

All but the first three inequalities obviously hold for positive integral sizes. In order to prove that the first three inequalities hold, we again evaluate the resulting inequalities and use the fact that the sizes are positive integers:

	$wn + \delta \geq s$ after delete	$wn + \delta \geq s$ after join	$ws + \delta \geq n$
$\omega = 2.5$	$s < \frac{125}{98}n + \frac{103}{98}$	$s < \frac{195}{98}n - \frac{1}{49}$	$n < \frac{7}{3}s + \frac{4}{3}$
$\omega = 3$	$s < \frac{27}{16}n + \frac{3}{8}$	$s < \frac{39}{16}n - \frac{9}{8}$	$n < 2s + \frac{5}{6}$
$\omega = 4$	$s < \frac{64}{25}n + \frac{28}{25}$	$s < \frac{84}{25}n - \frac{32}{25}$	$n < \frac{15}{8}s + \frac{5}{8}$

The linear coefficients are less or equal than the required ones and for small positive integral sizes the resulting inequalities imply the required ones, which concludes the proof.

6   BB-ω Trees Height

If the balance condition holds and $\delta \leq 1$, we know that the size of a tree decreases by at least a factor of $\frac{\omega}{\omega+1}$. Therefore the maximum height of a tree is $\frac{1}{\log_2(1+1/\omega)} \log_2 n$. But this is merely an upper bound – it is frequently not possible for the balance condition to be tight, because the tree sizes are integers.

To get an accurate estimate, we compute the maximum heights of BB-ω trees up to size of 1 million. We used the following recursive definition:

```
-- Returns the list [ max height of BB-w tree with n elements | n <- [1..] ].
heights :: Ratio Int -> Int -> [Int]
heights w d = result
  where
    result = 1 : 2 : compute_heights 3 1 result
    compute_heights n r rhs@(rhs_head : rhs_tail)
      | w*((n-1-(r+1))%1) + d%1 >= (r+1)%1 = compute_heights n (r+1) rhs_tail
      | otherwise = 1 + rhs_head : compute_heights (n+1) r rhs
```

The function compute_heights is given the size of the tree n, the size of the its right subtree r and also a list of maximum heights of BB-ω trees of r and more elements. It constructs the highest tree of size n by using the largest possible right subtree, and then using the highest tree of such size.

The resulting heights are presented in Fig. 6. The heights are divided by $\lceil \log_2 n \rceil$, so the optimal height is 1. Notice that the height of a BB-2.5 tree is always smaller than 2 for less than million elements – such height is better than the height of a red-black tree of the same size.

size of BB-ω tree	height divided by $\lceil \log_2 n \rceil$		
	$\omega = 2.5$	$\omega = 3$	$\omega = 4$
10	1.33	1.33	1.33
100	1.57	1.67	1.86
1 000	1.70	1.90	2.30
10 000	1.84	2.00	2.54
100 000	1.86	2.13	2.63
1 000 000	1.90	2.16	2.70
upper bound	2.06	2.41	3.11

Fig. 6. Maximum heights of BB-ω trees with $w = 2.5$, $w = 3$ and $w = 4$

7   The Performance of BB-2.5, BB-3 and BB-4 Trees

With various possible ω to use, a search for the optimum value is in order. Is some value of ω universally the best one or does different usage patterns call for specific ω values?

We know that smaller values of ω result in lower trees. That seems advantageous, because the time complexity of many operations is proportional to the tree height.

In order to compare different values of ω, we measured the number of invocations of balance function. We inserted and then deleted $10^{\{1..6\}}$ elements, in both ascending and uniformly random order, and measured the number of invocations of balance during each phase. The results are displayed in Fig. 7.

	insert			delete		
	$w = 2.5$	$w = 3.0$	$w = 4.0$	$w = 2.5$	$w = 3.0$	$w = 4.0$
consecutive 10 elements	25	25	26	11	12	10
random 10 elements	23	23	23	12	12	12
consecutive 10^2 elements	617	657	769	362	349	302
random 10^2 elements	542	549	562	377	376	413
consecutive 10^3 elements	10245	11439	13997	6554	6116	5500
random 10^3 elements	8700	8753	8953	7162	7177	7377
consecutive 10^4 elements	143685	163261	206406	94865	88487	79938
random 10^4 elements	121192	121623	124204	105251	105854	108362
consecutive 10^5 elements	1852582	2133997	2722419	1251621	1175569	1042398
random 10^5 elements	1554230	1562168	1595269	1395871	1402939	1434371
consecutive 10^6 elements	22701321	26336469	33878677	15492747	14429384	12974950
random 10^6 elements	18956075	19074599	19476673	17367930	17480730	17856278

Fig. 7. The number of `balance` calls during inserting and deleting elements

In case of ascending elements, smaller ω values perform better during insertion – the difference between $\omega = 2.5$ and $\omega = 4$ is nearly 50% for large number of elements. On the other hand, higher ω values perform better during deletion, although the difference is only 18% at most. In case of random elements, lower values of ω are always better, but the difference is less noticeable in this case.

We also performed the benchmark of running time of `insert`, `lookup` and `delete` operations. We used the `criterion` package [11], a commonly used Haskell benchmarking framework. All benchmarks were performed on a dedicated machine with Intel Xeon processor and 4GB RAM, using 32-bit GHC 7.0.1. The benchmarking process works by calling the benchmarked method on given input data and forcing the evaluation of the result. Because the benchmarked method can take only microseconds to execute, the benchmarking framework repeats the execution of the method until it takes reasonable time (imagine 50ms) and then divides the elapsed time by the number of iterations. This process is repeated 100 times to get the whole distribution of the time needed, and the mean and the confidence interval are produced.

The benchmarks are similar to our previous experiment – we insert, locate and delete $10^{\{1..6\}}$ elements of type `Int`, which are both in ascending and uniformly random order. We used the implementation of `balance` from the `containers` package – we already improved this implementation in [9]. The resulting execution times are normalised with respect to one of the implementations and presented as percentages. The overview is in Fig. 8. (Ignore the trees with `One` subscript, they are explained in the next section.) Here the geometric mean of running times for all input sizes 10^1 to 10^6 is displayed. The detailed results and the benchmark itself are available on the author's website `http://fox.ucw.cz/papers/bbtree`.

The findings are similar to the previous experiment – if the elements are in random order, the value of ω makes little difference, and smaller values perform slightly better. In case of ascending elements, smaller ω are better when inserting

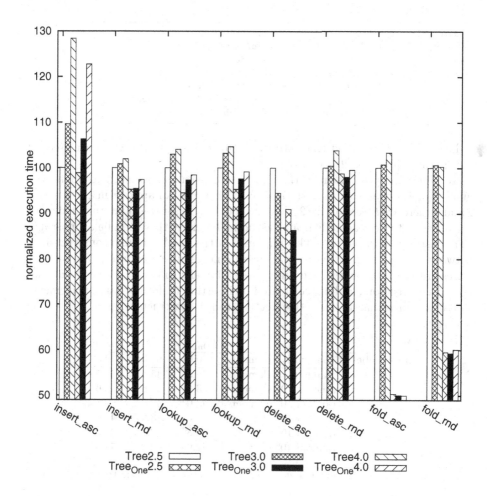

Fig. 8. The normalized execution times of BB-ω trees with various ω

and larger when deleting. As expected, the `lookup` operation runs faster for smaller values of ω, independently on the order of elements.

8   Reducing Memory by Introducing Additional Data Constructor

The proposed representation of a BB-ω tree provides room for improvements in terms of memory efficiency – if the tree contains n nodes, there are $n + 1$ `Nil` constructors in the whole tree, because every `Node` constructors contains two sub-trees. We can improve the situation by introducing additional data constructor representing a tree of size one:

```
data BBTree a = Nil           -- empty tree
            | One a           -- tree of size one
            | Node            -- tree node
                (BBTree a)    -- left subtree
                Int           -- size of this tree
                a             -- element stored in the node
                (BBTree a)    -- right subtree
```

Leaves are represented efficiently with this data-type. However, the trees of size 2 still require one `Nil` constructor.

To determine the benefit of the new data constructor we need to bound the number of `Nil` constructors in the tree. A `Nil` constructor appears in a tree of size 2 and if there are t trees of size 2, there need to be at least $(t-1)$ internal `Nodes` for these t trees to be reachable from the root. Therefore, there can be at most $n/3$ `Nil` constructors in the tree. This implies that the number of `One` constructors is between $n/3$ and $n/2$. Experimental measurements presented in Fig. 9 show that a tree created by repeatedly inserting ascending elements contains $n/2$ `One` and no `Nil` constructors, and a tree created by inserting uniformly random elements contains approximately $0.43n$ `One` and $0.14n$ `Nil` constructors.

	$T_{One}2.5$	$T_{One}3.0$	$T_{One}4.0$
any number of consecutive elements	50.0%	50.0%	50.0%
random 10 elements	45.5%	45.5%	45.5%
random 10^2 elements	43.6%	43.6%	43.6%
random 10^3 elements	43.0%	43.0%	42.8%
random 10^4 elements	43.0%	43.0%	43.0%
random 10^5 elements	42.8%	42.8%	42.9%
random 10^6 elements	42.9%	42.9%	42.9%

Fig. 9. The percentage of `One` constructors in a BB-ω tree

Considering the memory representation used by the GHC compiler, the `Node` constructor occupies 5 words and `One` constructor occupies 2 words, so the new representation takes 20-30% less memory. The time complexity of the new representation is also better as shown in Fig. 8. Especially note the speedup of the `fold` operation, which is the result of decreased number of `Nil` constructors in the tree. The only disadvantage is the increase of the code size – but this affects the library author only.

We could also add a fourth data constructor to represent a tree of size 2. That would result in no `Nil` constructors in a nonempty tree. The disadvantage is further code size increase ($4 \cdot 4 = 16$ cases in `join` operation) and also a noticeable time penalty – on 32bit machines GHC uses pointer tagging to distinguish data constructors without the pointer dereference, which is described in detail in [7]. This technique works with types with at most three data constructors (and up to 7 different constructors on 64bit machines), so it is not advantageous to add a fourth data constructor.

8.1   The Order of Data Constructors

When implementing the data-type with the `One` constructor, we found out that the order of data constructors in the definition of the data-type notably affects the performance. On Fig. 10, the time improvements in the benchmark from the previous section are displayed, when we reordered the constructors to the following order: `Node` first, then `One` and `Nil` last.

	$T_{One}2.5$	$T_{One}3.0$	$T_{One}4.0$
insert_asc	5.1%	6.8%	6.6%
insert_rnd	4.5%	5.2%	5.0%
lookup_asc	7.4%	6.1%	6.2%
lookup_rnd	6.1%	5.4%	5.4%
delete_asc	5.3%	8.4%	8.5%
delete_rnd	4.4%	4.8%	5.0%
fold_asc	8.9%	9.5%	13.1%
fold_rnd	10.1%	10.5%	9.4%

Fig. 10. The improvements of time complexity after reordering the data constructors

We believe the reason for the performance improvement is the following: When matching data constructors, a conditional forward jump is made if the constructor is not the first one from the data-type definition. Then another conditional forward jump is made if the constructor is not the second one from the data-type definition. In other words, it takes $i - 1$ conditional forward jumps to match the i-th constructor from the data-type definition, and these forward jumps are usually mispredicted (forward jumps are expected not to be taken). It is therefore most efficient to list the data constructor in decreasing order of their frequency.

9   Conclusions

We described balanced trees and explicitly proved their correctness for several representative parameter combinations. For these parameters we also measured their runtime performance. The resulting implementation (improved variant of `Data.Set` and `Data.Map`) is comparable to other available on Hackage (detailed list and measurements are in [9]). We also focused on memory complexity and improved it by changing the data-type representation. During this process we discovered the effect of the data constructors order in the data-type definition on the performance. The implementation and benchmarks used are available on author's website `http://fox.ucw.cz/papers/bbtree`.

Several goals remain for future work. In our further efforts, we will incorporate the improvements described here in the `containers` package. We will also benchmark the effect of reordering data constructors of other data structures from the `containers` package – especially the `IntMap`, `IntSet`, which also use three data constructors (preliminary measurements show 5-15% improvement). Also the benchmark of BB-ω trees could be extended to include set operations like `union`. We already described a benchmark with a `union` operation in [9].

9.1   Related Work

The original weight balanced trees were described in [8], with two parameters with values $1+\sqrt{2}$ and $\sqrt{2}$. Because these are not integers, the resulting algorithm is not very practical. Adams created a variant of balanced trees, the BB-ω trees, and described them in papers [1] and [2]. Unfortunately, the proof is erroneous – the paper concludes that for $\alpha = 2$ the valid parameters are $\omega \geq 4.646$.

The error in the proof was known by several people, but in 2010 a bug caused by the error in the proof was also found in the Haskell implementation – in the `Data.Set` and `Data.Map` modules from the `containers` package. The recent paper [5] deals with the correctness of the original weight balanced trees (equivalent to setting $\delta = \omega - 1$ in our definition) and proves in Coq, that for $\delta = \omega - 1$ the only integral valid parameters are $\omega = 3$ and $\alpha = 2$. Our proof on the other hand is explicit, and proves validity of only some chosen parameters. It covers both the original weighted trees and Adams' trees.

References

1. Adams, S.: Implementing sets efficiently in a functional language (Technical Report CSTR 92-10) (1992)
2. Adams, S.: Efficient sets – a balancing act. J. Funct. Program. 3(4), 553–561 (1993)
3. Adelson-Velskii, G.M., Landis, E.M.: An algorithm for the organization of information. Dokladi Akademia Nauk SSSR 146 (1962)
4. Guibas, L.J., Sedgewick, R.: A dichromatic framework for balanced trees. In: Annual IEEE Symposium on Foundations of Computer Science, pp. 8–21 (1978)
5. Hirai, Y., Yamamoto, K.: Balancing weight-balanced trees. J. Funct. Program 21(3), 287–307 (2011), http://dx.doi.org/10.1017/S0956796811000104
6. Knuth, D.: 6.2.2: Binary Tree Searching. In: The Art of Computer Programming, 3rd edn. Sorting and Searching, vol. 3, pp. 426–458. Addison-Wesley (1997)
7. Marlow, S., Yakushev, A.R., Jones, S.P.: Faster laziness using dynamic pointer tagging. In: Proceedings of the 12th ACM SIGPLAN International Conference on Functional Programming, ICFP 2007, pp. 277–288. ACM, New York (2007), http://doi.acm.org/10.1145/1291151.1291194
8. Nievergelt, J., Reingold, E.M.: Binary search trees of bounded balance. In: Proceedings of the Fourth Annual ACM Symposium on Theory of Computing, STOC 1972, pp. 137–142. ACM, New York (1972), http://doi.acm.org/10.1145/800152.804906
9. Straka, M.: The performance of the haskell containers package. In: Proceedings of the Third ACM Haskell Symposium on Haskell 2010, pp. 13–24. ACM, New York (2010), http://doi.acm.org/10.1145/1863523.1863526
10. The containers package, http://hackage.haskell.org/package/containers
11. The criterion package, http://hackage.haskell.org/package/criterion

A   Generating the Fig. 3

When generating the Fig. 3 of valid parameters for all trees up to size of 1 million, we used the following code:

```
max_n = 1000000
find_min x p | p x      = last $ x : takeWhile p [x-1, x-2 .. 0]
             | otherwise = head $ dropWhile (not . p) [x+1, x+2 ..]

test w a d = and [delete n m && join n m | n <- [0 .. max_n],
                                           let m = flr $ max 1 (w * n + d)]
  where
    delete n m = n == 0 || rebalance (n-1) m
    join n m = rebalance n (m+increment)
      where increment = max 1 $ ceil ((n+m+1-d) / (w+1) - 1)

    rebalance n m = and [rebalance' n m x | x <- nub [x_min, x_mid - 1,
                                             x_mid, m - 1 - x_min]]
      where x_min = find_min (flr $ m     / (w+1)) (\x -> balanced x (m-1-x))
            x_mid = find_min (flr $ m * a / (a+1)) (\x -> x >= a * (m-1-x))

    rebalance' n m x
      | x < a * y = balanced n x && balanced (n + 1 + x) y
      | otherwise = balanced n s && balanced t y && balanced (n+1+s) (t+1+y) &&
                    balanced n t && balanced s y && balanced (n+1+t) (s+1+y)
      where (y,s,t)=(m-1-x,find_min (flr$x/(w+1)) (\s->balanced s (x-1-s)),x-1-s)

    balanced n m = max 1 (w * n + d) >= m && n <= max 1 (w * m + d)

    flr, ceil :: Double -> Double
    flr = fromInteger . floor
    ceil = fromInteger . ceiling

results = [(w, a, d, test w a d) | w <- [2, 2.125 .. 5],
                                   a <- [1, 1.125 .. 3], d <- [0 .. 3]]
```

It relies on the fact that when there is a tree which cannot be balanced, there also exists a counterexample with a subtree as large as the balance condition allows. Therefore, for a fixed value of n it is enough to try the largest possible m and for a fixed value of m it is enough to verify that the balance condition is restored when considering the smallest and the largest subtree causing a single rotation and the smallest and the largest subtree causing a double rotation.

Functional Video Games in CS1 II

From Structural Recursion to Generative and Accumulative Recursion

Marco T. Morazán

Seton Hall University, South Orange, NJ, USA
morazanm@shu.edu

Abstract. The use of video games to teach introduction courses to programming and Computer Science is a trend that is currently flourishing. One of the most successful and promising approaches uses functional video games to get students interested and engaged in programming. This approach is successful, in part, because functional video games provide a domain of interest to most Computer Science undergraduates and remove the need to reason about designing state-based programs. A plethora of examples exist that have students develop games exploiting structural recursion which resemble such classics as Space Invaders and Snake. Once students master the basics of structural recursion the time comes to move beyond structural recursion to generative and accumulative recursion. It is up to the instructor to harness the enthusiasm and appetite that students have to develop more video games. This requires finding games that require the generation of subproblems in the same class as the input problem or that require accumulators to be successfully played or solved. This article presents a road map to make the transition from structural recursion to accumulative recursion using the N-puzzle problem as motivation to capture student enthusiasm and exploit what they have learned about program design. The N-Puzzle was also chosen to demonstrate that informed heuristic search strategies, traditionally the domain of undergraduate courses in Artificial Intelligence, are within the grasp of CS1 students. With proper guidance, CS1 students can reason such an algorithm into existence instead of simply using a textbook to study such algorithms. If the work described in this article is replicated elsewhere, there is no doubt that it will be an exciting time for Computer Science education and it will elevate the relevance of functional programming in the minds of future CS professionals.

1 Introduction

Based on the teaching philosophy of *program by design* (PBD) put forth in the textbook *How to Design Programs* (HtDP) [2], the use of functional video games to teach introduction courses to programming and Computer Science is a trend that is currently flourishing. At the heart of the PBD philosophy is the *design recipe*–a series of steps that students can follow to design and write programs.

R. Peña and R. Page (Eds.): TFP 2011, LNCS 7193, pp. 146–162, 2012.
© Springer-Verlag Berlin Heidelberg 2012

These steps include the development of data definitions based on problem analysis, the development of contracts and function headers, the development of function templates for all data definitions, the specialization of function templates to create functions, and the development and running of tests. One of the most successful and promising implementation approaches to a PBD-based course uses a hierarchy of successively richer student languages and functional video games to get students interested and engaged in programming. PLT's Dr-Racket [4] integrates such a hierarchy of student languages for use in conjunction with HtDP. The reader should note that students are not taught Racket, but do learn Racket-like syntax on a need-to-know basis. This approach is successful, in part, because the student languages allow for the generation of error messages that are meaningful for beginners. This approach is also successful, in part, because functional video games provide a domain of interest to most Computer Science undergraduates and remove the need to reason about designing state-based programs. A plethora of examples exist that have students develop games exploiting structural recursion which resemble such classics as Space Invaders and Snake [1,6].

At the beginning of an introduction course, the focus is on solving problems using primitive data, structures, and structural recursion. Once students master the basics of structural recursion, the time comes to explore other forms of recursion such as generative and accumulative recursion. In generative recursion, the subproblems generated are not derived from the data structure employed and are in the same class as the original problem (a typical example is quicksort). One of the important consequences of this that beginners must realize is that programs using generative recursion are not guaranteed to terminate like programs that employ structural recursion. Thus, generative recursion requires the development of termination arguments. In accumulative recursion, one or more accumulators are added as parameters to a function designed using structural or generative recursion to capture information that, otherwise, would be lost between recursive calls (a typical example is finding a path between two nodes in a cyclic graph). An important consequence of this for beginners is that they must realize that for each accumulator an accumulator invariant must developed to describe the value of the accumulator. The code students write must guarantee that the accumulator invariant holds for every recursive call. It is up to the instructor to harness the enthusiasm and appetite that students have to develop more video games to motivate these topics. This requires identifying games that can not be played nor solved by only using structural recursion. It is important to note, however, that the goal is not to make students masters at developing video games. Instead, the goal is to make students interested in generative and accumulative recursion by showing them how they are needed and/or used in a video game. Surprisingly, there are not many examples in an HtDP-based curriculum of video games that require students to go beyond structural recursion.

This article advocates the position that video games ought to be used to motivate the need to study generative and accumulative recursion in the CS1 classroom. It presents an example on how to make the transition from structural

Fig. 1. A Random 3-Puzzle Board   **Fig. 2.** Sample Winning 3-Puzzle Board

recursion to generative and accumulative recursion using the N-puzzle problem as motivation to capture student enthusiasm. This road map is used in the curriculum at Seton Hall University that has been previously described [6]. The primary goal is to introduce these topics in a context that exploits and reinforces lessons on program by design, structural recursion, and abstraction. Secondary goals are to expose students to ideas that they may encounter in upper-level courses such as heuristics in an Artificial Intelligence course and the use of random number generators. Section 2 briefly describes the N-puzzle game. Section 3 describes the first encounter of students with the N-puzzle game in the classroom and discusses opportunities the game presents to reinforce the lessons of program by design using structural recursion and abstraction. Section 4 discusses an initial strategy to finding a solution leading to the need for generative recursion. Section 5 discusses how the need for accumulators arises and how accumulative recursion is used in the N-puzzle game. Section 7 discusses related work and Section 8 draws some conclusions and briefly outlines future work.

2   The N-Puzzle Game

The N-puzzle game is one that is likely to be familiar to an international milieu of students and is simple enough that students can easily grasp how the game works. It consists of an $N \times N$ board with $N^2 - 1$ tiles[1] and an empty square or blank space that does not contain a tile. Each tile contains some form of symbolic or numeric data. Figure 1 displays a sample board using numeric tiles for the 3-puzzle[2] game in which the empty space is at the center of the board. Every N-puzzle game must also define a winning board. That is, a board that defines the solution to the puzzle. Figure 2 displays the traditional winning board for the numeric 3-puzzle problem.

A player can move tiles by swapping the blank space with one of its neighbors (i.e., right, left, up, or down). The goal of the game is to make a sequence of

---

[1] The choice of a square board is arbitrary, but facilitates developing a program.

[2] It is also common to refer to this version of the puzzle as the 8-puzzle.

```
A board is either:
    1. empty
    2. (cons number b), where b is a board

Template for functions on boards:
(define (f-on-board a-board)
    (cond   [(empty? a-board) ...]
            [else ...(first a-board)...(rest a-board)]))
```

Fig. 3. Data definition for boards and a template for functions on boards

moves that leads to the winning board. A player, of course, at some point during the game may feel stuck and the game should provide a mechanism, like a help button, to ask the computer to make the next move. The help button, of course, requires the program to first solve the puzzle before making a move towards the solution on behalf of the player.

To make the game more challenging and more interesting the game can be parameterized with a constant N. In this manner, students are free to make the board larger or smaller according to the level of the challenge they desire. A CS1 instructor should note, however, that as N increases the effective use of the help button decreases which can discourage some students.

3   The First Encounter with the N-Puzzle Game in CS1

Students that are presented with the N-puzzle game have gone through the first four parts of HtDP that cover program by design with structures, structurally recursive data types, and abstraction. They have experience designing programs that process, for example, lists and trees as well as familiarity with basic abstraction patterns that involve the use of higher-order functions such as map and filter.

When students are first presented with the N-puzzle game, they are asked what is changing while the game is played and how it can be represented. This leads to defining a board as a list of numbers[3] and to a template for functions on boards both of which are displayed in Figure 3. This brings the N-puzzle game into a realm that is familiar to the students and provides an opportunity to reinforce lessons on structural recursion.

To get students started, the first tasks they are asked to solve can be done using structural recursion and/or abstraction such as building the representation of the winning board, finding the position of the empty space, and swapping two tiles (eventually used to make moves). The solutions presented may vary with some students defining such functions using structural recursion and some

---

[3] The number in position i of the list corresponds the tile in row (quotient i N) and in column (remainder i N).

```
(define WIN (build-list N (lambda (n)
                          (cond [(< n (- N 1)) (+ n 1)]
                                [else 0])))))

; get-blank-pos: board --> number
; Purpose: To find the position of the blank
(define (get-blank-pos l)
  (cond [(empty? l) (error 'get-blank-pos "Blank not found")]
        [(= (car l) BLANK) 0]
        [else (add1 (get-blank-pos (cdr l)))]))

; swap-tiles: board natnum natnum --> board
; Purpose: To swap the given tiles in the given board
(define (swap-tiles w i j)
  (build-list N (lambda (n)
                  (cond [(= n i) (list-ref w j)]
                        [(= n j) (list-ref w i)]
                        [else (list-ref w n)]))))
```

Fig. 4. Auxiliary Functions Developed Using Structural Recursion and Abstraction

students using higher-order functions. Typical solutions for the game with numeric tiles are displayed in Figure 4.

The initial encounter with the N-puzzle game also provides an opportunity to perform data analysis that leads to the realization that more than structural recursion is required to implement the help button. Students are asked what does it mean to find a solution when the player requests the computer to make the next move. After some discussion, it becomes clear that finding a solution is finding a sequence of moves from the current board to the winning board. Students, in general, can grasp without too much trouble the idea that finding such a sequence of moves for board b means finding a solution for one of the possible successors of b, $child_b$, obtained by making a single move and adding the move that takes b to $child_b$. The question then becomes which move will be chosen to generate the child of b that is to be explored.

Observe that such a strategy is no longer in the domain of structural recursion. Structural recursion guarantees that the size of the subproblems (i.e., finding a solution starting from $child_b$) are smaller than the problem of finding a solution to the original problem (i.e., finding a solution starting at b) and are derived from the structure of the input. This is not the case, because in general some sequences starting at b are infinite as are sequences starting at any $child_b$ and $child_b$ is not used to build b. The question then becomes how do you solve problems that generate subproblems that are not guaranteed to be smaller than the original problem and are not part of the structure of the original problem. At this point, students have entered the realm of generative recursion by simply trying to implement a video game.

4   Finding a Solution

After using the N-puzzle game to discover the need for generative recursion, students are given several examples on how to design programs based on generative recursion. Examples outlined in HtDP include quicksort, fractals, binary search, Newton's method, and backtracking algorithms such as traversing a graph to find a path from node A to node C. Of these, the most relevant to finding a solution to an N-puzzle are the backtracking algorithms, because traversing a graph with cycles can lead to a path of infinite length precisely in the same manner that some sequences of moves are infinite in the N-puzzle problem. HtDP presents a solution to find a path from node A to node C in an acyclic graph using a depth-first traversal and postpones finding the solution for a graph with cycles to motivate accumulative recursion.

In the N-puzzle game, of course, we are for the most part unable to restrict our sequences of moves to those that are finite. Students, in general, are not aware at this point of this and can be led to develop a solution that seems reasonable. Class discussion is focused on how to choose a successor of the current board to find a solution. This presents the opportunity to introduce beginning students to heuristics. A heuristic can be used to choose which child of b is chosen to explore for a solution. It is important to remark to students that a heuristic is a rule that estimates how many moves away the current board is from the winning board and that is used hoping it will lead to a solution. At this point, most students will have no way to judge this statement and simply trust the professor. This trust opens the door for reinforcing lessons on the importance of testing and careful design in programming. As the reader knows, this approach is destined to immediate failure, but also to triumph after the process of iterative refinement is started.

There is a simple heuristic students can understand and implement for the N-puzzle problem. The heuristic chooses to explore the child of b that has the smallest Manhattan distance. The Manhattan distance of a board is the sum of how far away each tile is from its correct position. For example, the Manhattan distance of the board in Figure 2 is 0 given that all tiles are in the correct position. In Figure 1, tile 1 is in the right position and contributes 0 to the Manhattan distance while the blank space, in position 4 and whose correct position is 8, contributes 2 to the Manhattan distance. The code to compute the Manhattan distance of a board is displayed in Figure 5. Observe that the code only requires arithmetic and structural recursion on natural numbers which provides the opportunity to reinforce material students have already seen and to make this material relevant to their interests in video games.

Armed with the power of a heuristic, students can now delve into designing an N-puzzle solver to implement the help button. The basic idea is that given a board their program needs to return a non-empty list of boards, called a sequence, that contains all the boards in the sequence of moves from the given board to the winning board. These ideas lead quite naturally to the design of a depth-first search algorithm. If the given board is the same as the winning board,

```
; manhattan-distance: board --> number
; Purpose: To compute the Manhattan distance of the given board
(define (manhattan-distance b)
  (local
    [; distance: number number --> number
     ; Purpose: To compute the distance between the two tile positions
     (define (distance curr corr)
       (+ (abs (- (quotient curr (sqrt N)) (quotient corr (sqrt N))))
          (abs (- (remainder curr (sqrt N)) (remainder corr (sqrt N))))))
     ; adder: number --> number
     ; Purpose: To add all the distances of each tile
     (define (adder pos)
       (cond [(= pos 0) 0]
             [else (+ (distance (sub1 pos)
                                (correct-pos (list-ref b (sub1 pos))))
                      (adder (sub1 pos)))]))
     ; correct-pos: number --> number
     ; Purpose: To determine the correct position of the given tile
     (define (correct-pos n)
       (cond [(= n 0) (sub1 N)]
             [else (sub1 n)]))]
    (adder N)))
```

Fig. 5. Code for computing the Manhattan distance of a board

then the solution is trivial: a list containing the given board. Otherwise, create a list from the given board and the solution generated starting from the best child of the given board. The function to generate the children of a given board can either be done using structural recursion or map. It only entails swapping the blank space with its neighbors. Finding the best board from a list of boards also only requires structural recursion. A sample implementation is displayed in Figure 6.

The benefits of using the N-puzzle to reinforce lessons from structural recursion, to motivate generative recursion, and to capture the interest of students are likely to be self-evident to any instructor at the helm of a CS1 class. Clearly, this video game also provides the opportunity to introduce CS1 students quite naturally to depth-first search and to heuristics-based programming which is quite uncommon as far as the author knows. There are, however, two more benefits that deserve to be mentioned. These are reinforcing the value of testing and the value of iterative refinement. The instructor can strategically provide initial boards to test the game and the help button. The code in Figure 6 does, indeed, find a solution for some test boards while at the same time reveal that it fails to return a solution for some test boards. This leads to an exploration of why the program, which seems quite reasonable to most students, fails to return a solution for some boards and how it can be improved to guarantee that a solution is always returned (for a legal board).

```
; find-solution-dfs: board --> (listof boards)
; Purpose: To find a solution to the given board using DFS
(define (find-solution-dfs b)
  (cond [(equal? b WIN) (list b)]
        [else
          (local [(define children (generate-children b))]
            (cons b (find-solution-dfs (best-child children))))]))

; generate-children: board --> non-empty-list-of-boards
; Purpose: To generate a list of the children of the given board
(define (generate-children b)
  (local [(define blank-pos (get-blank-sq-num b))]
    (map (lambda (p)
            (swap-tiles b blank-pos p))
         (blank-neighs blank-pos))))

; best-child: non-empty-list-of-boards --> board
; Purpose: To find the board with the board with the smallest Manhattan
;          distance in the given non-empty list of boards
(define (best-child lob)
  (cond [(empty? (rest lob)) (car lob)]
        [else
          (local [(define best-of-rest (best-child (rest lob)))]
            (cond [(< (manhattan-distance (car lob))
                      (manhattan-distance best-of-rest))
                   (car lob)]
                  [else best-of-rest]))]))
```

Fig. 6. Code for depth-first search for a solution without backtracking

5   The Need to Remember Leads to Accumulators

The exploration of why the program fails to return a solution to some boards leads to the discussion of a situation like the one depicted in Figure 7. If the current board is the one in the root of the tree, it has two children both of which have a Manhattan distance of 18. The algorithm chooses the right child as the board to explore. This board has three children that, from left to right, have Manhattan distances of 20, 20, and 16. The rightmost child is chosen for exploration as it has the smallest Manhattan distance. At this point, all students can see the problem. The algorithm cycles through the same set of boards never choosing a different board to escape the cycle. In other words, students understand why there is an infinite recursion and why it is impossible to argue that the algorithm terminates as is required by the design recipe for programs based on generative recursion. Some readers may argue that developing a termination argument ought to always be done before implementing an algorithm. At Seton Hall, we have discovered that this is not always true. Much of it depends on the CS-maturity that students bring to the classroom. In our CS1 course, it is

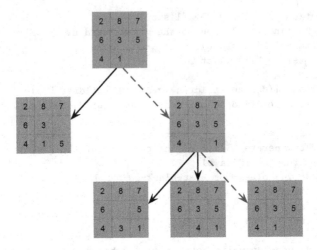

Fig. 7. Illustration of why a depth-first path (dashed) does not lead to a solution

assumed that students have little or no background in Computer Science when they start. For such students, theoretical termination arguments do not easily flow. Understanding why an implemented algorithm fails, on the other hand, presents an excellent learning experience and brings home the importance of developing termination arguments. We conjecture that as students gain experience it becomes easier for them to visualize, before implementation, termination arguments.

After understanding why the algorithm does not always terminate, students are guided to think that a solution to this problem requires that all sequences starting at the given board must be explored instead of choosing to only explore the sequence of best children. This requires that all paths explored so far be remembered. Through this analysis, students have entered the realm of accumulative recursion and this is used as motivation to return to HtDP and study how to design programs that exploit this new kind of recursion.

One of the functions students can develop while exploring how to design programs that use accumulative recursion is a function to present a player with an initial board to solve in the N-puzzle problem. This presents an interesting task, because not all possible orderings of tiles in a board are valid boards in the N-puzzle game. In the 3-puzzle game, for example, the ordering that has 1, 2, 3 in the 0th row, 4, 5, 6, in the 1st row, and 8, 7, 0 in the 2nd row is an invalid board. The challenge, therefore, is to design a strategy to compute an initial board that does not simply randomly assign tiles to positions in the board. After some discussion, a natural strategy to follow is to start from the winning board and randomly make k valid moves. This strategy is a good one to choose in CS1 for three reasons. The first is that it provides students at this

```
; make-moves: natnum board --> board
; Purpose: To create a board by making the given number of moves
;           in the given board.
; ACCUMULATOR INVARIANT: b is the board created by making
;                         (- NUM-INIT-MOVES nummoves) moves from WIN
(define (make-moves nummoves b)
  (cond [(= nummoves 0) b]
        [else (make-moves (sub1 nummoves) (make-a-move b))]))


; make-a-move: board --> board
; Purpose: To make a random move in the given board
(define (make-a-move b)
  (local [(define blank-index (get-blank-index b))
          (define neighs-indices (neighs-of blank-index))
          (define move-to-index
            (list-ref neighs-indices (random (length neighs-indices))))]
    (swap-tiles w move-to-index blank-index)))


(define NUM-INIT-MOVES 200)
(define INIT-BOARD (make-moves NUM-INIT-MOVES WIN))
```

Fig. 8. An implementation for creating an initial N-puzzle board

early stage in their studies with an example of where the use of randomness is useful. The second is that it requires an accumulator to "remember" the board created so far. That is, after every random move a new board is created and the new board needs to be used to make any further moves. The third is that it brings accumulative recursion into the domain of structural recursion on natural numbers–a familiar world for students that have followed an HtDP-based curriculum. This approach, for example, is implemented by students as displayed in Figure 8. The function make-moves is written using the design recipe for structural recursion on natural numbers to which an accumulator has been added. As per the design recipe for designing functions using accumulative recursion, students must develop an accumulator invariant. Although the invariant in this case may seem straightforward to an experienced programmer, its development by beginning students usually requires some coaching. One effective strategy is to have students trace an example, before writing any code, to help them visualize what characteristics of the parameters remain unchanged for every recursive call. For the function make-moves in Figure 8, for example, the parameter b is an accumulator. Initially, students are led to reason that b is the board obtained by making a number of random moves starting from WIN. This reasoning is then refined to precisely define the number of moves: (- NUM-INIT-MOVES nummoves). Students can now argue that for every recursive call a move is made and the number of moves is reduced by 1. Thus, they can conclude that the accumulator invariant holds for every recursive call and that when nummoves is 0 the initial board has been computed.

5.1   Developing a Breadth-First Solution

The heuristic-based depth-first N-puzzle solver assumed a solution can be found by always exploring the best successor of the current board. This assumption is removed and all possible sequences starting at a given board are explored. This requires that a list of all sequences generated so far be maintained. It is important during the exploration of this idea in the classroom to have students realize that this list of sequences must be maintained in order by length. Otherwise, the strategy may degenerate into a depth-first search that leads to an infinite recursion. The experienced reader will recognize that such a list is, in essence, a queue. It presents an opportunity to develop an interface for queues, but our success with having students reason about queues is mixed. CS1 students need to work on several queue-based solutions to different problems to internalize what a queue is. Therefore, we usually only mention queues in passing and allow students to structure their reasoning using a list of sequences ordered by length.

The implementation builds on the work done for the heuristic-based depth-first N-puzzle solver. The function find-solution-bfs takes as input a board, b, and returns a sequence from b to WIN. To accomplish this, a helper function, search-paths, is called that takes as input an accumulator that stores the list of all sequences generated so far. Initially, this list of sequences contains a single list that contains b. The function search-paths is a combination of generative recursion and accumulative recursion. Each time the function is called, it checks if the first board in the first sequence is WIN and, if so, it returns the first sequence. Otherwise, the successors of the first board in the first sequence are generated and a new sequence is generated for each successor by adding it to the front of the first sequence. To maintain the accumulator invariant, the list of sequences that does not include the first sequence is appended with the new sequences generated for the recursive call. A sample implementation is displayed in Figure 9.

Students must develop an accumulator invariant as well as an argument for termination. The accumulator invariant is developed, as mentioned above, during the exploration of the idea to search all possible sequences. The argument for termination hinges on having students realize that as paths get longer the number of moves required for one or more paths to reach the winning board gets smaller. Thus, the number of moves required to reach the winning board will eventually reach 0 for some path and the algorithm returns the appropriate sequence as long as the initial board is valid.

5.2   Refining the Solution: Deriving an A*-like Algorithm

The breadth-first N-puzzle solver does find a solution for any given board, but students soon discover that the help button is very sluggish and in some cases extremely so. The problem, of course, is that exploring all possible sequences starting at a given board is a great deal of work. Students can be led to realize

```
; find-solution-bfs: board --> lseq
; Purpose: To find a solution to the given board
(define (find-solution-bfs b)
  (local
    [; search-paths: lseq --> seq
     ; Purpose: To find a solution to b by searching all possible paths
     ; ACCUMULATOR INVARIANT:
     ;   paths is a list of all seqs generated so far starting at b from
     ;   from the shortest to the longest in reversed order
     (define (search-paths paths)
       (cond [(equal? (first (first paths)) WIN) (car paths)]
             [else
              (local [(define children (generate-children
                                          (first (first paths))))
                      (define new-paths (map (lambda (c)
                                               (cons c (first paths)))
                                             children))]
                (search-paths (append (rest paths) new-paths)))]))]
    (reverse (search-paths (list (list b))))))
```

Fig. 9. A breadth-first N-puzzle solver

that the number of sequences being searched surpasses 2^9 after 10 moves and surpasses 2^{19} after 20 moves[4]. This provides an opportunity to expose students to the problems of exponential growth. At this point, students are asked if searching all possible sequences and searching all possible sequences at the same time is necessary. This is a difficult question for them to answer. Most students will say yes to both questions, because all possible sequences must be searched. In other words, most students at this level are unlikely to realize on their own that not all sequences need to be searched and that not all sequences that ought to be searched have to be simultaneously searched.

There are two main ideas that must be planted in students' minds. The first idea is that not every sequence needs to be explored. We draw on the experience obtained from the depth-first N-puzzle solver. If any successor, s, of a given board, b, has been explored (i.e., the successors of s have been generated), then the path through b to s need not be explored. The reason is that a sequence, of equal or shorter length, to s has already been generated. The second idea is that we can choose to explore the most "promising" sequence first instead of blindly exploring all possible sequences at the same time. This leads the class discussion back to the Manhattan distance heuristic as a mechanism for deciding which sequence is the most promising. The idea to always explore the most promising sequence first is one that students in CS1 can grasp and implement.

---

[4] 2^9 and 2^{19} are, respectively, the number of leaves in a binary tree that describes the search space after 10 and 20 moves if all boards only had two successors.

```
(define (find-solution-a-star b)
  (local
    [(define (find-best-seq seqs)
       (cond [(empty? (rest seqs)) (first seqs)]
             [else
              (local [(define best-of-rest (find-best-seq (rest seqs)))]
                (cond [(< (manhattan-dist (first (first seqs)))
                          (manhattan-dist (first best-of-rest)))
                       (first seqs)]
                      [else best-of-rest]))]))
     (define (search-paths visited paths)
       (local [(define bstseq (find-best-seq paths))]
         (cond [(equal? (first best-path) WIN) bstseq]
               [else
                (local
                  [(define children
                     (filter (lambda (c) (not (member c visited)))
                             (generate-children (first bstseq))))
                   (define new-seqs (map (lambda (c) (cons c bstseq))
                                         children))]
                  (search-paths
                   (cons (first bstseq) visited)
                   (append new-seqs (rem-path bstseq paths))))])))]
    (reverse (search-paths '() (list (list b))))))
```

Fig. 10. An A* N-puzzle solver

Figure 10 displays an implementation of this strategy[5]. The function search-paths requires two accumulators each with its own invariant. The accumulator visited is a list of all the boards whose successors/children have been generated. The accumulator paths is a list of all the sequences starting at b that may need to be explored and that have no repeated boards in them. Both invariants, with some guidance, can be developed by students. The development of these invariants is likely to be the most time-consuming exercise in class. The rest of the implementation flows faster. The code finds the best sequence in paths. If the winning board has been reached by the best sequence, then the best sequence is returned. Otherwise, the program filters the successors of the last board[6] in the most promising sequence to remove boards that have already been explored. New sequences are generated using map to add each remaining successor to the most promising sequence. Notice that both of these computations are achieved by reinforcing lessons on abstraction that students have been exposed to in the near past. Finally, to maintain the two accumulator invariants, the last board of the

---

[5] Due to figure size limitations, all comments including contracts, purpose statements, and accumulator invariants have been omitted.

[6] Note that sequences are reversed making the last board in the sequence the first in the list.

most promising sequence is added to visited and the new sequences are appended with sequences obtained from removing the most promising sequence from paths. The only remaining tasks students must implement is finding the most promising sequence and removing a sequence from a list of sequences. The first can be done either by using accumulative recursion with an accumulator that remembers the best sequence so far or using structural recursion. The implementation in Figure 10 displays the latter and redesigning such a function using accumulative recursion is left as an exercise to give students more practice. The second is a straightforward exercise using structural recursion[7].

The algorithm developed is in essence an A*-like algorithm [8,9]. That is, it is a combination of a breadth-first strategy and a depth-first with backtracking strategy. Such algorithms are commonly referred to as *informed heuristic search strategies* [9]. What is most noteworthy is the fact that the development flows naturally from following the steps of the design recipe and iterative refinement. Students reason the algorithm into existence instead of being told about an algorithm. Such a development challenges the tacit assumption that A*-like algorithms are too complex for beginning students to understand and, therefore, are left as material restricted to more advanced courses such as an Introduction to Artificial Intelligence. There is, of course, one important observation about the N-puzzle domain that allowed us to simplify the design. Once a board is encountered there is no need to change its predecessor, because the cost of reaching it through the sequence of a previous encounter is always as good or better than the cost through the new sequence. In a full-fledged A* algorithm, the costs of the different sequences to a board must be examined to always maintain the sequence with the least cost.

6   Facilitating Deployment in the Classroom

The most important computational components of the presented N-puzzle solver have been developed in this article. The remaining components have to deal with the development of the interface with a player. The developers of HtDP have implemented a library (or teachpack as referred to by HtDPers), called *universe*, that allows students to easily develop interactive programs such as a video game [3]. Universe envisions an animation as a series of snapshots of an evolving world. There is a clock that at every tick displays the next snapshot of the world. Students must define the elements of the world and define functions for computing the next snapshot of the world when the clock ticks or when an external event, such as a keystroke or a mouse movement, occurs. Students must also define functions for drawing the world and for detecting the end of the game/animation.

It is important to carefully gauge the amount of work that beginning students are asked to do. Although the universe library truly simplifies the development of video games, sometimes students feel overburdened by the fine details of deciding on what tile a mouse click has occurred or of drawing the N-puzzle with a help

---

[7] This function does not appear in Figure 10 due to space limitations for figures.

button. If such is the case, invariably students get bogged down by writing drawing and mouse processing functions which leads them to relegate to the back burner the important lessons about generative and accumulative recursion. After all, in the mind of a beginning student nothing makes sense if you can not play the game. When faced with such a problem, the best course of action may be to eliminate the need for students to develop these low-level functions. This can be achieved by writing a library/teachpack specifically for the N-puzzle problem. The teachpack ought to include all the functions necessary for drawing the puzzle with the help button and for processing mouse events as well as the interface with the universe teachpack. In this manner, students can focus on the important lessons of generative and accumulative recursion. The downside of this approach, of course, is that it reduces the opportunities to reinforce previous lessons. An instructor must decide what the right balance is for the students in the classroom.

7   Related Work

The most closely related work on teaching generative and accumulative recursion to beginners is presented in HtDP. HtDP presents generative recursion as programs that have recursive calls that do not operate on part of the input. Instead, they generate a new instance of the problem. The examples used include, among others, moving a ball across a canvas, quicksort, fractals, and the computation of the greatest common divisor (gcd) of two numbers. Of these, the only example that truly captures the imagination of students is fractals. The reason is that fractals allow for a student to personalize their solutions to problems. Problems like quicksort and gcd, although important to be exposed to, do not permit for the personality of the student to be incorporated into their programs. Fractals and the N-puzzle video game, allow students to personalize solutions to their liking and that seems to be a great motivator by giving students a creative outlet to distinguish themselves and their work. The important lesson is to strike a balance between problems that allow personalization and those that do not. Both need to be included in a CS1 course. Problems that do not allow personalization, force students to focus on the lessons of designing functions that use generative recursion. Once those lessons have been presented and practiced, it is important to give students a chance to have a little fun with problems that allow personalization like the N-puzzle problem. In the N-puzzle problem, students can personalize the board (e.g., letters, number, images, etc.), the color of the tiles, and the definition of the winning board.

HtDP introduces accumulative recursion as a solution to the loss of knowledge between recursive calls. This can lead to efficiency issues in the case of programs designed using structural recursion or to problems not being solved in the case of generative recursion. The examples developed include finding a path in a graph and reversing a list. HtDP also outlines exercises that, like the work presented in this article, require students to combine skills to design programs that exploit structural, generative, and accumulative recursion. None of the problems are video-game-based, but, in fairness, HtDP was published before the development of the universe teachpack.

To the best knowledge of the author, there have been no published attempts to have beginning students work on the N-puzzle problem nor on developing A*-like algorithms. The N-puzzle game has been used to motivate topics in Artificial Intelligence and Machine Learning [5]. In addition to using the N-puzzle in an undergraduate AI course, the authors report using the N-puzzle game in a data structures and an algorithms course. In contrast, the approach presented in this article targets beginning students.

8   Concluding Remarks

The teaching philosophy of *program by design* put forth by HtDP when applied to the design of functional video games is a powerful combination that allows CS1 students to receive a solid introduction to programming while at the same time to become enthusiastic about the field of Computer Science. The enthusiasm comes from seeing in practice that what they are learning in the classroom is directly applicable to a domain that is of interest to them. In addition, the video game domain allows students to personalize solutions which means that students are not all producing the exact same solution to problems. Contrast this to solving problems in a Mathematics, Physics, or Chemistry course and it is easy to see why students find working with video games fun, personally rewarding, and enlightening. There are examples in the literature that illustrate how to design animations and video games that require the use of primitive data, structures, and structural recursion. The work described in this article is an example of how, in the CS1 classroom, to make the transition from structural recursion to generative and accumulative recursion using a video game as motivation to capture student enthusiasm. The choice of game, the N-puzzle, was made to also demonstrate that informed heuristic search strategies, traditionally the domain of undergraduate courses in Artificial Intelligence, are within the grasp of CS1 students. Students do not simply study such an algorithm. Instead, the full power of program by design allows CS1 students to reason such an algorithm into existence. If this work is replicated elsewhere, there is no doubt that it will be an exciting time for Computer Science education and it will elevate the relevance of functional programming in the minds of future CS professionals.

Future work includes demonstrating how functional video games can be an effective pedagogical tool for motivating and teaching distributed/parallel programming to CS1 students. Functional programming has been identified as providing a clear and concise way to program parallel computers and distributed computations [7,10]. It is time for this knowledge to reach down to the CS1 classroom. The approach will assume that students have a foundation using different forms of recursion as well as abstraction and will use the universe teachpack as in the work described in this article. A second line of future work is to extend the work presented in this article to other, more complex, games such as checkers and chess. The biggest challenge in this second line of future work is identifying heuristics that can be understood and implemented by CS1 students. Finally, a third line of future work focuses on the impact the use of video games in CS1 has on detecting plagiarism. The hypothesis underlining this line of work is that a programming medium that allows for the personalization of solutions, such as the development of video games, may make it easier for instructors to detect plagiarized code.

References

1. Felleisen, M., Findler, R.B., Fisler, K., Flatt, M., Krishnamurthi, S.: How to Design Worlds (2008), http://world.cs.brown.edu/1/
2. Felleisen, M., Findler, R.B., Flatt, M., Krishnamurthi, S.: How to Design Programs: An Introduction to Programming and Computing. MIT Press, Cambridge (2001)
3. Felleisen, M., Findler, R.B., Flatt, M., Krishnamurthi, S.: A Functional I/O System or, Fun for Freshman Kids. In: ICFP, pp. 47–58 (2009)
4. Findler, R.B., Clements, J., Flanagan, C., Flatt, M., Krishnamurthi, S., Steckler, P., Felleisen, M.: DrScheme: A Programming Environment for Scheme. Journal of Functional Programming 12(2), 159–182 (2002)
5. Markov, Z., Russell, I., Neller, T., Zlatareva, N.: Pedagogical Possibilities for the N-Puzzle Problem. In: Proceedings of the Frontiers in Education Conference, pp. S2F1–S2F6 (November 2006)
6. Morazán, M.T.: Functional Video Games in the CS1 Classroom. In: Page, R., Horváth, Z., Zsók, V. (eds.) TFP 2010. LNCS, vol. 6546, pp. 166–183. Springer, Heidelberg (2011)
7. Peyton-Jones, S.: Parallel Implementations of Functional Programming Languages. The Computer Journal 32(2) (1989)
8. Rich, E., Knight, K.: Artificial Intelligence. McGraw-Hill, New York (1991)
9. Russell, S.J., Norvig, P., Candy, J.F., Malik, J.M., Edwards, D.D.: Artificial intelligence: A Modern Approach. Prentice-Hall, Inc., Upper Saddle River (1996)
10. Szymanski, B.K.: Parallel Functional Languages and Compilers. Frontier Series. ACM Press, New York (1991)

GiN: A Graphical Language
and Tool for Defining iTask Workflows

Jeroen Henrix, Rinus Plasmeijer, and Peter Achten

Institute for Computing and Information Sciences
Radboud University Nijmegen, P.O. Box 9010, 6500 GL Nijmegen, The Netherlands
j.henrix@science.ru.nl, {rinus,p.achten}@cs.ru.nl

Abstract. Workflow Management Systems (WFMSs) are software applications that coordinate business processes. The coordination is based on a workflow model, expressed in a domain-specific Workflow Description Language (WDL). WDLs are typically graphical languages because the specification has to be understandable for domain experts as well as workflow application developers. Commonly, only simple workflows can be described while additional coding is needed to turn the description into a running application. The iTask system is a combinator library, embedded in Clean, to construct WFMSs. Complex workflows can be defined declaratively from which a complete web-based application is generated. However, the textual specification is less suitable for domain experts who are used to graphical notations. In this paper we address this problem and present GiN: a graphical notation for iTask workflows, as well as a prototype implementation of a tool to construct GiN workflows interactively and graphically. The tool is fully integrated in the iTask system: it is just another iTask component, and workflows created with GiN can be subsequently added and executed dynamically as part of other workflows.

1 Introduction

In this paper we present *GiN* (*Graphical iTask Notation*). GiN is both a graphical notation for the iTask system as well as a tool to construct iTask workflows in an interactive and graphical way. The iTask system [18] is a combinator library, embedded in the pure and lazy functional programming language Clean, to construct Workflow Management Systems (WFMSs) in a functional style. WFMSs are software applications that coordinate business processes. This coordination is based on a workflow model: a formal description in a Workflow Description Language (WDL) of the tasks that comprise a business process.

Conventional WDLs have a graphical nature. This has as advantage that their notation is perceived as intuitive and can be used in the development process by both workflow engineers and domain experts. Frequently, these WDLs are based on (colored) Petri nets [2]. In contrast, the iTask EDSL uses a textual WDL. To understand and appreciate an iTask workflow model, one needs to be trained in

R. Peña and R. Page (Eds.): TFP 2011, LNCS 7193, pp. 163–178, 2012.
© Springer-Verlag Berlin Heidelberg 2012

functional programming. It is our goal to make the iTask system and formalism accessible for the workflow community. GiN is the first step in this project to achieve this goal.

The GiN *language* is a hybrid language that combines graphical elements with textual elements. Where suitable, the graphical elements are borrowed from graphical WDLs used in the workflow community. GiN adds a few new graphical elements that are particular to iTask. Right from the beginning we have decided that GiN *is not* a visual programming language substitute for Clean. That would defeat the purpose of GiN of being an accessible tool for domain experts who are not trained in functional programming. Furthermore, in contrast with conventional systems, the iTask system can generate a complete web-based application from a workflow specification. In conventional systems, the graphical definition of a workflow is only a partial specification that defines the control flow between tasks, and hence, a significant programming effort is required to implement the data dependencies and data flow. For these reasons we think it is reasonable that in GiN not all parts of a workflow can be expressed graphically. The current version of GiN is restricted to the 'classic' iTask combinator language core [18]. Recent extensions of the iTask API, such as run-time changes [19] and support for GUIs and shared data [15] are not supported yet. This is future work.

The GiN *tool* is an interactive and graphical editor to create iTask workflows. It supports the user with direct feedback about mistakes in the workflow under construction. The GiN tool is integrated in the iTask system, and can be used like any other task in a workflow. We envision that this integration is particularly useful in the presence of change [19] when workflow engineers or managers need to design alternative workflows quickly and correctly.

The contributions of our work are:

- We define and motivate a new hybrid WDL, GiN, that combines the salient features of iTask with elements from the workflow community.
- We design and implement a prototype GiN tool that allows users to construct GiN workflows while being continuously informed about the correctness of the workflows under construction.
- We integrate the GiN tool in the iTask system. Workflows can invoke the tool, and use the output subsequently.

The remainder of this paper is organized as follows. First, we define the GiN language in Section 2. The GiN tool and its design choices are described in Section 3. Section 4 defines the formal semantics and explains how to compile GiN specifications to executable workflow applications. Related work is discussed in Section 5. Section 6 presents conclusions and future work.

2   The GiN WDL

In this section we introduce the GiN language. We first give a concise introduction to the iTask WDL (Section 2.1), followed by the GiN WDL (Section 2.2), and give an example of a higher-order workflow (Section 2.3).

2.1 The iTask WDL

The iTask WDL is a combinator language, constructing basic and composite tasks of abstract type Task a. Figure 1 shows an excerpt of the signatures of basic tasks and task combinators. The iTask WDL is generic: the generic type class constraint | iTask allows the framework to automatically derive a fully operational web-based GUI for any value of any first-order data type. In Clean both overloaded and generic constraints are placed at the end of a type signature. For instance, in Figure 1, descr is a type constructor class, and iTask is a generic class. The semantics of iTask is formally defined [11,19].

```
updateInformation :: d a                      → Task a    | descr d & iTask a
showMessage       :: d                        → Task Void | descr d
return            :: a                         → Task a    | iTask a
(>>=)  infixl 1   :: (Task a) (a → Task b)    → Task b    | iTask a & iTask b
(>>|)  infixl 1   :: (Task a)   (Task b)      → Task b    | iTask a & iTask b
(-||-) infixr 3   :: (Task a)   (Task a)      → Task a    | iTask a
(-&&-) infixr 4   :: (Task a)   (Task b)      → Task (a,b)| iTask a & iTask b
anyTask           :: [Task a]                  → Task a    | iTask a
allTasks          :: [Task a]                  → Task [a]  | iTask a
(@:)   infix 3    :: User       (Task a)      → Task a    | iTask a
```

Fig. 1. Excerpt of basic tasks and task combinators of the iTask WDL

The basic task (updateInformation descr init) generates a GUI to allow the user to update an initial value init; the task (showMessage descr) shows a message descr to the user and returns the Void value when terminated. The iTask WDL is monadic, and provides the usual monadic core combinators: return lifts a value to the task domain and >>= binds two tasks sequentially. a >>| b is shorthand for a >>= λ_ → b, which will discard the value of task a. Tasks can be composed in parallel. Either the result of the first completed task is returned (-||- and anyTask combinators) or the results of all parallel tasks are collected and returned as a whole (-&&- and allTasks). Finally, a task t can be assigned to a user u with u @: t.

2.2 The GiN WDL

Although the iTask library is a textual formalism, a graphical notation comes naturally. We have studied a number of graphical WDLs for defining workflows to see what graphical notation is used. These WDLs are *workflow nets* [1], *YAWL* [3], *event-driven process chains* [9], and *UML activity diagrams* [5]. Visual elements commonly found in these languages are workflow units, depicted as boxes, control flow relations indicated by arrows, and decision and parallel structures indicated by separate split and merge connectors. We refer to [8] for a detailed discussion.

In order to make GiN appealing for workflow engineers, we have adapted graphical notation from the above mentioned WDLs. Figure 2 shows the result.

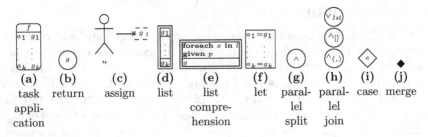

Fig. 2. Graphical GiN elements

In a GiN project, a workflow is defined by means of a collection of *host language modules* and *task definition diagrams*. The names of task definitions and host language modules must not overlap. A task definition diagram (see picture to the right) introduces a task function of name f that uses parameters a_i of types α_i $(i \geq 0)$. The parameter-names a_i are simple variable names. There are no restrictions on the types, and they can be (higher-order) task types as well (the example in Section 2.3 illustrates this). The body g of the task definition diagram is a directed graph, consisting of the nodes that are summarized in Figure 2 and edges that are optionally labeled with host-language pattern expressions. Figure 3 enumerates the way in which the graph can be constructed by means of production rules, denoted as (pattern ⇒ substitution). In the production rules, variables a, b match individual nodes, p, q match (possibly empty) host-language pattern expressions on edges, and e denotes a literal host-language expression. GiN graphs are semi-block structured: rules PARALLEL and PARALLEL LIST, when applied at nesting level n, introduce subgraphs at nesting level $n + 1$. Any part of the top-level graph or a parallel subgraph which matches the pattern and concerns elements at the same nesting level, can be replaced by its substitution. The rules may be applied any number of times. We informally discuss the semantics of the individual elements as we go along. The formal semantics and scope rules are presented in Section 4.

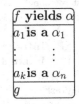

All GiN graphs are constructed from INIT. The SEQ rule composes tasks sequentially: $\cdot \xrightarrow{p} \cdot$ corresponds with $\cdot \text{ >>= } \lambda p \to \cdot$, and $\cdot \to \cdot$ corresponds with $\cdot \text{ >>| } \cdot$. The tasks enumerated in Figure 2 (**a** - **c**) can be put in sequence without restriction. A *task application* node applies a task function f to all of its arguments. The arguments g_i are GiN graphs or host-language expressions. If f is defined by means of a task definition diagram or f is an iTask API function (such as updateInformation or showMessage), then the names a_i of its parameters are repeated to guide the user to fill in the correct arguments. The names are absent in any other case, for instance when invoking a task passed as an argument to a higher-order task. The *return* node corresponds directly with the return combinator from Figure 1. Its argument is a host-language expression or GiN graph, so it is possible to return tasks. Similarly, the *assign* node corresponds directly

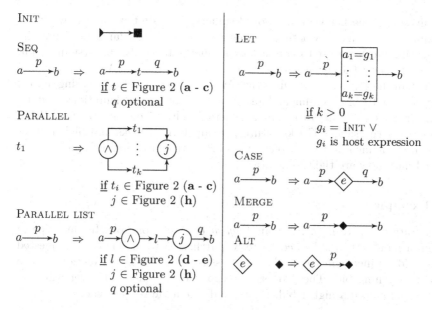

Fig. 3. GiN graph production rules

with the @: combinator from Figure 1. Here u must be a host-language expression of type User, and g is a GiN graph.

One can replace a single task t_1 by a group of parallel tasks $t_1 \ldots t_n$ ($n > 0$) by means of the PARALLEL rule. Each of these tasks is evaluated in parallel. The termination behavior of this group is determined by means of the join node value j which corresponds one-to-one with the parallel combinators from Figure 1: $j = \vee_{1st}$ corresponds with anyTask, $j = \wedge_{[]}$ corresponds with allTasks, and $j = \wedge_{(,)}$ corresponds with -&&-. The group of parallel tasks can also be supplied as a list, in which case rule PARALLEL LIST applies. Either a static list can be used, or a list comprehension, in which x, l and the optional predicate p are host-language expressions.

Edge-patterns introduce identifiers. Identifiers can be used or also introduced with the LET rule and bind to either host-language expressions or new GiN graphs. Within a let, $a_i = g_i$ precedes $a_j = g_j$ if $i < j$.

With the CASE, MERGE, and ALT rules loops can be constructed using guarded choice. A *case* node has indegree one and positive outdegree, and a *merge* node has positive indegree and outdegree one. Edges starting from a case node are labeled with a host-language pattern expression that must have the same type as the host-language expression inside the case node. It is allowed that the 'last' edge is not labeled, which corresponds with the default case. Note that 'last' is determined in left-to-right, top-to-bottom order of edges.

Evaluation. The GiN language has been designed to make the iTask WDL more accessible for workflow engineers and domain experts. The question needs to be answered whether we have moved sufficiently close towards the workflow community, and, dually, whether we have not moved too far away from the iTask WDL. We have yet to conduct experiments to verify the first question, but we can answer the second question affirmatively. The GiN WDL is arguably simpler than the full-blown textual iTask WDL: we do not allow currying in task applications, pattern-matching and guards are absent in task definitions, and list comprehensions are limited to a single generator-filter. However, the GiN WDL still preserves the salient iTask features: parameterized tasks and higher-order tasks can be defined and used, recursive workflows can be defined, and control flow and data flow are tightly integrated.

2.3   Example

To illustrate GiN, we implement an *English auction* workflow. In this type of auction, a number of bidders compete to purchase a ware. They are requested to place bids of increasing price. This process is controlled by an auctioneer who starts the opening bid. The process is terminated by the auctioneer when no bidder puts forward a higher bid. First, we define a Bid record type:

```
:: Bid = { user   :: User     // bid is done by bidder or terminated by auctioneer
         , ware   :: String   // name of merchandise (≠ "")
         , price  :: Int      // price (> 0)
         }
```

The auction workflow is defined in a task definition diagram (Figure 4). The auction workflow yields a bid. The first parameter of auction, bidf, abstracts over the concrete way of bidding (an example could be updateInformation "Make your bid") and illustrates the use of higher-order tasks. The auctioneer parameter is a User who is in charge of the auction process, and starts with the opening bid. The bidders parameter is a list of users [User] who compete to purchase a ware. Finally, current is the currently pending Bid.

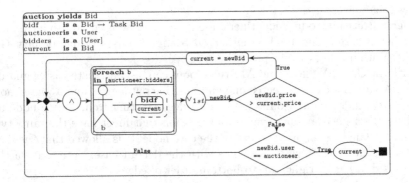

Fig. 4. Auction workflow example in GiN

The auction workflow is an iterative process in which bidders and auctioneer interact. With a list comprehension the participants (the auctioneer and all bidders, denoted as [auctioneer:bidders]) are collected. Each participant is assigned the same task (using the assign node): to enter a new bid according to the higher-order task function bidf (using task application). The parallel list node uses the $\vee_{1st}$ parallel join node to determine the first person who enters a new bid. The value of the bid is identified with the variable newBid (using a pattern-edge). The topmost case distinction needs to inspect the new value newBid.price. If the price is higher, it becomes the current bid (using let and looping back to the start of the auction graph). If not, the person newBid.user who placed the bid is checked. If she was not the auctioneer, the bid is invalid, and the process loops back to the start of the auction graph without changing any value. Otherwise, the workflow terminates and returns the most recent bid (using return).

3   The GiN Tool

In order to investigate whether the GiN language is useful in practice, we have implemented a proof-of-concept tool to create and compile GiN diagrams. In this section we discuss the editor component with which users can create and maintain GiN diagrams. The compiler component is discussed in Section 4.

The GiN editor is based on the *Oryx editor*, which is part of the *Oryx platform* [4]: an academic open source framework for business process management. We use Oryx because it offers the standard editing functionality one expects from such a graphical editor such as arranging and manipulation of graph elements. Reimplementing this is a duplication of effort. Besides, Oryx uses similar web technologies as iTask, like the Ext JS web framework and the JSON data interchange format, which facilitates integration.

Figure 5 shows a screenshot of the GiN tool. The editor consists of a drawing canvas and a repository. The drawing canvas shows the *task definition diagram* under construction. The repository shows the available node types from Figure 2. Other task functions in the iTask API are available as *task application* nodes. Workflows are compositional: both from textual and graphical workflow definitions, one can import other (textual or graphically defined) modules.

While the user is constructing a workflow, the editor continuously provides her with informative feedback. GiN diagrams can contain two sorts of errors: either the diagram does not conform to the GiN graph structure or (combinations of) literal host language expressions are erroneous. The first sort of error is detected by the compilation process of a GiN diagram under construction to iTask code, and the second sort of error by invoking the Clean compiler on the generated code. Due to the speed of the Clean compiler, this process is not excessively time-consuming. On a test system (Intel Core 2 Duo, 2.1 GHz), we measure response times in the order of 100 milliseconds, which is acceptable for interactive use. The GiN tool parses error messages that may have been generated in the two steps and indicates the source of the error on the right spot in the GiN diagram under construction. An example indication is visible in Figure 5, where the diagram contains an undefined variable name.

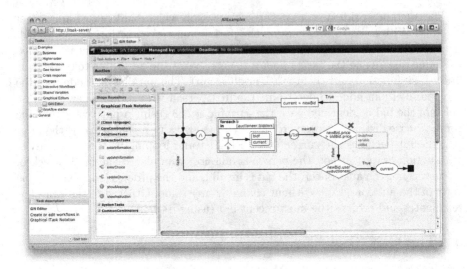

Fig. 5. Editing the auction example in the GiN tool embedded in the iTask system

The GiN tool is integrated in the iTask system. This has several consequences. First, from the point of view of the iTask system, the GiN tool 'is just another editor' for values of type `GiNDiagram` (the internal data structure that is used to represent GiN diagrams). By adding (`updateInformation "Create your workflow!" myGiNDiagram`) in any workflow definition results in the creation of the GiN tool to allow the user to work on a GiN diagram with initial value `myGiNDiagram`. As a consequence, it can be used in a meta workflow: an iTask workflow which defines how new workflows have to be constructed. One can think of scenarios where some people construct workflows with the GiN tool, while others have to approve the workflow thus designed. Second, as part of such a scenario one also wants to use such a new workflow once it has been approved. This means that the resulting code corresponding to the new workflow has to be dynamically plugged in into the running iTask application. Clean facilitates this by making use of dynamic types [17] and the ability to link any value of a dynamic type into a running application [23]. Third, this technology allows the user to browse her repository of created workflows, and use them to build new workflows, just by drag-and-drop in the user interface of the tool. Fourth, in the iTask project, a first step towards adaptability has been set, by making the technical abilities to make changes to running tasks [19]. We envision that the GiN tool is particularly useful to make changes right on the spot, in an understandable way for end users.

4   The GiN Compiler

In this section we discuss the compilation process of GiN diagrams under construction to iTask workflows. The basic idea is that the GiN tool serves as a

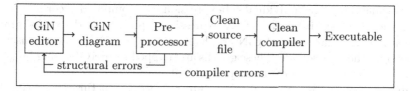

Fig. 6. Compilation steps

preprocessor for the Clean compiler (Figure 6). The preprocessor detects ill-structured diagrams and generates error messages. Well-structured diagrams are compiled to textual iTask source files. The Clean compiler detects remaining errors and generates error messages. Correct iTask programs are compiled to an executable that generates a dynamic on disk that can be used for further processing, as described in Section 3.

Internally, a diagram is represented as a graph structure of type GiNDiagram, consisting of a set of nodes and a set of edges. In order to represent iTask source files, we define an abstract syntax tree (AST) containing only the elements needed for the mapping. These elements are function definitions, literals, variables, prefix and infix applications, lambda abstractions, case expressions, let-expressions, tuples, lists and simple (one-generator) list comprehensions. Literal Clean expressions found in diagrams are stored as literal text in the AST. By pretty-printing the AST, we obtain an iTask source file.

The preprocessor transforms the nodes and edges in the GinDiagram graph to expressions in the AST. We have seen in Section 2 that the parallel constructs consist of separate split and join nodes. These nodes are mapped pair-wise to a single iTask expression. Given the fact that constructs may be arbitrarily combined, the question is how to identify the corresponding nodes that should map to an expression. A complicating factor is that the graph structure may contain cycles to express loops.

A similar problem is more widely known in the workflow community. Many WDLs used in business modeling are *graph based*: these WDLs use a graph structure which allows arbitrary unstructured connections between nodes. Execution-oriented WDLs are often *block based*, allowing only structured compositions of properly nested blocks. When mapping a graph-based WDL onto a block-based WDL, the structured subgraphs need to be identified in order to map them. A structured subgraph has a unique entry node and a unique exit node.

In [22], Vanhatalo *et al* describe a linear time algorithm that decomposes a graph into a tree structure, named *Process Structure Tree* (PST). The branches in the PST are the structured subgraphs, while the leaves contain the individual nodes from the original graph.

The mapping $[\![g]\!]_{graph}$ of a GiN graph g to an iTask expression takes three steps. First, g is decomposed into a process structure tree, consisting of subgraphs. Second, each subgraph is classified into one out of four categories. Third, each subgraph is mapped to a subexpression. For each category, we define a different mapping. The individual subexpressions are composed according to the tree structure, resulting in an iTask expression representing the entire graph. Note that individual *nodes* of GiN graphs may contain GiN graphs themselves, for instance the *return* node. These graphs are mapped recursively using $[\![g]\!]_{graph}$. We will now discuss each of the steps in detail.

First, we decompose the GiN graph into a process structure tree, using the algorithm mentioned above. We add two restrictions: the exit node of a subgraph cannot be a *case* node (to ensure each case alternative has an expression), and individual *let, parallel split, parallel join, case* and *merge* nodes (Figure 2 **f** - **j**) are not decomposed to subgraphs. As an example, we show the identified subgraphs of the auction workflow (labeled $A \ldots D$), the individual nodes (labeled $e \ldots l$), together with its corresponding PST in Figure 7.

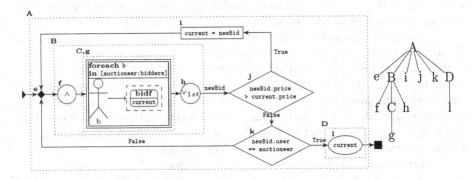

Fig. 7. Subgraph decomposition and corresponding PST in the auction example

Second, we classify each subgraph in the PST decomposition, with entry node s and exit node t, into in one of these four categories:

- *Trivial subgraphs*, which consist only of a single node, so $s = t$.
- *Structured parallel subgraphs*, in which s is a parallel split node, t is a parallel join node, s splits to nodes a_i, and nodes a_i join to t.
- *Sequential subgraphs*, which do not contain any parallel split or parallel join nodes. Hence, these graphs are purely sequential, but may contain non-block structured branches and arbitrary cycles.
- *Other subgraphs*, which do not fit any of the above categories.

In the auction example, subgraph A is a sequential subgraph, B a structured parallel subgraph, and C and D are trivial subgraphs. Graphs in the first three categories can be mapped to iTask expressions. Other graphs from the fourth category are rejected, and an error is reported to the user. Such graphs may contain parallel branches which are not properly block structured, and thus cannot be expressed in terms of the 'classic' set of core iTask combinators. These cases could possibly be expressed using recent extensions of the iTask API [15], but this belongs to future work.

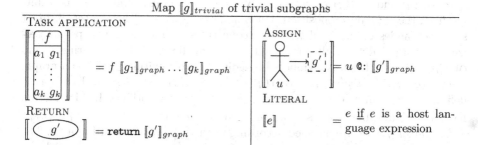

Map $[\![g]\!]_{trivial}$ of trivial subgraphs

TASK APPLICATION

$$\left[\!\!\left[\begin{array}{cc} \boxed{f} \\ a_1\ g_1 \\ \vdots\ \ \vdots \\ a_k\ g_k \end{array}\right]\!\!\right] = f\ [\![g_1]\!]_{graph} \ldots [\![g_k]\!]_{graph}$$

RETURN

$$\left[\!\!\left[\ \boxed{g'}\ \right]\!\!\right] = \texttt{return}\ [\![g']\!]_{graph}$$

ASSIGN

$$\left[\!\!\left[\begin{array}{c} \text{(person)} \to \boxed{g'} \\ u \end{array}\right]\!\!\right] = u\ @:\ [\![g']\!]_{graph}$$

LITERAL

$$[\![e]\!] = \begin{array}{l} e\ \underline{\text{if}}\ e\ \text{is a host lan-} \\ \text{guage expression} \end{array}$$

Map $[\![g]\!]_{parallel}$ of parallel subgraphs

PARALLEL

$$\left[\!\!\left[\begin{array}{c} \boxed{\wedge} \\ g_1\ \cdots\ g_k \\ \boxed{j} \end{array}\right]\!\!\right] = \begin{cases} \texttt{anyTask}\ [[\![g_1]\!]_{graph}, \ldots, \\ \quad [\![g_k]\!]_{graph}]\ \underline{\text{if}}\ j = \vee_{1st} \\ [\![g_1]\!]_{graph}\ \texttt{-\&\&-}\ [\![g_2]\!]_{graph} \\ \quad \underline{\text{if}}\ j = \wedge_{(,)}\ \text{and}\ n = 2 \\ \texttt{allTasks}\ [[\![g_1]\!]_{graph}, \ldots, \\ \quad [\![g_k]\!]_{graph}]\ \underline{\text{if}}\ j = \wedge_{[]} \end{cases}$$

PARALLEL LIST

$$\left[\!\!\left[\begin{array}{c} \boxed{\wedge} \\ \downarrow \\ \boxed{l} \\ \downarrow \\ \boxed{j} \end{array}\right]\!\!\right] = \begin{cases} \texttt{anyTask}\ [\![l]\!]_{list}\ \underline{\text{if}}\ j = \vee_{1st} \\ \texttt{allTasks}\ [\![l]\!]_{list}\ \underline{\text{if}}\ j = \wedge_{[]} \end{cases}$$

Map $[\![l]\!]_{list}$ of lists

LIST

$$\left[\!\!\left[\begin{array}{c} \boxed{g_1} \\ \vdots \\ \boxed{g_k} \end{array}\right]\!\!\right] = \begin{array}{l}[\ [\![g_1]\!]_{graph} \\ ,\ \ldots \\ ,\ [\![g_k]\!]_{graph} \\ ]\end{array}$$

LIST COMPREHENSION

$$\left[\!\!\left[\begin{array}{l} \boxed{\textbf{foreach}\ x\ \text{in}\ l'} \\ \boxed{\textbf{given}\ p} \\ \boxed{g} \end{array}\right]\!\!\right] \begin{array}{l} [[\![g]\!]_{graph}\ \backslash\backslash\ x \leftarrow l'\ |\ p] \\ = \text{Note: if } \textbf{given}\ p \text{ is absent:} \\ \quad [[\![g]\!]_{graph}\ \backslash\backslash\ x \leftarrow l'] \end{array}$$

Map $[\![n]\!]_{node}$ of nodes in sequential subgraphs

CASE

$$\left[\!\!\left[\ \boxed{\diamondsuit_e}\ \right]\!\!\right] = \begin{array}{l} \textbf{case}\ e\ \textbf{of} \\ \quad p_1 = [\![n_1]\!]_{node} \\ \quad \vdots\ \ \ \ \vdots \\ \quad p_k = [\![n_k]\!]_{node} \\ \quad \_\ = [\![o]\!]_{node} \\ \underline{\text{if}}\ succ(n) = \{n_1, \ldots, n_k, o\} \\ \wedge n \xrightarrow{p_1} n_1 \wedge \ldots \wedge n \xrightarrow{p_k} n_k \\ \wedge n \to o \end{array}$$

MERGE

$$\left[\!\!\left[\ \boxed{\blacklozenge_i}\ \right]\!\!\right] = \begin{array}{l} f_i\ \overrightarrow{\text{IN}(n) \setminus \{f_i\} \setminus env} \\ \underline{\text{if}}\ \neg ends(n) \end{array}$$

LET

$$\left[\!\!\left[\ \boxed{a = g}\ \right]\!\!\right] = \begin{array}{l} (\lambda a \to [\![n']\!]_{node})[\![g]\!]_{graph} \\ \underline{\text{if}}\ succ(n) = \{n'\} \\ \wedge \neg ends(n') \end{array}$$

BIND

$$[\![\ n\ ]\!] = \begin{array}{l} [\![n]\!]_{graph}\ \texttt{>>=}\ \lambda p \to [\![n']\!]_{node} \\ \underline{\text{if}}\ succ(n) = \{n'\} \\ \wedge n \xrightarrow{p} n' \wedge \neg ends(n') \end{array}$$

SEQUENCE

$$[\![\ n\ ]\!] = \begin{array}{l} [\![n]\!]_{graph}\ \texttt{>>|}\ [\![n']\!]_{node} \\ \underline{\text{if}}\ succ(n) = \{n'\} \\ \wedge n \to n' \wedge \neg ends(n') \end{array}$$

TERMINAL

$$[\![\ n\ ]\!] = \begin{array}{l} [\![n]\!]_{graph} \\ \underline{\text{if}}\ succ(n) = \emptyset \\ \vee(\ succ(n) = \{n'\} \\ \quad \wedge ends(n')) \end{array}$$

Fig. 8. Map of graphs and nodes to host language expressions

Third, we map each of the subgraphs to a subexpression. For a subgraph g, let $entry(g)$ and $exit(g)$ be respectively the entry and exit node of g, as resulting from the PST decomposition. For a node n, let $succ(n)$ be the set of direct successor nodes of n. We define the scope rules by means of two parameterized sets: $\text{IN}(n)$ defines all known symbols immediately before entering n and $\text{OUT}(n)$ defines all known symbols immediately after exiting n. If g is a graph, then $\text{IN}(g) = \text{IN}(entry(g))$ and $\text{OUT}(g) = \text{OUT}(exit(g))$. Suppose we have a task definition diagram in an environment env that defines identifiers. If this diagram has name f, arguments $\overrightarrow{a_i \text{ is a } \alpha_i}$, and body g, then $\text{IN}(g) = env \cup \{f\} \cup \{\overrightarrow{a_i}\}$.

Trivial subgraphs are mapped according to the $[\![g]\!]_{trivial}$ map of Figure 8. The TASK APPLICATION node n has a name f and parameters $g_1 \ldots g_k$, which are GiN graphs or Clean expressions. This node is mapped to a function application, in which the arguments are mapped recursively. The scope of the task application is closed, hence $\text{OUT}(n) = \text{IN}(n)$. The RETURN node n maps to the monadic **return** combinator. The argument g' is mapped recursively. Its scope is closed: $\text{OUT}(n) = \text{IN}(n)$. The ASSIGN n node, which assigns a graph g' to a user u, maps to the **@:** iTask operator. The graph g' is mapped recursively. We have $\text{IN}(u) = \text{IN}(g') = \text{IN}(n)$ and $\text{OUT}(n) = \text{OUT}(g')$. A LITERAL e allows the embedding of literal host language expressions. Its scope is closed, so $\text{OUT}(e) = \text{IN}(e)$.

In *structured parallel subgraphs*, the parallel split node and parallel join node j are mapped pair-wise to a corresponding iTask combinator, according to the map $[\![g]\!]_{parallel}$ of Figure 8. Each of the graphs g_i in the parallel branches is mapped recursively and put in a list. Alternatively, if there is only one branch consisting of a LIST or LIST COMPREHENSION node l, that branch is mapped straightforwardly to respectively a list or list comprehension, according to $[\![l]\!]_{list}$ in Figure 8. The scope of list (comprehension) is closed, so $\text{OUT}(l) = \text{IN}(l)$. The scope of variables bound within a parallel branch is limited to that branch only. This restriction avoids scope conflicts (what is the value of x if x was bound in two parallel branches, after completion of both of them?). Hence, the scope of a parallel graph g is closed: $\text{OUT}(g) = \text{IN}(g)$.

Sequential subgraphs may contain arbitrary cycles. The idea is to unfold the paths starting from merge nodes ($\blacklozenge$) into separate functions, defined in a let-expression. Each edge entering such a merge node is translated to a tail-recursive call of the corresponding function. More formally: let g be a sequential subgraph. We define the predicate $ends(n) = n$ is a merge node and either $n = exit(g)$, or there is a path from n to $exit(g)$ consisting only of merge nodes. Let $\{m_i\}$ denote the set of merge nodes in g for which $ends(m_i)$ does not hold. g is mapped to **let** $\overrightarrow{f_i \ \text{IN}(m_i) \setminus \{f\} \setminus env} = [\![succ(m_i)]\!]_{node}$ **in** $[\![entry(g)]\!]_{node}$.

We define $[\![n]\!]_{node}$ as a map from a node n to an expression, depending on the context in which n occurs. $[\![n]\!]_{node}$ is shown in Figure 8.

A CASE node n is a direct visualization of the **case-of** in the host language: given the literal expression e in node n, perform case distinction by means of the literal patterns labeled on the outgoing edges of the node. At most one unlabeled edge is allowed, which maps to the default case. The successor nodes denote the alternatives, which are mapped recursively by $[\![n]\!]_{node}$. They are ordered from left to right, top to bottom, followed by the default case. The scope rules are $\text{OUT}(e) = \text{IN}(e) = \text{IN}(n)$, and for each pattern p_i: $\text{IN}(p_i) = \text{OUT}(e)$ and alternative n_i: $\text{IN}(n_i) = \text{OUT}(e) \cup \textit{free}(p_i)$; the optional default case has $\text{IN}(o) = \text{IN}(e)$.

A MERGE node m_i for which $\neg ends(m_i)$ holds, maps to a tail-recursive call of the corresponding function f_i in the let-expression, with arguments $\text{IN}(n) \setminus \{f_i\} \setminus env$. Since m_i can have multiple incoming edges, $\text{IN}(m_i)$ is defined as the *intersection* of the sets of known symbols on each incoming edge. Hence, a variable can only be passed across a merge node if it is known in all of its incoming edges. The scope of MERGE is closed: $\text{OUT}(m_i) = \text{IN}(m_i)$.

A LET node n suggests a mapping to the **let** host language construct. We wish to allow LET-nodes in GiN which can be read like an assignment, e.g. $\boxed{x = x + 1}$, which requires LET to have a non-recursive semantics. However, let-expressions in the host language Clean are always recursive; Clean does not have a separate **letrec** expression In order to get a non-recursive semantics, we map LET nodes to a lambda abstraction and application, as shown in LET in $[\![n]\!]_{node}$. LET nodes containing multiple definitions are simplified to a sequence of singleton lets. The argument g of each LET node is mapped recursively. The scope rules are $\text{IN}(g) = \text{IN}(n)$, $\text{OUT}(n) = \text{IN}(n) \bigcup \{a\}$.

According to the BIND rule, a labeled edge $n \overset{p}{\to} n'$ maps to the monadic bind operator and a lambda: $n \mathbin{>\!>=} \lambda p \to n'$. Its scope rules are $\text{IN}(p) = \text{IN}(n)$, $\text{OUT}(n') = \text{IN}(n') = \text{IN}(n) \cup \textit{free}(p)$. Likewise, the SEQUENCE rule omits the pattern: an unlabeled edge $n \to n'$ maps to the monad sequence operator $n \mathbin{>\!>|} n'$. Its scope rules are $\text{OUT}(n') = \text{IN}(n') = \text{IN}(n)$. Finally, the TERMINAL rule ensures that if a node n is on a path with only merge nodes and leading to an exit node, we stop after recursively mapping n.

For completeness, we show the translation of the auction example:

```
auction :: (Bid → Task Bid) User [User] Bid → Task Bid
auction bidf auctioneer bidders current =
    let g bidf auctioneer bidders current =
          anyTask [b @: bidf current \\ b ← [auctioneer : bidders]] >>= λnewBid →
              case newBid.price > current.price of
                 True  = (λcurrent → g bidf auctioneer bidders current) newBid
                 False = case newBid.user = auctioneer of
                            True  = return current
                            False = g bidf auctioneer bidders current
    in g bidf auctioneer bidders current
```

This is different from a typical task function manually written by an iTask programmer. The local function **g** is redundant here; instead auction could have been called directly. Besides, the Clean language allows us to express the conditions more compactly using guards, which are not available in GiN.

5 Related Work

Many graphical WDLs are based on directed graphs and primarily model control flow. Data flow is added as an additional layer, in which all data is often globally accessible and stored in databases. Specifications are often partial, and hence require a significant additional software engineering effort in order to create a complete executable WFMS. There exist numerous graphical WDLs: industry standards like Event-driven Process Chains (EPCs) [13], UML activity diagrams [5], BPMN [16], and proprietary WDLs from WFMS vendors. As explained in Section 2, the GiN language adopts notational conventions found in these graphical WDLs. Because GiN is based on the underlying iTask WDL, GiN diagrams have an executable semantics and express both control flow and data flow. Workflow data is strongly typed. Recursive and higher-order workflows can be defined graphically. GiN diagrams are hybrid, and can embed Clean code to express more complex business rules.

BPEL is a text-only, XML-based industry standard for expressing executable workflows based on web services. Several vendors invented their own (different) graphical tools for BPEL, like ActiveBPEL designer and Eclipse BPEL designer. Another approach is mapping BPEL to an existing graphical notation, like EPCs [14] or a subset of BPMN [21]. These systems focus on the coordination of web services. In the GiN/iTask system, web services can be included as basic tasks as well. The expressive power of the BPEL coordination language is, compared to GiN/iTask, relatively simple. Specification of user interaction and form handling is not part of BPEL.

We may consider the GiN language to be a visualization of a subset of a functional language, with the intent to make the language more accessible for users with limited programming knowledge. In this respect, it is similar to projects like Visual Haskell [20], VFPE [10], Vital [7], Eros [6], and Sifflet [24]. However, these visualizations are designed to be complete visual functional programming languages. Therefore their granularity of diagram language is much more fine-grained than that of GiN, which is designed specifically to support the iTask WDL in a graphical way.

The way the GiN tool provides immediate feedback to inform the user about errors in the GiN diagrams is very much related to the *continuous validation* approach by Kühne *et al* [12]. They define a formalism in which a set of validation rules can be specified that are checked against an EPC model under construction. In our approach syntactic mistakes are detected in the preprocessor, and semantic mistakes by the Clean compiler.

6   Conclusions and Future Work

The GiN language is a new WDL that mixes graphical elements (inspired by the workflow community WDLs) with textual elements (inspired by the functional host language) and that connects control flow with data flow. With the GiN tool users can create GiN workflows. During this process, they are continuously given feedback about the correctness of the diagrams under construction. The next step in this project is to verify whether the GiN language and tool is indeed appreciated by domain experts when it is used in concrete projects. However, experienced programmers may prefer to create workflows directly in iTask. In order to visualize these workflows, it would be interesting to investigate a reverse mapping from iTask to GiN.

GiN workflows are complete: when the specification is approved by the compiler, a runnable workflow is generated from it. Such newly defined approved workflows can be dynamically added to a running WFMS. The GiN tool is 'just another iTask editor'. This allows one to define meta workflows: workflows for defining workflows. Consequently, the construction, approval and use of new workflows can be formally defined for a particular organization.

Acknowledgement. This research is supported by a grant from Stichting IT Projecten.

References

1. van der Aalst, W.M.P.: The application of petri nets to workflow management. Journal of Circuits, Systems and Computers 81, 21–66 (1998)
2. van der Aalst, W.M.P.: Chapter 10: Three good reasons for using a Petri-net-based Workflow Management System. Information and Process Integration in Enterprises: Rethinking Documents 428, 161–182 (1998)
3. van der Aalst, W.M.P., ter Hofstede, A.H.M.: YAWL: Yet Another Workflow Language. Technical Report FIT-TR-2002-06, Queensland University of Technology (2002)
4. Decker, G., Overdick, H., Weske, M.: Oryx – An Open Modeling Platform for the BPM Community. In: Dumas, M., Reichert, M., Shan, M.-C. (eds.) BPM 2008. LNCS, vol. 5240, pp. 382–385. Springer, Heidelberg (2008)
5. Dumas, M., ter Hofstede, A.H.M.: UML Activity Diagrams as a Workflow Specification Language. In: Gogolla, M., Kobryn, C. (eds.) UML 2001. LNCS, vol. 2185, pp. 76–90. Springer, Heidelberg (2001)
6. Elliot, C.: Tangible functional programming. In: Proceedings of the 12th International Conference on Functional Programming, ICFP 2007, Freiburg, Germany, October 1-3, pp. 59–70. ACM Press (2007)
7. Hanna, K.: A Document-Centered Environment for Haskell. In: Butterfield, A., Grelck, C., Huch, F. (eds.) IFL 2005. LNCS, vol. 4015, pp. 196–211. Springer, Heidelberg (2006)
8. Henrix, J.: A graphical workflow editor for iTask. Master's thesis, Radboud University Nijmegen, Number 638 (2010)
9. Keller, G., Nüttgens, M., Scheer, A.-W.: Semantische Prozeßmodellierung auf der Grundlage "Ereignisgesteuerter Prozeßketten (EPK)". Veröffentlichungen des Instituts für Wirtschaftsinformatik (IWi), Universität des Saarlandes, Heft 89 (January 1992)
10. Kelso, J.: A Visual Programming Environment for Functional Languages. PhD thesis, Murdoch University (2002)
11. Koopman, P., Plasmeijer, R., Achten, P.: An Executable and Testable Semantics for iTasks. In: Scholz, S.-B., Chitil, O. (eds.) IFL 2008. LNCS, vol. 5836, pp. 212–232. Springer, Heidelberg (2011)
12. Kühne, S., Kern, H., Gruhn, V., Laue, R.: Business Process Modelling with Continuous Validation. In: Ardagna, D., Mecella, M., Yang, J. (eds.) BPM 2008 Workshops. LNBIP, vol. 17, pp. 212–223. Springer, Heidelberg (2009)
13. Mendling, J., Neumann, G., Nüttgens, M.: Towards workflow pattern support of event-driven process chains (EPC). In: Proceedings of the 2nd Workshop XML4BPM 2005, pp. 23–38 (2005)

14. Mendling, J., Ziemann, J.: Transformation of BPEL processes to EPCs. In: Nüttgens, M., Rump, F.J. (eds.) Proceedings of the 4th GI Workshop on Business Process Management with Event-Driven Process Chains (EPK 2005), pp. 41–53 (2005)
15. Michels, S., Plasmeijer, R., Achten, P.: iTask as a New Paradigm for Building GUI Applications. In: Hage, J., Morazán, M.T. (eds.) IFL 2010. LNCS, vol. 6647, pp. 153–168. Springer, Heidelberg (2011)
16. Object Management Group. Business process model and notation (BPMN) version 1.2. Technical report, Object Management Group (2009)
17. Pil, M.: Dynamic Types and Type Dependent Functions. In: Hammond, K., Davie, T., Clack, C. (eds.) IFL 1998. LNCS, vol. 1595, pp. 169–185. Springer, Heidelberg (1999)
18. Plasmeijer, R., Achten, P., Koopman, P.: iTasks: executable specifications of interactive work flow systems for the web. In: Hinze, R., Ramsey, N. (eds.) Proceedings of the International Conference on Functional Programming, ICFP 2007, Freiburg, Germany, pp. 141–152. ACM Press (2007)
19. Plasmeijer, R., Achten, P., Koopman, P., Lijnse, B., van Noort, T., van Groningen, J.: iTasks for a change - Type-safe run-time change in dynamically evolving workflows. In: Khoo, S.-C., Siek, J. (eds.) Proceedings of the Workshop on Partial Evaluation and Program Manipulation, PEPM 2011, Austin, TX, USA, pp. 151–160. ACM Press (2011)
20. Reekie, H.J.: Realtime Signal Processing – Dataflow, Visual, and Functional Programming. PhD thesis, University of Technology at Sydney, Australia (1995)
21. Schumm, D., Karastoyanova, D., Leymann, F., Nitzsche, J.: On visualizing and modelling BPEL with BPMN. In: GPC 2009: Proceedings of the 2009 Workshops at the Grid and Pervasive Computing Conference, pp. 80–87. IEEE Computer Society, Washington, DC, USA (2009)
22. Vanhatalo, J., Völzer, H., Koehler, J.: The Refined Process Structure Tree. In: Dumas, M., Reichert, M., Shan, M.-C. (eds.) BPM 2008. LNCS, vol. 5240, pp. 100–115. Springer, Heidelberg (2008)
23. Vervoort, M., Plasmeijer, R.: Lazy Dynamic Input/Output in the Lazy Functional Language Clean. In: Peña, R., Arts, T. (eds.) IFL 2002. LNCS, vol. 2670, pp. 101–117. Springer, Heidelberg (2003)
24. Weber, G.D.: Sifflet home page (2011),
http://mypage.iu.edu/~gdweber/~software/sifflet/home.html

Applicative Shortcut Fusion

Germán Andrés Delbianco[1], Mauro Jaskelioff[2], and Alberto Pardo[3]

[1] IMDEA Software Institute, Spain
[2] CIFASIS-CONICET/Universidad Nacional de Rosario, Argentina
[3] InCo, Universidad de la República, Uruguay

Abstract. In functional programming one usually writes programs as the composition of simpler functions. Consequently, the result of a function might be generated only to be consumed immediately by another function. This potential source of inefficiency can often be eliminated using a technique called shortcut fusion, which fuses both functions involved in a composition to yield a monolithic one. In this article we investigate how to apply shortcut fusion to applicative computations. Applicative functors provide a model of computational effects which generalise monads, but they favour an applicative programming style. To the best of our knowledge, this is the first time shortcut fusion is considered in an applicative setting.

1 Introduction

One of functional programming much advocated benefits is the possibility of easily constructing large and complex programs through the combination of smaller or simpler ones [12]. This modular approach, however, often results in programs which are quite inefficient when compared to their monolithic counterparts: compositional design often involves creating an *intermediate* data structure which is immediately consumed. In order to alleviate this problem, several formal techniques have been developed that allow the derivation of efficient programs from simpler modular ones. The way these techniques are usually discovered is by identifying common patterns in programs, analyzing these patterns, and obtaining algebraic laws for programs that fit the pattern [18].

Among these techniques lies *shortcut fusion* [11,20] which is concerned with the elimination of unnecessary list traversals. It is based on a single transformation: the `foldr/build` rule which fuses the application of a uniform list-consuming function, expressed as a *fold* on lists, to the result of a uniform list-generating function, expressed in terms of the *build* combinator. This *fusion rule* can be generalised to any inductive datatype, yielding the following generic rule:

$$fold\ k \circ build\ g = g\ k$$

Shortcut fusion has been extended to cope with cases where the intermediate structure is produced in certain contexts. For example, shortcut fusion has been considered for monadic computations [6,13,14], unstructured functors [7], accumulations [15] and circular programs [5,19].

R. Peña and R. Page (Eds.): TFP 2011, LNCS 7193, pp. 179–194, 2012.

A recent development is the notion of applicative functor [16]. Applicative functors provide a novel manner in which effectful computations can be constructed that has gained a rapid acceptance among functional programmers. However, shortcut fusion under an applicative context has not yet been studied. Precisely, in this article, we investigate shortcut fusion under the context of an applicative computation, we identify common patterns in which many applicative programs are written, and give algebraic laws that apply to programs that fit those patterns. Concretely, the contributions of this article are:

- We show how to do shortcut fusion on applicative computations.
- We identify a common pattern in applicative programs which shows the importance and generality of traversals for generating applicative structures and their fundamental role in applicative shortcut fusion.
- We provide a combinator (*ifold*) which models the uniform consumption of applicative computations.

The paper is organised as follows. In Section 2 we review the concept of shortcut fusion. In Section 3 we present the notions of applicative and traversable functors. Section 4 develops the notions of applicative shortcut fusion and applicative structural recursion. In Sections 2 to 4 our motivating examples are on lists. In Section 5 we show the datatype-generic formulation of the concepts and laws presented in previous sections. Finally, in Section 6 we conclude and discuss future work.

Throughout the paper we asume we are working in the context of a functional language with a Haskell-like syntax and with a set-theoretic semantics in which types are interpreted as sets and functions as set-theoretic functions.

2   Shortcut Fusion

Shortcut fusion [11] is a program transformation technique for the elimination of intermediate data structures generated in function compositions. It is a consequence of parametricity properties, known as "free theorems" [21], associated with polymorphic functions. Given a composition $fc \circ fp$, where fc is called the *consumer* and fp the *producer* of the intermediate structure, shortcut fusion requires for its application that both consumer and producer definitions conform to determinate structural requirements. Like other fusion laws of its kind, shortcut fusion requires that the consumer be expressible as a *fold* [4]. The producer, on the other hand, is required to build the intermediate data structure using uniquely the constructors of the datatype. This is expressed in terms of a function, called *build*, which carries a "template" that abstracts from the function body the occurrences of those constructors. For example, when the intermediate structure is a list, *fold* and *build* are given by the following definitions:

$$foldr :: (a \rightarrow b \rightarrow b) \rightarrow b \rightarrow [a] \rightarrow b$$
$$foldr \; f \; e \; [\,] \quad = e$$
$$foldr \; f \; e \; (x : xs) = f \; x \; (foldr \; f \; e \; xs)$$

$$build \quad :: (\forall b.(a \to b \to b) \to b \to c \to b) \to c \to [a]$$
$$build \; g = g \; (:) \; []$$

where *foldr* is a well-known function pattern in functional programming [4].

The essential idea of shortcut fusion is then to replace, in the template of *build*, the occurrences of the constructors of the intermediate structure ((:) and [] in the case of lists) by the corresponding operations carried by the *fold*. The second-order polymorphism of *build* ensures that the argument can only manufacture its result by using its two arguments. For lists, shortcut fusion is expressed by the following law, usually referred to as the *fold/build law*.

Law 1 (FOLDR/BUILD [11])

$$foldr \; f \; e \circ build \; g = g \; f \; e$$

As a result of the application of this law one obtains an equivalent definition that computes the same as the original consumer-producer composition but avoiding the construction of the intermediate data structure.

Example 1. To see an application of Law 1 we define a function that computes the sum of the positionwise differences between two lists of numbers.

$$sumDiff \quad :: Num \; a \Rightarrow ([a],[a]) \to a$$
$$sumDiff \; ys = sum \circ diffList$$

$$diffList \qquad\qquad :: Num \; a \Rightarrow ([a],[a]) \to [a]$$
$$diffList \; (xs,[]) \qquad = []$$
$$diffList \; ([], y : ys) \qquad = []$$
$$diffList \; (x : xs, y : ys) = (x - y) : diffList \; (xs, ys)$$

Function *sum* has the usual definition as a foldr: $sum = foldr \; (+) \; 0$. When applied to a pair of lists (xs, ys), *diffList* computes the list of differences between values in xs and ys, up to the shorter of the two lists. This function is a *good producer* in the sense that it can be expressed in terms of *build*:

$$diffList = build \; gdiff$$
$$\textbf{where}$$
$$gdiff \; cons \; nil \; (\_, []) \qquad = nil$$
$$gdiff \; cons \; nil \; ([], \_) \qquad = nil$$
$$gdiff \; cons \; nil \; (x : xs, y : ys) = cons \; (x - y) \; (gdiff \; cons \; nil \; (xs, ys))$$

Once we have consumer and producer expressed in terms of *foldr* and *build* we are in a position to apply Law 1, obtaining the following definition for *sumDiff*:

$$sumDiff = gdiff \; (+) \; 0$$

Inlining the definition,

$$sumDiff \; (\_, []) \qquad = 0$$
$$sumDiff \; ([], \_) \qquad = 0$$
$$sumDiff \; (x : xs, y : ys) = (x - y) + sumDiff \; (xs, ys)$$

In this paper we are also interested in a generalised form of shortcut fusion which captures the case where the intermediate data structure is generated as part of another structure. This generalisation has been a fundamental tool for the formulation of shortcut fusion laws for monadic programs [14,7], and for the derivation of (monadic) circular and higher-order programs [19,5]. In this paper our aim is to analyse this generalisation in the case when the effects are given by applicative functors.

The generalisation of shortcut fusion [7] is based on an extended form of build. For lists, it has the following definition:

$$ebuild \quad :: Functor\ f \Rightarrow (\forall b.(a \rightarrow b \rightarrow b) \rightarrow b \rightarrow c \rightarrow f\ b) \rightarrow c \rightarrow f\ [a]$$
$$ebuild\ g = g\ (:)\ []$$

where f acts as a container of the generated list. The type requires f to be an instance of the *Functor* class, which ensures that f has an associated function $fmap :: (a \rightarrow b) \rightarrow f\ a \rightarrow f\ b$ that preserves composition and identity.

Law 2 (FOLDR/EBUILD [7])

$$fmap\ (foldr\ f\ e) \circ ebuild\ g = g\ f\ e$$

The use of *fmap* means that fusion acts on the occurrences of the list type within the context structure, maintaining the context structure unchanged.

3   Applicative Functors

An *applicative functor* (or *idiom*) [16] is a type constructor $f :: * \rightarrow *$, equipped with two operations:

```
class (Functor f) ⇒ Applicative f where
   pure :: a → f a
   (⊛) :: f (s → t) → f s → f t
```

Intuitively, *pure* lifts a pure computation into the effectful context defined by f and ⊛ performs an effectful application. Instances of *pure* and ⊛ must verify certain laws (see e.g [16] for details).

Example 2 (Maybe). The *Maybe* applicative functor models *failure* as a computational effect.

```
instance Applicative Maybe where
   pure             = Just
   (Just f) ⊛ (Just x) = Just (f x)
   _       ⊛ _       = Nothing
```

All monads are applicative functors, taking ⊛ to be monadic application and *pure* to be *return*. However, there are applicative functors which are not monads, such as the one in the following example.

Example 3 (Ziplists). The list functor has an *Applicative* instance other than the one obtained from the list monad [16]. This applicative functor models a *transposition* effect, and is defined as follows:

instance *Applicative* [] **where**
$$pure\ x \qquad\qquad = x : pure\ x$$
$$(f : fs) \circledast (x : xs) = f\ x : (fs \circledast xs)$$
$$\_ \quad \circledast \quad \_ \qquad = []$$

An *applicative action* is a function of type $a \to f\ b$ where f is an applicative functor. Applicative actions can be used to perform traversals over a certain class of data structures, threading an effect through the data structure. This class of data structures is called *Traversable*:

class *(Functor t)* $\Rightarrow$ *Traversable t* **where**
$$traverse :: (Applicative\ f) \Rightarrow (a \to f\ b) \to t\ a \to f\ (t\ b)$$

Alternatively, this class can be defined by means of a distributive law *dist* :: $f\ (c\ a) \to c\ (f\ a)$ which pulls the effects out of the data structure. The functions *dist* and *traverse* are interdefinable, with *dist* = *traverse id* and *traverse* $\iota = dist \circ fmap\ \iota$. The latter definition gives a concise description of what an effectful traversal does: first populate the structure with effects by mapping the applicative action and then collect them using the distributive law.

Example 4 (Lists). Lists are *Traversable* data structure, as witnessed by the following instance:

instance *Traversable* [] **where**
$$traverse\ \iota\ [] \qquad = pure\ []$$
$$traverse\ \iota\ (x : xs) = pure\ (:) \circledast \iota\ x \circledast traverse\ \iota\ xs$$

Example 5 (Reciprocal List). We want to define a function that computes the reciprocals of a given list of numbers, failing if there is any 0 value in the list. We can think of the computation of the reciprocal of a value as an *applicative action*: if the value is nonzero then a computation that produces its reciprocal is returned, else we fail *via Nothing*.

$$recipM \quad :: Fractional\ a \Rightarrow a \to Maybe\ a$$
$$recipM\ x = \textbf{if}\ (x \not\equiv 0)\ \textbf{then}\ pure\ (recip\ x)\ \textbf{else}\ Nothing$$

where *recip* :: *Fractional* $a \Rightarrow a \to a$ is such that *recip* $x = 1 / x$. We can use this applicative action to define *recipList* by structural recursion:

$$recipList \qquad :: Fractional\ a \Rightarrow [a] \to Maybe\ [a]$$
$$recipList\ [] \qquad = pure\ []$$
$$recipList\ (x : xs) = pure\ (:) \circledast recipM\ x \circledast recipList\ xs$$

In this definition, we recognise the application of *recipM* to each element in the list, and therefore it clearly can be expressed in terms of *traverse*:

$$recipList = traverse\ recipM$$

On lists as well as on other *Traversable* inductive datatypes function *traverse* can be seen both as a good consumer and good producer: similar to the map function on the datatype, it traverses its input and generates its output in a uniform way. In the remainder of this section we focus on its quality as a consumer; in the next section we show that it is a good producer as well.

Any *Traversable* inductive datatype is a good consumer because it can easily be defined as a *fold*. For example, for lists,

$$traverse\ \iota = foldr\ (\lambda x\ t \rightarrow pure\ (:) \circledast \iota\ x \circledast t)\ (pure\ [])$$

From this fact, we can state the following law in connection with *build*.

Law 3 (TRAVERSE/BUILD FOR LISTS)

$$traverse\ \iota \circ build\ g = g\ (\lambda x\ t \rightarrow pure\ (:) \circledast \iota\ x \circledast t)\ (pure\ [])$$

Proof. By the definition of *traverse* as a *fold* and Law 1.   □

Example 6 (Hermitian transpose). Given a type for complex numbers *Comp*, we will define an algoritm which calculates the *Hermitian or conjugate transpose* of a complex matrix.

data $Real\ x \Rightarrow Comp\ x = x + x\,\mathbf{i}$

The algorithm is quite simple: first calculate the conjugate matrix and then transpose it. The conjugate matrix is defined elementwise, taking the complex conjugate of each entry:

$hermitian :: (Real\ a) \Rightarrow [[Comp\ a]] \rightarrow [[Comp\ a]]$
$hermitian = transpose \circ map\ (map\ scalarconj)$
　　　　where $scalarconj\ (a + b\,\mathbf{i}) = a + (-b)\,\mathbf{i}$

In Example 3, we stated that the ziplists applicative function models a transposition effect. In fact, matrix transposition is a traversal with the identity function i.e. $transpose = traverse\ id$ [16]. Then, by the application of Law 3 the following definition of the Hermitian transpose is obtained, avoiding the construction of the intemediate matrix:

$hermitian :: (Real\ a) \Rightarrow [[Comp\ a]] \rightarrow [[Comp\ a]]$
$hermitian = foldr\ (\lambda xs\ xss \rightarrow pure\ (:) \circledast fmap\ scalarconj\ xs \circledast xss)\ (pure\ [])$
　　　　where $scalarconj\ (a + b\,\mathbf{i}) = a + (-b)\,\mathbf{i}$

4   Applicative Shortcut Fusion

In this section we analyse situations where the production and consumption of a data structure is performed in the context of an applicative effect. Our aim is to obtain a shortcut fusion law for those cases. As with monads [14,7], the extension of shortcut fusion presented in Section 2 turns out to be an appropriate device to achieve this goal. Again, our development in this section is performed on lists; the datatype-generic constructions are shown in Section 5.

Applicative shortcut fusion works on those cases where the container of the generated intermediate data structure is an applicative functor. The *build* function in this case is simply an instance of the *extended build* that we call *ibuild* (for *idiomatic build*):

$$ibuild \quad :: Applicative\ f \Rightarrow (\forall b.(a \rightarrow b \rightarrow b) \rightarrow b \rightarrow c \rightarrow f\ b) \rightarrow c \rightarrow f\ [a]$$
$$ibuild\ g = g\ (:)\ []$$

The corresponding instance of extended shortcut fusion (Law 2) is the following:

Law 4 (FOLDR/IBUILD)

$$fmap\ (foldr\ f\ e) \circ ibuild\ g = g\ f\ e$$

Example 7 (traverse). As mentioned at the end of Section 3, function *traverse* may not only be considered a good consumer but also a good producer since it generates its output list in a uniform way as the result of an effectful computation. In fact, it is very simple to express *traverse* in terms of *ibuild*:

$$traverse\ \iota = ibuild\ gtrav$$
$$\quad \textbf{where}$$
$$\quad\quad gtrav\ cons\ nil\ [] \quad\quad = pure\ nil$$
$$\quad\quad gtrav\ cons\ nil\ (x : xs) = pure\ cons \circledast \iota\ x \circledast gtrav\ cons\ nil\ xs$$

which is the same as,

$$traverse\ \iota = ibuild\ gtrav$$
$$\quad \textbf{where}$$
$$\quad\quad gtrav\ cons\ nil = foldr\ (\lambda x\ t \rightarrow pure\ cons \circledast \iota\ x \circledast t)\ (pure\ nil)$$

It is also interesting to see that the composition *traverse* $\iota \circ$ *build g*, which is the subject of Law 3, can also be expressed as an *ibuild*:

$$traverse\ \iota \circ build\ g = ibuild\ g'$$
$$\quad \textbf{where}\ g'\ f\ e = g\ (\lambda x\ t \rightarrow pure\ f \circledast \iota\ x \circledast t)\ (pure\ e)$$

A common pattern of computation using applicative functors is the one that applies a *fold* after having performed an applicative traversal over a data structure. We identify this pattern with a new program scheme that we call *idiomatic fold*, which specifies an applicative notion of structural recursion. For lists,

$$ifoldr :: Applicative\ f \Rightarrow (b \to c \to c) \to c \to (a \to f\ b) \to [a] \to f\ c$$
$$ifoldr\ f\ e\ \iota = fmap\ (foldr\ f\ e) \circ traverse\ \iota$$

Using the fact that *traverse* can be expressed as an *ibuild* we can apply Law 4 obtaining as result that an *ifoldr* is a *foldr*:

$$ifoldr\ f\ e\ \iota = foldr\ (\lambda x\ t \to pure\ f \circledast \iota\ x \circledast t)\ (pure\ e) \tag{1}$$

Inlining,

$$ifoldr\ f\ e\ \iota\ [\,] \qquad = pure\ e$$
$$ifoldr\ f\ e\ \iota\ (x : xs) = pure\ f \circledast \iota\ x \circledast ifoldr\ f\ e\ \iota\ xs$$

Example 8 (Sum of reciprocal list). In Example 5 we defined the function *recipList* that computes the reciprocals of a list of numbers. We used the *Maybe* applicative functor to model the possibility of failure originated by the occurrence of some 0 in the input list. Now we want to compute the sum of the reciprocals of a list:

$$sumRecips :: Fractional\ a \Rightarrow [a] \to Maybe\ a$$
$$sumRecips = fmap\ sum \circ recipList$$

Since $sum = foldr\ (+)\ 0$ and $recipList = traverse\ recipM$, *sumRecips* corresponds to an *ifold*:

$$sumRecips = ifoldr\ (+)\ 0\ recipM$$

Inlining,

$$sumRecips\ [\,] \qquad = pure\ 0$$
$$sumRecips\ (x : xs) = pure\ (+) \circledast recipM\ x \circledast sumRecips\ xs$$

Having introduced a notion of applicative structural recursion, we can state a shortcut fusion law associated with it.

Law 5 (IFOLDR/BUILD)

$$ifoldr\ f\ e\ \iota \circ build\ g = g\ (\lambda x\ y \to pure\ f \circledast \iota\ x \circledast y)\ (pure\ e)$$

Proof

$$\quad ifoldr\ f\ e\ \iota \circ build\ g$$
$$\equiv \{\ \text{definition } ifoldr\ \}$$
$$\quad fmap\ (foldr\ f\ e) \circ traverse\ \iota \circ build\ g$$
$$\equiv \{\ \text{Example 7, } g'\ f\ e = g\ (\lambda x\ t \to pure\ f \circledast \iota\ x \circledast t)\ (pure\ e)\ \}$$
$$\quad fmap\ (foldr\ f\ e) \circ ibuild\ g'$$
$$\equiv \{\ \text{Law 4}\ \}$$
$$\quad g\ (\lambda x\ t \to pure\ f \circledast \iota\ x \circledast t)\ (pure\ e) \qquad\qquad \square$$

Example 9 (Sum of reciprocals of list differences). We now want to compose the function that calculates the sum of reciprocals of a list of numbers, given in Example 8, with the function that computes the differences of two list of numbers, given in Example 1.

$$sumRecipsDiff :: Fractional\ a \Rightarrow ([a], [a]) \rightarrow Maybe\ a$$
$$sumRecipsDiff = sumRecips \circ diffList$$

Since $sumRecips = ifoldr\ (+)\ 0\ recipM$ and $diffList = build\ gdiff$, by Law 5 we get a monolithic definition that avoids the construction of the intermediate lists:

$$sumRecipsDiff = gdiff\ (\lambda x\ t \rightarrow pure\ (+) \circledast recipM\ x \circledast t)\ (pure\ 0)$$

Inlining,

$$
\begin{aligned}
sumRecipsDiff\ (\_, [\,]) \quad &= pure\ 0 \\
sumRecipsDiff\ ([\,], \_) \quad &= pure\ 0 \\
sumRecipsDiff\ (x : xs, y : ys) &= pure\ (+) \circledast recipM\ (x - y) \\
&\qquad \circledast sumRecipsDiff\ (xs, ys)
\end{aligned}
$$

We conclude this section by showing an example that, unlike the previous one, does not fit the pattern *fold/traverse/build*: it is a case where we cannot factor an occurrence of *traverse*. The example, however, needs extra structure on the applicative functor, namely to be an instance of the *Alternative* class.

Example 10 (Parsing). Suppose we want to compute the exclusive OR of a sequence of bits that we parse from an input string. It is in the parsing phase that effects will come into play, as we will use an applicative parser.

```
newtype Parser a = P { runP :: String → [(a, String)] }
instance Functor Parser where
    fmap f p = P $ λcs → [(f a, cs') | (a, cs') ← runP p cs]
instance Applicative Parser where
    pure a = P $ λcs → [(a, cs)]
    p ⊛ q  = P $ λcs → [(f v, cs'') |  (f, cs') ← runP p cs
                      ,  (v, cs'') ← runP q cs']
class Applicative f ⇒ Alternative f where
    empty :: f a
    (⟨|⟩)  :: f a → f a → f a
instance Alternative Parser where
    empty = P $ const []
    p⟨|⟩q  = P $ λcs → case runP p cs ++ runP q cs of
                      []   → []
                      x : xs → [x]
pSym :: Char → Parser Char
pSym x = P $ λcs → case cs of
```

$$c : cs \mid x \equiv c \rightarrow [(c, cs)]$$
$$otherwise \quad \rightarrow [\,]$$

Alternatives are represented by a choice operator ($\langle | \rangle$), which, for simplicity, returns at most one result. The parser *pSym* parsers a determinate character.

Using these combinators we define parsers for bits and bit strings.

$$bitstring = pure \; (:) \circledast bit \circledast bitstring$$
$$\langle | \rangle$$
$$pure \; [\,]$$

$$bit = pure \; (const \; False) \circledast pSym \; {}'0{}'$$
$$\langle | \rangle$$
$$pure \; (const \; True) \circledast pSym \; {}'1{}'$$

$$listXor \qquad :: [Bool] \rightarrow Bool$$
$$listXor \; [\,] \qquad = False$$
$$listXor \; (b : bs) = b \; {}`xor{}` \; listXor \; bs$$

$$xor \qquad :: Bool \rightarrow Bool \rightarrow Bool$$
$$b \; {}`xor{}` \; b' = (b \wedge \neg \, b') \vee (\neg \, b \wedge b')$$

We want to compute the composition: $xorBits = fmap \; (listXor) \circ bitstring$.

Since $listXor = foldr \; xor \; False$ and *bitstring* can be expressed as an *ibuild*:

$$bitstring = ibuild \; gbits$$
$$\textbf{where} \; gbits \; cons \; nil = pure \; cons \circledast bit \circledast gbits \; cons \; nil$$
$$\langle | \rangle$$
$$pure \; nil$$

we can apply Law 4 obtaining that $xorBits = gbits \; xor \; False$. Inlining,

$$xorBits = pure \; xor \circledast bit \circledast xorBits$$
$$\langle | \rangle$$
$$pure \; False$$

5   The Datatype-Generic Formulation

In the previous sections, we focused our presentation on the list datatype in order to give a comprehensive explanation of the main concepts. However, constructions such as *fold*, *build* and *ebuild*, and laws like shortcut fusion can be formulated for a wide class of datatypes using a datatype-generic approach [2,3,9].

5.1   Inductive Data Types

The structure of data types can be captured using the concept of a *functor*. A functor consists of a type constructor f and a map function:

$$\textbf{class} \; Functor \; f \; \textbf{where}$$
$$fmap :: (a \rightarrow b) \rightarrow f \; a \rightarrow f \; b$$

where *fmap* must preserves identities and compositions: $fmap\ id = id$ and $fmap\ (f \circ g) = fmap\ f \circ fmap\ g$. A standard example of a functor is that formed by the list type constructor and the well-known *map* function.

Inductive data types correspond to least fixed points of functors. Given a data type declaration it is possible to derive a functor f, which captures the structure of the type, such that the data type can be seen as the least solution of the equation $x \cong fx$ [1]. In Haskell, we can encode this isomorphism defining a type constructor $\mu :: (* \to *) \to *$ as follows:

newtype $\mu\ f = In\ \{\ unIn :: f\ (\mu\ f)\}$

Example 11 (Naturals). Given a data type for natural numbers,

data $Nat = Zero \mid Succ\ Nat$

its signature is given by a functor *FNat* defined as follows:

data $FNat\ x = FZero \mid FSucc\ x$
instance *Functor FNat* **where**
$\quad fmap\ f\ FZero \quad\ = FZero$
$\quad fmap\ f\ (FSucc\ n) = FSucc\ (f\ n)$

So, alternatively, we can say that $Nat = \mu\ FNat$.

For polymorphic types, it is necessary to use functors on multiple arguments to capture their signature in order to account for type parameters. For example, for types with one parameter we need a functor on two arguments, usually called a *bifunctor*, to represent their structure.

class *Bifunctor f* **where**
$\quad bimap :: (a \to b) \to (c \to d) \to f\ a\ c \to f\ b\ d$

Example 12 (Lists). The structure of polymorphic lists, $[a]$, is captured by a bifunctor *FList*,

data $FList\ a\ b = FNil \mid FCons\ a\ b$
instance *Bifunctor FList* **where**
$\quad bimap\ f\ g\ FNil \quad\quad = FNil$
$\quad bimap\ f\ g\ (FCons\ a\ b) = FCons\ (f\ a)\ (g\ b)$

By fixing the bifunctor argument corresponding to the type parameter a (the type of the list elements) we get a functor *FList a* which represents the signature of lists of type a:

instance *Functor (FList a)* **where**
$\quad fmap\ f\ FNil \quad\quad\ = FNil$
$\quad fmap\ f\ (FCons\ a\ b) = FCons\ a\ (f\ b)$

Thus, $[a] = \mu\ (FList\ a)$.

5.2 Fold

Given a functor f that captures the signature of a data type and a function $k :: f\ a \to a$ (called an *f-algebra*), we can define a program scheme, called *fold* [3], which captures function definitions by structural recursion on the type $\mu\ f$.

> $fold :: Functor\ f \Rightarrow (f\ a \to a) \to \mu\ f \to a$
> $fold\ k = k \circ fmap\ (fold\ k) \circ unIn$

The signature corresponding to a type T with n constructors is a functor that has also n cases. The same occurs with the algebras for that functor; they are essentially a tuple $(k_1, \ldots, k_n)$ of n component operations, each one with the appropriate type. For example, an algebra for the functor *FList a* is a function $k :: FList\ a\ b \to b$ of the form:

> $k\ FNil\qquad\ \ = e$
> $k\ (FCons\ a\ b) = f\ a\ b$

with components $e :: b$ and $f :: a \to b \to b$. This is the reason why *foldr*, the *fold* for lists, has type $(a \to b \to b) \to b \to [a] \to b$.

5.3 Shortcut Fusion

The shortcut-fusion law of Section 2 can be generalised from list to all datatypes expressible as the (least) fixpoint of a functor [8,20]. The generic *build* can be defined as follows.

> $build\ \ :: (Functor\ f) \Rightarrow (\forall a.(f\ a \to a) \to c \to a) \to c \to \mu\ f$
> $build\ g = g\ In$

Notice that the abstraction of the datatype's constructors is represented in terms of an f-algebra. As explained before, the idea of shortcut fusion is then to replace, in the producer, the occurrences of the abstracted constructors by corresponding operations in the algebra of the fold that appears as consumer. The datatype-generic *fold/build law* is then:

Law 6 (FOLD/BUILD [8,20])

$$fold\ k \circ build\ g = g\ k$$

5.4 Extended Shortcut Fusion

The generic formulation of the extended build [7] is as follows:

> $ebuild :: (Functor\ f, Functor\ h) \Rightarrow (\forall a.(f\ a \to a) \to c \to h\ a) \to c \to h\ (\mu\ f)$
> $ebuild\ g = g\ In$

where h is a functor that represents the container structure of the generated datatype. As we saw for lists, this is a natural extension of the standard build function. Using *ebuild* we can state the extended shortcut fusion law:

Law 7 (EXTENDED FOLD/BUILD **[7,14]**)

$$fmap \; (fold \; k) \circ ebuild \; g = g \; k$$

Fusion acts on the occurrences of the internal structure, while the context structure is maintained unchanged.

5.5   Generic Traversals

It is possible to define *datatype-generic* traversals for parametric data structures corresponding to fixpoints of a parametric bifunctors. In order to define *traverse* generically, we must first establish when the signature of a datatype can be traversed:

class *Bifunctor* $s \Rightarrow$ *Bitraversable* s **where**
  $bitraverse :: (Applicative \; f) \Rightarrow$
    $(a \rightarrow f \; c) \rightarrow (b \rightarrow f \; d) \rightarrow s \; a \; b \rightarrow f \; (s \; c \; d)$

Gibbons and Oliveira [10] present an equivalent characterisation: a bifunctor s is *Bitraversable* if for any applicative functor c there exists a *natural transformation* $bidist :: s \; (c \; a) \; (c \; b) \rightarrow c \; (s \; a \; b)$ which serves as a distributive law between the signature bifunctor and the applicative functor. Such distributive law exists for any given regular datatype and it can be defined *polytipically* i.e. by induction on the structure of the signature bifunctor [2,17]. As in the case of *traverse* and *dist* above, *bitraverse* and *bidist* are also interdefinable as $bidist = bitraverse \; id \; id$ and $bitraverse \; f \; g = bidist \circ bimap \; f \; g$. Thus, *traverse* can be defined generically for all fixed points of *Bitraversable* functors.

  $traverse :: (Applicative \; f, Bitraversable \; s) \Rightarrow$
    $(a \rightarrow f \; b) \rightarrow \mu \; (s \; a) \rightarrow f \; (\mu \; (s \; b))$
  $traverse \; \iota = fold \; (fmap \; In \circ bitraverse \; \iota \; id)$

Gibbons and Oliveira [10] also claim that the *traverse* operator captures *"the essence of the Iterator pattern"* and have studied some calculational properties of idiomatic traversals. In Section 4, we saw that traversals play an important role in the characterisation of some common applicative forms of computation, like applicative structural recursion, and are well suited for fusion because of the fact of being good producers and good consumers simultaneously.

5.6   Applicative Shortcut Fusion

We define an idiomatic build to be an extended build where the container is an applicative functor.

  $ibuild \quad :: (Applicative \; f) \Rightarrow (\forall b.(s \; a \rightarrow a) \rightarrow c \rightarrow a) \rightarrow c \rightarrow f \; (\mu \; s)$
  $ibuild \; g = g \; In$

The corresponding instance of extended shortcut fusion (Law 7) results:

Law 8 (FOLD/IBUILD)

$$fmap \; (fold \; \phi) \circ ibuild \; g = g \; \phi$$

5.7   Applicative Structural Recursion

Given a bitraversable bifunctor s, an algebra $\phi :: s\ b\ c \to c$ for the functor $(s\ b)$ and an applicative action $\iota :: a \to f\ b$ for an applicative functor f, we define *ifold* by the following equation:

$$
\begin{aligned}
&ifold \quad :: (Applicative\ f, Bitraversable\ s) \Rightarrow \\
&\qquad\qquad (s\ b\ c \to c) \to (a \to f\ b) \to \mu\ (s\ a) \to f\ c \\
&ifold\ \phi\ \iota = fmap\ (fold\ \phi) \circ traverse\ \iota
\end{aligned}
$$

which in turn, is equivalent to the following generalization of (1):

$$ifold\ \phi\ \iota = fold\ (fmap\ \phi \circ bitraverse\ \iota\ id) \qquad (2)$$

Associated with *ifold* we have the following shortcut fusion law which gives a monolithic expression for the pattern *fold/traverse/build*:

Law 9 (IFOLD/BUILD)

$$ifold\ \phi\ \iota \circ build\ g \qquad\qquad (I)$$

$$=$$

$$fmap\ (fold\ \phi) \circ traverse\ \iota \circ build\ g \qquad\qquad (II)$$

$$=$$

$$g\ (fmap\ \phi \circ bitraverse\ \iota\ id) \qquad\qquad (III)$$

Proof. $(I) = (II)$ by the definition of *ifold*. By the definition of *ifold* in terms of *fold*, (2), and Law 6, $(I) = (III)$. □

Note that in the *fold/traverse/build* pattern there is no need to use generalised shortcut fusion. The traversal takes care of creating and collecting the extra structure.

5.8   Composite Functors

Applicative Functors are closed under functor composition. Gibbons and Oliveira [10] exploit this fact to define the *sequential composition* of applicative actions:

$$
\begin{aligned}
&\textbf{data}\ (m \boxdot n)\ a = Comp\ \{ unComp :: m\ (n\ a) \} \\
&(\odot)\quad :: (Functor\ m, Functor\ n) \Rightarrow (b \to n\ c) \to (a \to m\ b) \to a \to (m \boxdot n)\ c \\
&f \odot g = Comp \circ fmap\ f \circ g
\end{aligned}
$$

The $\odot$ operator can not only be used to compose traversals but also to show they are, in fact, closed under sequential composition i.e.

$$traverse\ (f \odot g) = traverse\ f \odot traverse\ g \qquad (3)$$

Using this equation, we can derive a shortcut fusion law for the sequential composition of *ifold* and *traverse* as follows.

Law 10 (IFOLD/$\odot$/TRAVERSE)

$$ifold\ \phi\ \iota \odot traverse\ \kappa = ifold\ \phi\ (\iota \odot \kappa)$$

Proof (Sketch). By expanding definitions of $\odot$ and *ifold*, using functoriality and composition of traversals (3).

6   Conclusions and Future Work

We have presented two approaches to shortcut fusion for applicative computations. One is based on the extended shortcut fusion law tailored to applicative computations. We aimed at obtaining a more structured fusion law that took into account the way applicative computations are written. By analysing several examples we found that traversals are at the core of applicative computations. Based on this fact we proposed the pattern *fold/traverse/build* as the core of structural applicative computations and introduced a law for those patterns. This pattern elegantly separates the pure part of the computation from the one producing computational effects. We also introduced a notion of applicative structural recursion as the composition of a fold with a traversal.

Future Work. The proposed pattern arose as a result of the study of several examples found in the literature (e.g. [16,10]). Despite the elegance of the results, we would like to obtain a more theoretically founded justification for them such as an initial algebra semantics for *ifold*. Related to this is the notion of a category of applicative computations, but this notion is still missing. Additionally we would like to extend our results to applicative functors with extra structure, such as the one in Example 10.

Acknowledgements. We thank the anonymous reviewers for their helpful commments and suggestions.

References

1. Abramsky, S., Jung, A.: Domain Theory. In: Abramsky, S., Gabbay, D., Maibaum, T.S.E. (eds.) Handbook of Logic in Computer Science, vol. 3, pp. 1–168. Oxford University Press (1994)
2. Backhouse, R., Jansson, P., Jeuring, J., Meertens, L.: Generic Programming — An Introduction. In: Swierstra, S.D., Oliveira, J.N. (eds.) AFP 1998. LNCS, vol. 1608, pp. 28–115. Springer, Heidelberg (1999)
3. Bird, R., de Moor, O.: Algebra of programming. Prentice-Hall, Inc., Upper Saddle River (1997)
4. Bird, R.S.: Introduction to Functional Programming Using Haskell. Prentice-Hall (1998)
5. Fernandes, J.P., Pardo, A., Saraiva, J.: A shortcut fusion rule for circular program calculation. In: Keller, G. (ed.) Haskell, pp. 95–106. ACM (2007)
6. Ghani, N., Johann, P.: Monadic augment and generalised short cut fusion. Journal of Functional Programming 17(6), 731–776 (2007)
7. Ghani, N., Johann, P.: Short cut fusion of recursive programs with computational effects. In: Achten, P., Koopman, P., Morazán, M. (eds.) Trends in Functional Programming. Trends in Functional Programming, Intellect, vol. 9, pp. 113–128 (2009) ISBN 978-1-84150-277-9
8. Ghani, N., Uustalu, T., Vene, V.: Build, Augment and Destroy, Universally. In: Chin, W.-N. (ed.) APLAS 2004. LNCS, vol. 3302, pp. 327–347. Springer, Heidelberg (2004)

9. Gibbons, J.: Datatype-Generic Programming. In: Backhouse, R., Gibbons, J., Hinze, R., Jeuring, J. (eds.) SSDGP 2006. LNCS, vol. 4719, pp. 1–71. Springer, Heidelberg (2007)
10. Gibbons, J., Oliveira, B.C.d.S.: The essence of the iterator pattern. Journal of Functional Programming 19(3-4), 377–402 (2009)
11. Gill, A., Launchbury, J., Peyton Jones, S.: A short cut to deforestation. In: FPCA 1993: Proceedings of the Conference on Functional Programming Languages and Computer Architecture, pp. 223–232. ACM Press, New York (1993)
12. Hughes, J.: Why functional programming matters. Comput. J. 32(2), 98–107 (1989)
13. Johann, P., Ghani, N.: Monadic fold, monadic build, monadic short cut fusion. In: Proceedings of the 10th Symposium on Trends in Functional Programming (TFP 2009), pp. 9–23 (2009)
14. Manzino, C., Pardo, A.: Shortcut fusion of monadic programs. Journal of Universal Computer Science 14(21), 3431–3446 (2008)
15. Martínez, M., Pardo, A.: A shortcut fusion approach to accumulations. In: Simpósio Brasileiro de Linguagens de Programacao, SBLP 2009 (2009)
16. McBride, C., Paterson, R.: Applicative programming with effects. Journal of Functional Programming 18(01), 1–13 (2008)
17. Meertens, L.: Functor pulling. In: Backhouse, R., Sheard, T. (eds.) Proc. Workshop on Generic Programming (1998)
18. Meijer, E., Fokkinga, M.M., Paterson, R.: Functional Programming with Bananas, Lenses, Envelopes and Barbed Wire. In: Hughes, J. (ed.) FPCA 1991. LNCS, vol. 523, pp. 124–144. Springer, Heidelberg (1991)
19. Pardo, A., Fernandes, J.P., Saraiva, J.: Shortcut fusion rules for the derivation of circular and higher-order monadic programs. In: Puebla, G., Vidal, G. (eds.) PEPM, pp. 81–90. ACM (2009)
20. Takano, A., Meijer, E.: Shortcut deforestation in calculational form. In: Proc. Conference on Functional Programming Languages and Computer Architecture, pp. 306–313. ACM Press (1995)
21. Wadler, P.: Theorems for Free! In: Proceedings of the 4th ACM Conference on Functional Programming Languages and Computer Architecture, FPCA 1989, pp. 347–359. ACM Press, New York (1989)

Author Index